MW01180745

Health Economics
for Developing Countries

A PRACTICAL GUIDE

Sophie Witter
Tim Ensor
Matthew Jowett
Robin Thompson

BUPA

THE UNIVERSITY *of York*

CENTRE FOR HEALTH ECONOMICS
INTERNATIONAL PROGRAMME

MACMILLAN

Macmillan Education
Between Towns Road, Oxford OX4 3PP
A division of Macmillan Publishers Limited
Companies and representatives throughout the world

www.macmillan-africa.com

ISBN 0 333 75205 8

Text © S. Witter, T. Ensor, M. Jowett, R. Tompson, 2000
Design and illustration © S. Witter, T. Ensor, M. Jowett, R. Tompson, 2000

First published 2000

All rights reserved; no part of this publication may be
reproduced, stored in a retrieval system, transmitted in any
form or by any means, electronic, mechanical, photocopying,
recording, or otherwise, without the prior written permission
of the Publishers.

Cover Photographs courtesy of John Walley and TALC

Printed and bound in Malaysia

2006 2005 2004 2003 2002
10 9 8 7 6 5 4 3 2

Contents

PART 3   Allocating resources for health and health care

PART 4   The organisation of health services

Preface and acknowledgements

The motivation for producing this book was an immediate practical need. Since 1986 the International Programme at the Centre for Health Economics in York has been running short courses in health economics and financing for participants from developing countries. Most of these participants have in-depth experience of working in health systems but no formal education as economists. Their needs are for skills and techniques which they can use when they return to their posts – as doctors, managers and planners. We found, however, that there was no introductory 'textbook' which we could give them, which would explain health economics in an accessible, applied way in the context of their countries. There is a growing body of health economics literature, but most of it is produced by and for the richer Western nations, which face a different set of challenges. A lot of it is very specialised and theoretical.

What we have tried to produce is an introduction to health economics and finance for low income countries which does not assume any prior training in economics and which is easy to read and use. It is designed for lone students, for use on short courses, or as an introduction for more in-depth studies.

In a book of this size, we have had to be very selective about what we cover: we have gone into greater detail on what we consider to be 'core' areas for health economists, with brief discussion and references for areas which are linked but fall more commonly under other related disciplines (such as health management policy or public health). Underlying the problem of drawing lines around the subject is the fact that people will come to this book with very different needs. There are few people practising as 'health economists' in developing countries, but a very large number of people in a variety of roles who need to know about it in order to be effective in their jobs.

Just as drawing lines around the subject is to some degree arbitrary, so too is drawing lines within it. The structure of the book, explained in Chapter 1, divides health economics into a number of topics, but there are many connections between them, to which we draw attention by cross-referencing. Although each chapter can stand alone, the book is designed to be read as a whole.

Each chapter introduces the topic and explains what will be covered. The material is then explored, with the aid of a group of characters in a hypothetical country. (To avoid suggesting a particular region or country, we have used unusual names, which we hope will amuse the reader.) Each chapter ends with a summary, some questions or an exercise for the reader, and a list of references and further reading. At the end of the book is a glossary of health economics terms and some web-site addresses which will be of use to readers who have access to the Internet.

Health economists, both in the West and in developing countries, tend to have a poor image. At worst, they are seen as a mean-minded, heartless group, with little to contribute to everyday decision making. The message of this book is, we hope, positive:

- health economics can be practical and usable for a wider group of people
- it is concerned with getting as much benefit for society as possible, not just with cutting costs
- it should be at the heart of planning and managing health systems
- it can and should serve public goals – it does not dictate them.

Read on...

Acknowledgements

This book has been a team effort by the staff of the International Programme at the Centre for Health Economics in the University of York. I would like to thank them all for their many contributions, both in their own chapters and in commenting on other parts of the book. Thanks also to Alan Maynard and Alan Williams for their useful comments on chapters.

We would also like to thank course participants of 1998 for their comments on the draft chapters. We hope that these comments have helped to make the book of use to future generations of would-be health economists.

We would also like to acknowledge the financial assistance of BUPA, which has helped to keep down the price of this book so that it can reach a wider audience.

PART I

Introduction to Health Economics

1

Introduction to health economics

Sophie Witter

What is health economics?

All around the world people fall ill, and all around the world resources are used to try to make them better. This is the area that health economics is concerned with: the connection between health and the resources which are consumed in promoting it. Resources here means not just money, but also people, materials, and time which could have been put to some other use. The underlying problem is that people have almost infinite needs – not just for health, but also for food, shelter, entertainment, and other types of consumption – but finite (limited) resources with which to satisfy them. They therefore have to make choices, as individuals and as groups, about which needs are most important and how to use available resources. Health economics attempts to illuminate those choices.

So what are the kinds of questions that health economics is used to answer? They can be grouped into a number of different areas. Starting with examples of the most general:

- What is health? How (how much) should we invest in it?
- How do we define and measure health?
- How much value do people set on it?
- What are the different channels for producing health, both within and outside the health sector?
- How do we make overall allocations of resources?
- What criteria do we use to guide us?

This sounds quite theoretical and much of the work around it is academic. However, there is a practical point, which is that health economists are involved in setting overall allocations to

2

3

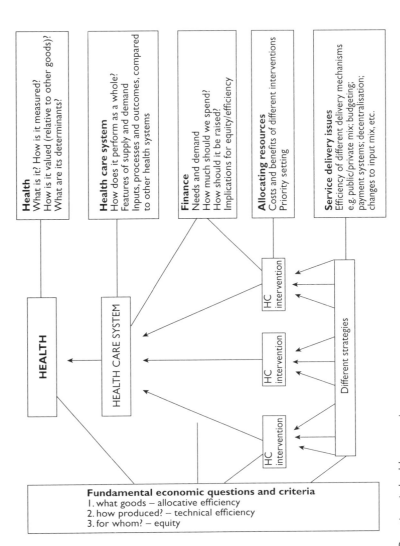

Health
What is it? How is it measured?
How is it valued (relative to other goods)?
What are its determinants?

Health care system
How does it perform as a whole?
Features of supply and demand
Inputs, processes and outcomes, compared
to other health systems

Finance
Needs and demand
How much should we spend?
How should it be raised?
Implications for equity/efficiency

Allocating resources
Costs and benefits of different interventions
Priority setting

Service delivery issues
Efficiency of different delivery mechanisms
e.g. public/private mix: budgeting;
payment systems; decentralisation;
changes to input mix, etc.

HEALTH

HEALTH CARE SYSTEM

HC intervention

HC intervention

HC intervention

Different strategies

Fundamental economic questions and criteria
1. what goods – allocative efficiency
2. how produced? – technical efficiency
3. for whom? – equity

Fig. 1.1 Questions in health economics

the health sector and in determining ways of judging the success of policies. In doing so they have to consider these questions. They should be particularly mindful of the importance of activities outside the health sector in influencing health status. These issues will be discussed in Part 1 of this book.

- How does our health service as a whole perform?
- How much are we spending on health care?
- Is it the right amount?
- What are we getting for that money?
- How does our health system compare with others?
- How does our health compare with others?

This second group of questions takes a broad view of the health system as a whole and compares it with other health systems in terms of the inputs (of money) and the outputs (of health). It tries to make some general judgements about the health sector which can inform more detailed questions, outlined later. We can call this function *system-level evaluation*. It is pursued in Chapter 2 on health and development, Chapters 4 and 5 on financing health care and Chapter 13 on technical efficiency.

- What is the best way (or mix of ways) of raising money for health care?
- What are the advantages and disadvantages of general taxation as opposed to payroll taxes, social insurance, private insurance or user fees?
- What are the implications of different financing systems for efficiency and equity (see later for discussion of these terms)?
- Does it matter if fees are informal rather than formal?
- How much are patients spending on health as a whole, including drugs?
- How can problems of access for low income groups be mitigated under these different financing systems?

These questions, which deal with *health financing*, are of particular relevance for developing countries. These typically have to grapple with (a) high health needs; (b) particularly acute resource shortages; (c) administrative problems in collecting revenue; and (d) real access problems for a sizeable proportion of the population. They will form the heart of Part 2 of this book, on health financing.

• Given the resources available, which health activities should be given priority?
• Should we focus on prevention or cure?
• Should we focus on diseases faced by children or adults/old people?
• How should money be divided between the different regions?
• Is tuberculosis control more important than malaria?
• Should we deliver these services in the health centres or through outreach teams? In hospitals or primary care centres?
• How much of each service should be provided?

These difficult and varied questions all relate to how best to spend money on health – choosing services and service mix and method. This involves a number of techniques. First, *needs assessment*, looking at the disease patterns in a country or region and how these are being handled by existing services. Secondly, *evaluation of health interventions*: how much do they cost and what benefit do they bring? Finally, all of these considerations and other issues relating to social preferences are brought together in a process of *priority setting*, in which difficult choices are made. Part 3 of this book deals with costs and benefits in health care programmes, priority setting in health care and project or programme appraisal.

• Having agreed priorities, what are the best ways of implementing them?
• Should the state or the private sector provide these services?
• Within the state sector, which decisions should be taken at the centre, and which at other levels of the administrative system?
• How should institutions and doctors be paid?
• What are the best management structures/budgeting systems within health care units?
• What mix of inputs (such as staff) is most efficient?

These questions all relate to the organisation of the provision of health services. They focus on the issue of *technical efficiency* – in other words, getting the most gain for the resources which are invested in a given activity. By contrast, the questions in Part 3 focus on what economists call *allocative efficiency* (see Box 1.1). Given severe resource constraints and their typically heavy burden of disease, developing countries need to focus on both of these last two groups of questions.

Box 1.1   Concepts of efficiency

What does 'efficiency' mean? Economists commonly distinguish between two different types: *technical* and *allocative* efficiency.

Technical efficiency means carrying out agreed activities using the least possible resources – or carrying out the maximum activities possible using a fixed pot of resources. For example, if you alter the procedures in your clinic so that you can increase the number of patients you see (with quality remaining constant), then you have increased your technical efficiency. (If you see more patients but provide a poorer service to each one, then you have increased activity rates but probably decreased efficiency.)

Allocative efficiency means directing resources to their most productive use. In health care terms, it means assessing which intervention will produce greatest health gains for a given investment of resources, and focusing on that activity.

A hospital may be technically efficient, for example, in that all procedures are carried out using the minimum of resources necessary for those procedures. However, it may well be focusing on allocatively inefficient activities – expensive, high technology activities which benefit a small minority, rather than measures which offer more significant health gains.

The last part of the book (Part 4) looks at these issues, which relate to technical efficiency in the provision of services. The chapters on changing views of public and private roles in the provision of health services, decentralisation within public services, changes to payment systems and general measures to increase efficiency all try to answer the last group of questions.

Finally, the conclusion summarises key points from the book and looks at the reasons why health economics in developing countries has developed a different agenda, compared with health economics as practised in the West.

Health, public goals and health economics

If we are to measure costs and benefits of a health care strategy, we need to have a clear idea of the overall objective which is being served and the criteria for judging success. This section will discuss the different types of public goals which can be set and how they may be measured.

At the most general level, economists argue that the goal should be to maximise social welfare. This in turn means maximising production as a whole (efficiency, in the broadest sense), but also allocating it in a way which produces most welfare (which is where notions of equity come in – see later in the chapter). What, for example, is the relative contribution of good health to an individual's welfare, in comparison with adequate food, clothing, or shelter? There is also debate around how we measure and aggregate individual welfares, which is discussed in Appendix 1 (the ethical and philosophical basis of health economics).

If we set the goal as maximising health, then the question is which sectors or kinds of intervention can deliver greatest health improvement at least cost, and in a way which meets society's understanding of fairness.

Within the health care sector, we need to ask the same question, but also to consider the other benefits of health care. Better health may be a significant motivation for providing health services, but there are other values too, such as reassurance and increasing social cohesion. The distribution of gains may often matter to members of the public more than the absolute amount of gains (see sections on equity later in this chapter and Appendix 1). Knowing that health care will be available in case of catastrophic illness may be considered more important than getting maximum health gain from money spent. The value of different criteria for judging the health sector as a whole also has to be assessed (for example, to what extent are we prepared to trade off improved quality against increased cost?).

Similarly, at the level of evaluating a single health care intervention, we need to consider not only health outcome gains but also the relief of pain, reduction of anxiety, reassurance to relatives and the impact of the process itself (was it empowering and informing? Or did the patient feel embarrassed, undignified, etc?).

For health economists it is often a useful simplification to think that the overriding goal is the improvement in health for the population as a whole. Ways of measuring that goal and the implications of different strategies for achieving it then occupy most of our time. However, it is important in each particular context to discuss and agree on what the goal is, and to reflect as far as possible the variety of impacts that each intervention is likely to have (both positive and negative) (see Table 1.1).

Table 1.1 Setting objectives: different levels

Level of objective	Example	Important considerations
General	Maximising social welfare	1. Assume we can aggregate individual welfares 2. How to measure value of, e.g., health vs nutrition, secure employment or leisure time
Specifying a particular basic good	Maximising health	1. How is this achieved? E.g., value of increasing female literacy vs disease control measures? 2. These interventions will have a wider impact, too, which needs to be assessed (e.g., reduction in fear)

Sector specific	Maximising health gain from health care activities within given budget	1. This will involve targeting between different disease groups OR by region OR by level or type of services.
		2. In doing so, it is important to agree on the relative importance of basic criteria such as:
		  – cost control
		  – efficiency
		  – quality
		  – equity

Disease group specific	Reducing illness and deaths from diarrhoeal disease	What is the right mix of strategies, e.g., between promoting ORS (oral rehydration solution) and improving sanitation?
Strategy specific	Increasing awareness and correct use of ORS by mothers of children with diarrhoeal diseases	Improving implementation of a given strategy, e.g., by increasing the role of community workers in this aspect of health promotion, versus clinic-based contact.

Equity

We will be referring to equity in a number of places as an important goal. It is also one of the most important criteria for judging the success of policies in the health sector. But what does it mean and how can it be applied? This section looks at this question.

At its most basic, equity implies some notion of 'fairness'. Fairness is integral to our perspective on the world, as human beings are sociable animals and judge things in relative terms: we only know what we have by looking at what our neighbour has. This influences our judgement of our position in the social hierarchy, our expectations and ultimately, our happiness. Fairness, however defined, is therefore fundamental, and is particularly so when applied to health, which is itself basic to our well-being.

There are however many possible interpretations of equity.

1 *Equal resources/use of services.* It could be argued, for example, that everyone should receive the same services or have the same resources spent on them. This would make little sense though, from an efficiency point of view, as health needs differ widely.
2 *Equal health.* Alternatively, does everyone have a right to equal health? That is ambitious and possibly misguided. People have very different health endowments and some look after themselves less well than others. If I want to drink myself to an early death, is it the duty of the state to pour resources into preserving me?
3 *Fair innings.* Another possible interpretation of this version is the 'fair innings' argument, that we might set a target age which people are in some way entitled to reach. Health activities would then be focused on enabling as many as possible to reach that age. The implication of this, however, is that people whose genetic inheritance and/or behaviour predisposes them to early death or disability would receive a disproportionate share of health resources, while people beyond the target age would be neglected, however cost-effective a treatment for them. It could be argued that this is neither fair nor efficient.
4 *Equal access/utilisation according to need.* This can be interpreted narrowly, as in equal geographic proximity to health facilities, or more broadly to include quality of services and their affordability. If the broader approach is taken, differential fees or some income redistribution would be needed to ensure that the real costs of using services is evened out between income groups. If equal utilisation is the goal, then that would also imply dis-

mantling cultural barriers which prevent certain groups (sexual, ethnic, religious, etc.) from making full use of available services.
Equal treatment for equal needs is the ethical basis for doctors' clinical work. It follows the principle of *'horizontal equity'* that people with the same problems be treated in the same way. This is important, but it does not illuminate decisions about *vertical equity*, or how to treat unlikes. The most difficult issue is how to prioritise between groups with different health problems (e.g., which is more important, reducing maternal mortality or dealing with mental health problems?)

5 *Treatment according to capacity to benefit.* This goes beyond needs to the question of whether someone is likely to benefit from treatment. It will depend both on the availability of effective technologies and the characteristics of the patient which make successful treatment likely or unlikely. This is a definition favoured by economists as it links fairness with effectiveness and maximises health gain. The assumption is that money would be spent on those with the greatest marginal capacity to benefit, moving down the scale until all health gains are exhausted or funds run out.

This provides a technical rule of thumb which avoids delicate decisions between social and disease groups. However, in practice we are unlikely to be able to measure marginal capacity to benefit, and will have to exercise judgement in operating this rule. Moreover, this approach could appear harsh, if people who have less capacity to benefit are excluded from treatment. For example, if someone is a smoker and less likely to benefit from an operation, should they be denied it? Or should we invest in stopping them smoking thus increasing their capacity to benefit?

These are some of the definitions of equity which have been proposed. The first three are arguably too egalitarian, not taking account of the differing needs and behaviour of different people. Equal access according to need probably accords most closely with the common interpretation of equity. However, it provides little guidance on how to set priorities between groups with different needs. The last definition is appealing in a theoretical sense, but may be hard to use in practice.

Does it matter which one we use? Different societies will have different priorities, but a clear consensus is needed if equity goals are to be realised. It is also helpful to clarify whether achieving equity is going to cost you more money, and if so, how much you are able and prepared to spend.

It may be, for example, that a mountainous region with low population density lacks health facilities. The government's priority is to extend infrastructure into that area in order to reduce health inequalities. The capital investments will be great and the benefits relatively low, because of low population density. Greater health needs could be met at lower cost in the lowlands by investing in cost-effective health programmes. However, the government takes a legitimate decision on equity grounds to go ahead.

More commonly, though, equity and efficiency can go hand in hand. Some of the most cost-effective interventions (such as promoting the use of oral rehydration solution for diarrhoea) benefit the less well off more than the wealthy. The common pattern of spending a large proportion of the health budget on tertiary care in the capital city is neither efficient (in an allocative sense) nor equitable. There does not have to be a trade-off between equity and efficiency; we should be concerned with both.

See Box 1.2 for common indicators of inequity in practice.

Mrs Foresight, a Ministry of Health planner in Ebul, has been asked to develop a plan to provide health insurance for civil servants. This is intended to provide a perk to induce more of them to stay in their jobs, rather than leaving for the growing private sector. It is also being presented as a way of alleviating the burden on the public health service. What concerns, if any, might she have about the equity of this proposed arrangement?

If health insurance for civil servants is to be funded out of general taxation, the first question to consider is: who pays the taxes? Are they progressive (i.e., the rich pay more as a proportion of their income than the poor) or regressive (i.e., the poor pay more than the rich as a proportion of income)? Secondly, what is the position of the beneficiaries of this scheme (the civil servants) relative to the rest of society? If taxes are regressive and civil servants well off relative to the rest of society, then the scheme will constitute a transfer of resources from the poor to the rich, generating increased inequity.

The second issue is how the money will be spent. Will it be used to stimulate small businesses at home, or are the funds likely to be used to purchase private treatment abroad? Are the knock-on economic effects progressive or regressive?

There is also a very important question about the knock-on effect of such a scheme on public health services. It is quite likely that if an influential group of people stops using them, they will lose political profile and, ultimately, funding. This could leave

Box 1.2   Equity checklist

How do we identify equity concerns in practice?

Resources

- The funding base: is it progressive (higher relative burden on richer households) or regressive (higher on poorer households)?
- What proportion of household disposable income (after tax) is being spent on health?
- Is there evidence of inability to pay for fees, drugs, etc. (e.g., borrowing; non-use of services; alternative strategies, such as self prescription or use of traditional medicine)?
- What is the balance of public funding between primary and secondary/tertiary care?
- What is the balance between private and public funding of health care in general?
- Is there evidence of differential use of services by different income groups, adjusted for need?
- Is the allocation of resources between regions carried out according to need?
- Are exemption mechanisms for fees/drugs or differential charges being targeted effectively at those in most need?

Infrastructure

- Are services evenly distributed in different parts of the country, or according to need?
- Is the quality of services even between different areas?
- Are supplies, drugs, manpower, etc. equally available?

Health status

- Are there significant variations in health indicators between income groups, the sexes, ethnic minorities or other significant groups?

the bulk of the population with access to an even more under-funded and poor quality service.

Finally, equity here could be considered in terms of health status. What is the evidence of the health needs of civil servants versus the rest of the population? If their health status is better than average, then the case for transferring resources to them will be weak; it would be likely to result in increased rather than decreased health disparities.

In this case, Mrs Foresight's concerns about equity may more than outweigh the job perk argument (which might not have been effective anyway, in terms of retaining staff).

Summary

This introductory chapter has covered three main areas:

• what is health economics (and hence this book) about?
• how can it serve general public or health sector goals?
• what are the common criteria which are used for judging success and failure in this field?

Health economics covers a range of topics, from how to judge the performance of your health sector, to raising finance for it, evaluating different health care interventions, informing priority setting and the allocation of resources, and improving the performance of service providers. All of these will be covered in this book.

Health economics provides some tools of analysis to inform decision makers, but it can only do so usefully if there is some agreement on what the overall social goals are. Economists often make simplifying assumptions, such as that the goal is to maximise health gain, but these should be tested against reality by finding out where public preferences lie. Different levels of objective can then be established, and progress monitored against them.

A number of criteria are used here to test the effects of policies:

• Technical efficiency. Activities use the minimum of resources
• Allocative efficiency. Resources are put to their best possible use (allocated to more productive uses before less productive ones)
• Equity. This can be defined in a number of ways, embodying different notions of fairness. There is no one 'right' definition, but any approach should be clear, command support and be thought through in its implications
• Quality. To be considered both in relation to the process of care (politeness of staff, convenience of service, etc.) and its outcomes (effectiveness of treatments, etc.)

References and further reading

Culyer, A. and Wagstaff, A. (1993). Equity and equality in health and health care, *Journal of Health Economics*, 12.
Lee, K. and Mills, M. (1982). Developing countries, health and health economics, in K. Lee and M. Mills, (eds), *The Economics of Health in Developing Countries*. Oxford: Oxford University Press.
Le Grand, J., Propper, C. and Robinson, R. (1992). Social objectives, allocation of resources, in *The Economics of Social Problems*. Basingstoke: Macmillan.
Williams, A. (1987). A cheerful face of the dismal science? In A. Williams, (ed.) *Health and Economics*. Basingstoke: Macmillan.
World Health Forum, (1997), volume 8, Round table on equity.

2

Health and development: the broad issues

Sophie Witter

Introduction

This chapter looks at some broad questions about the nature of growth, the nature of health, and how the two interact. This is a very complicated area, but we try to give it a short and simple treatment. On a day-to-day level, health economists rarely deal with such 'big' questions. However, it is helpful to be aware of the general conclusions that have been drawn by a number of cross-country and historical studies. We will structure this short chapter around the three questions in the following scenario.

The Ministry of Health of Ebul finds its budget under attack from the Ministry of Finance, which is seeking to make cuts to re-allocate to other sectors. Mr Datum, a health economist, is sent three testing questions to answer. The answers will go to the Council of Ministers to help with their decision making.

1 What is the relationship between health and growth: why should we invest in health?
2 Aren't there better ways of producing good health than investing in health care?
3 What is the relationship between spending on health and good health itself?

Health and growth

Let us start with some definitions. What is health? The broadest and most commonly used definition is the World Health Organization (WHO) one: 'Health is a state of complete physical, mental and social well-being and not merely the absence of disease or infirmity' (WHO, 1993). This positive conception of health has fairly radical implications. 'Complete social well-being' suggests housing, jobs, civil rights – almost anything. It is clearly a normative statement, rather than one which we would expect to see implemented in the short term.

Growth is interpreted in more varying ways. For a mainstream economist, growth means an increase in the goods and services produced by a society, which can be measured in various ways. The most commonly cited indicators are gross domestic product (GDP) and gross national product (GNP). GDP is the value of all the goods and services produced in a country, plus its exports and minus its imports. GNP is similar, but includes rents from factors owned abroad (such as repatriated profits from overseas factories), minus the equivalent payments to foreigners for factors which they own in the home country.

These indicators are relatively easy to use, but do not in themselves tell us about welfare in that society. For example, GDP may increase, but if it accompanied by an increase in inequality of income distribution, the society may be less 'well off' in a broader sense. This and other criticisms of these narrow indicators has motivated the search for an index of 'development', which incorporates features such as income distribution; levels of education and skills; health status measurements; gender imbalances; and political representation. The Human Development Report, produced annually by United Nations Development Programme is a good example of a broader index. Similarly, environmentalists have put together indexes which value natural resources and reflect the extent to which these are being maintained or degraded.

If an economy is growing, in the narrow economic definition of growth, what impact is that likely to have on health (viewed here in narrow terms too, for simplicity)? In general, we would expect that economic growth will contribute to better health and that better health will contribute to economic growth – i.e., that there is positive relationship between them.

In terms of the impact of the economy on health, the negative effects are well documented. Poverty at the household level often leads to poor diet, poor housing and insanitary conditions. This in turn encourages the spread of diseases (particularly infectious ones). Poverty can also induce individual or group attitudes which reduce life expectancy. If you have a high discount rate (i.e., you care about present needs much more than future ones – see Chapter 7), then giving up smoking may not be an attractive option. Economic stagnation or decline also reduces the resources available to governments to invest in public health programmes or poverty mitigation.

However, economic growth on its own does not guarantee improvements in health status development. How growth takes place, and how the benefits of growth are distributed and reinvested is crucial, too. In a 38-country study looking at the relationship between absolute poverty and child mortality rates, it was found that under-five mortality for the non-poor was an average of 41 per 1,000, while for the poor (i.e., under $1 per capita per day, adjusted for purchasing power parity) it was 215 (Jamison, 1998). How is public spending used? And within households, who controls the resources and what are their priorities?

There is also one group of diseases which increase as 'development' progresses: diseases of affluence, such as cancer, heart disease, stress-related problems and depression. These are encouraged by a number of facets of modernity, such as work patterns, social fragmentation, obesity and increased consumption of drugs, such as cigarettes and alcohol. Industrial pollution is also a concern, particularly in transitional economies, which may rely on heavy industries, with low standards of environmental protection.

Many developing countries are currently suffering a 'double burden of disease', with continuing high rates of 'old' diseases, such as malaria and tuberculosis, and a growth in the 'new' diseases such as cancer and heart problems. The projected burden of ill health in the developing world by the year 2020 reveals this pattern, with some diseases of affluence rising up the list, but not totally displacing the current major killers, such as respiratory infections, diarrhoeal diseases and tuberculosis (see Table 2.1).

What of the impact of improved health on the economy? We would expect a healthier population to be more productive, both in terms of attendance (i.e., being well enough to work) and skill levels (because ill-health affects educational achievement negatively). With longer life expectancies, individuals' time preference should also decrease and savings and investment increase.

The effect on population structure is more complicated. Good health prolongs life. Where this is productive working life, the economic effects should be positive. Where it is old age, it increases the ratio of dependants to working population and creates a financial burden (unless outweighed by increased personal savings, as mentioned earlier).

The impact on population size is even harder to predict. Reductions in infant mortality rates would be expected to reduce

Table 2.1   Projected burden of ill health in the developing world

Rank in 2020	Cause of ill health	Rank in 1990
1	Depression	4
2	Road traffic accidents	11
3	Ischaemic heart disease	8
4	Chronic obstructive pulmonary disease	12
5	Cerebrovascular disease	10
6	Tuberculosis	5
7	Lower respiratory infections	1
8	War	16
9	Diarrhoeal diseases	2
10	HIV/AIDS	–

Source: Murray and Lopez, 1996.

fertility after a period, on the assumption that families aim for a target number of surviving children. This phenomenon, known as *demographic transition*, has also been connected historically with economic development, changing employment patterns and advances in education, though the relative impact and sequencing of these various factors is still debated. The whole question of whether a large population size is an economic asset or liability, and what is a sustainable rate of population growth, is both politically and economically contentious.

It is important, though, to be clear about the fundamental philosophical question: does the population exist to serve some higher ends (such as the advancement of the wealth of the state) or are they the goal in themselves? Economics takes the view that maximising the aggregate welfare of individuals is the goal. To justify health in terms of production is to ignore the fact that health is fundamental to individual well-being in many ways and is therefore independently valid.

Figure 2.1 demonstrates that there is a broad correlation between life expectancy and GNP per head, although there are also outliers, which suggest that there is scope for influencing the relationship. Why, for example, is Vietnam's life expectancy so much higher than that of Guinea-Bissau, which has roughly the same GNP per capita? The same holds true if we use infant mortality rates or under five mortality rates as an indicator for health. There is a broadly positive relationship, but with certain notice-

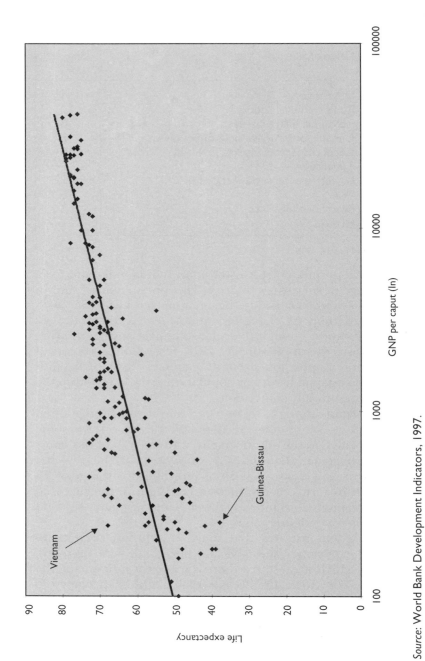

Source: World Bank Development Indicators, 1997.

Fig. 2.1 Relationship between income and life expectancy

able outliers. Recent evidence from transitional economies supports this relationship, too. In transitional economies where income levels have improved (such as China) there generally has been an improvement in health status; in contrast, economic decline in countries like Russia have been accompanied by worsening health indicators.

There is also strong evidence that health is negatively related to the proportion of a population in absolute poverty (Carrin and Politi, 1996). This reinforces the point that wealth distribution, as well as wealth creation, is important to social welfare (see the discussion of equity in Chapter 1).

Health care and health

If health is an important goal in itself, then how is it best achieved? As Figure 2.2 demonstrates, formal health sector activities are only one of a host of areas influencing health. Some, such as education and rural development spending, are within the power of government to alter. Others, such as savings or fertility rates, are partly influenceable and partly independent of government. Others again, such as individual genetic inheritance or the social environment, both of which can be crucial to health, are beyond its control almost altogether.

Because these linkages are so complicated, it is not possible to make a sensible general statement about which investment is more productive of health. In the West, historically, economic and social developments are attributed with producing more health gains than specific medical interventions, like vaccination. However, this may be partly because many medical technologies followed rather than predated industrial and economic changes. In developing countries, medical progress has often preceded socio-economic change, and is therefore responsible for more of the health gains which have been achieved (Over, 1991).

The difficulty of measuring the impact on health of alternative strategies should not distract health economists from their goal, which is improved health. The focus on health services and indicators of activity is so strong that we often miss opportunities for intersectoral work. We need reminding that health services are not a goal in themselves – just a means to improved health. Where possible, we should collect and compare information about outcomes: information about health gain, either as a result of health care activities or some other programme or policy.

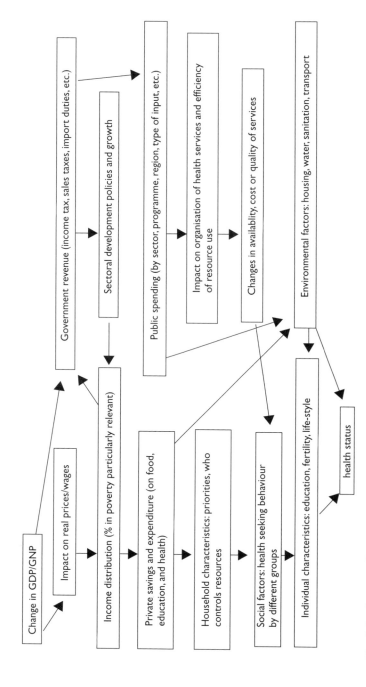

Fig. 2.2 Factors influencing health: an example starting with a macroeconomic change

Health expenditure and health

Within the health sector, can we assume that more spending will produce more health? The answer has to be: it depends on how it is spent. In Figure 2.3, after controlling for their general level of development, countries fall into four categories: those that are spending more than expected on health and achieving higher levels of health; those that are spending more and achieving less than expected; those that are spending less and gaining more; and those that are spending less and achieving less. There is no clear pattern – no necessary link, in other words, between spending more on your health sector and having better health as a nation.

The US is a good example: it spends more than any other country on health, yet has worse health indicators than most other OECD (Organisation for Economic Co-operation and Development) countries. One explanation is that its system of private health insurance has encouraged cost escalation, while leaving a large minority uncovered. There are other factors too, related to other determinants of health. At the other end of the spectrum, Sri Lanka managed for many years to maintain better social development indicators than expected for its level of national income by pursuing policies to promote health, education and fairer income distribution (i.e., 'human capital development', to use the economic jargon). Maintaining this investment over the long term, in the absence of economic growth, is very difficult however.

While there may be no clear relationship between expenditure and effectiveness, there is evidence that as a country's income levels rise, its share of expenditure on health will increase too. Average expenditure on health in developing countries was 4.7 per cent of GDP in 1993; by contrast, OECD countries were spending double that at 9.2 per cent of their anyway much larger economies (WDR, 1993). There is also a tendency for the proportion of health care funded out of public sources to rise as income levels rise. This is significant not only in terms of equity and access to services, but also because public finance is more likely than private to pay for valuable public health interventions (Musgrove, 1996).

Health care in aggregate is what economists call a luxury good (see Chapter 3 for further explanation of this term): the higher your level of income, the more you want to invest in your health. (Note though that patterns of health care will change with changing income levels, and that some elements may be inferior.) This

22

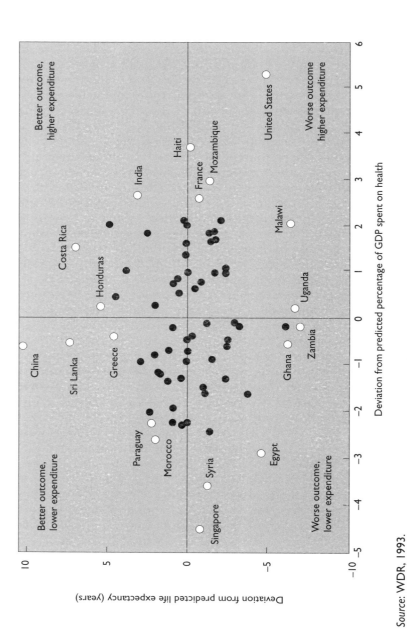

Source: WDR, 1993.

Fig. 2.3 Life expectancies and health expenditures in selected countries; deviations from estimates based on GDP and schooling

is partly because rising income and education levels lead to increased awareness of health needs; and partly because of cost escalation in health systems where costs are borne largely by third parties (such as insurance companies or governments), rather than individual users.

This makes it all the more important to ensure that health systems are organised to produce maximum benefit for the money invested. For while health costs and health expenditure tend to rise with income, the marginal product of health spending is likely to decline. For every additional dollar spent on health per capita in low income countries there is a decrease of 1 death per 1,000 live births, or a reduction of 1.25 in years of life lost. By contrast in high income countries no improvement can be expected as a result of the same additional expenditure (Shmueli, 1995). This is largely because the main causes of premature death in richer countries are accidents and non-communicable diseases, for which prevention and cure are difficult. At higher levels of income, health expenditure is likely to impact more on quality of life indicators (such as increased mobility in old age, or reduced suffering), rather than mortality.

Summary

This is a complex area, to which this chapter aims to give a simple introduction. Let us return to the three original questions.

1 There should be a positive relationship generally between economic development and health, though the pattern of development and distribution of its benefits will matter as much as growth itself. Ill-health is strongly linked to household poverty, so that growth which favours the poor will be the most effective in improving health.
2 There are many channels for investing in health. Which one is most cost-effective in producing better health will depend on the context.
3 Spending on health care is not inherently a good thing, although it may be regarded as such in countries where absolute levels of expenditure are too low. What is important is the productivity of health expenditure. Typically this will be higher in poorer areas than in rich, and will be higher for public expenditure than for private.

Many developing countries face challenges on all three levels: first, to move along the life expectancy/GDP curve (Figure 2.1) through socio-economic development; secondly, to shift that curve to the left by investing in effective health technologies; and, finally, to 'join' the curve (for low performers) by improving the organisation of and access to services (Jamison, 1998). These themes will be developed in this book.

Questions for discussion

1 Where does your country fall in terms of Figure 2.3?
2 Can you think what the main causes of over- or under-achievement in health might be? Think of issues relating to:

- income levels or distribution
- public investment and safety nets
- social or cultural features
- issues relating to the financing and organisation of health services?

References and further reading

Berman, P. (1995). Health sector reform: making health development sustainable, *Health Policy*, 32, 13–28.

Carrin, G. And Politi, C. (1996). Exploring the health impact of economic growth, poverty reduction and public health expenditure. Technical Paper 18. Geneva: WHO.

Gertler, P. and Van der Gaag, J. (1990). The willingness to pay for medical care. Ch. 2 in *Health, Health Care and Development.* Washington, DC: World Bank.

Jamison, D. (1998). Poverty, inequality and health. Presentation to DFID Health and Population Day, 13 October 1998.

Murray, C. and Lopez, A. (1996). *The Global Burden of Disease.* Cambridge, MA: Harvard University Press for WHO and World Bank.

Musgrove, P. (1996). Public and private roles in health: theory and financing patterns. Washington: World Bank Discussion Paper 339.

Over, M. (1991). The health sector in a developing economy, from *Economics for Health Sector Analysis: Concepts and Cases.* Washington, DC: EDI/World Bank.

Shmueli, A. (1995). Cost effective outlays for better health outcomes, *World Health Forum*, 16, 287–92.

United Nations Development Programme. Human Development Report (published annually). New York: UNDP.

WDR (World Development Report) (1993). *Investing in Health.* Washington, DC: World Bank.

World Health Organisation (1993). *Macroeconomic Environment and Health, with Case Studies for Countries in Greatest Need.* Geneva: WHO.

3

Economics and health care markets

Sophie Witter

Introduction

One of the important roles of a health economist is to analyse how health care markets work. We need to be able to answer questions such as: what do people value, in terms of health care? How much are they prepared to pay (or sacrifice, in terms of time, for example) in order to get it? How do suppliers behave? How much competition do they face? The answers to these and other questions will determine the pattern of care which is provided in our area.

This chapter introduces the way that economists analyse markets, explains key economic terms which health economists should be familiar with, and discusses some peculiar aspects of health markets which call for outside intervention. It will cover the following questions:

- Demand: what is it? What do consumers take into account when seeking health services?
- Supply: what influences the sellers of health care (doctors, clinics, pharmacies, etc.)?
- How do supply and demand adjust to changes in price, income and other important factors?
- What is the effect of intervening in markets?
- What is required for markets to work perfectly?
- Do health markets meet those conditions?
- What can be done to deal with market failure in health?

Markets and health

Demand

> *Lula lives in a small village, Gombi, in Rungara Province of Ebul country. There is a government hospital in the district capital at Gamlan, some 20 miles away from her village. The service there is free, but staff are often not at their posts and so waiting times can be long. When a family member falls sick, Lula sometimes buys medicines from the drugs sellers who come through the village. Recently a retired doctor has set up a private clinic in the village. His fees are high, but he seems to be attracting quite a lot of patients. Lula's daughter develops a fever. Where should her mother take her for diagnosis and treatment?*

What we have described here is a market in health care. There are several suppliers: the government post; the drugs sellers; the private clinic. Demand comes from sick people who decide which services to buy. Their decision will be influenced by a number of factors. First, *availability:* does that supplier offer the relevant service? Secondly, *price:* how much does it cost? Other things being equal, buyers tend to prefer the least expensive service or product, which leaves them with more money to spend on other things.

But if price is so important, why is the private clinic attracting patients in Lula's village? The answer is that we have to look not just at the fees charged, but all costs incurred by the patient. The government clinic may not charge fees, but Lula would have to pay to make the journey there, would have to wait for a number of hours, and might well be expected to give a present to the staff there in order to ensure that her daughter got the best treatment. How do these compare, as a total package, with the fees charged by the local doctor, who sees patients promptly and without the need to travel, or with the local drug sellers, who charge a modest amount for a swift and concrete treatment?

Then there is the question of *quality* to consider. If the quality of a 'good' or service is thought to be better, then a buyer may be prepared to pay a higher price for it. But judging quality is not always straightforward, especially in health markets.

> *Lula takes her daughter to see the assistant doctor in Gamlan health post. She wants a prescription for a drug which will make the fever go away. The assistant doctor, however, says that it is just a passing fever. He*

recommends rest and plenty to drink. Dissatisfied, Lula goes to the market in Gamlan and buys some pills recommended by the drug seller. The next time I need treatment, she thinks, I will visit that private doctor in the village. He is kindly and listens more to what patients want.

Health economists would distinguish here between what Lula and her daughter *need*, what they *want*, and what they *demand*. Need is what is objectively best suited to their medical condition. This is commonly judged by a doctor, but doctors are only as good at judging need as their training, equipment and abilities allow, and they may be influenced by factors other than need, such as fee schedules or the views of their patients. Wants are what the patient believes to be best for them – what they would like (in this case, a fast-acting drug). This may or may not be the same as what they need. Finally, what they demand is what they actually purchase. This is influenced by medical opinion, commonly, but also by other factors, such as whether they can afford the recommended treatment or whether they are convinced by the advice offered. Again, demand may or may not overlap with need (see Figure 3.1).

The distinction is important, if our aim is to meet people's health needs as far as possible. To do so, we need to improve the ability of medical staff to recognise and respond to actual needs (through training, support, payment systems, etc.). Equally, we need to influence wants and demand so that they overlap as much as possible with needs (by public education about treatments,

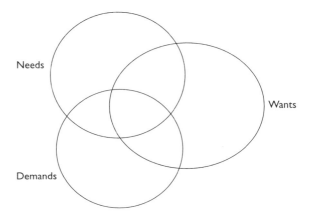

Fig. 3.1   Needs, wants and demand

for example, or ensuring that appropriate treatments are affordable).

Lula's daughter is still feverish a few days later. Lula decides this time to consult the local private clinic. The doctor there recommends an antibiotic and a return visit to see him in a few days. It is expensive, but Lula trusts his judgement and pays for the course of treatment.

Is she right? It is hard to say. If Lula were buying bread in the market, she would know exactly what she should do. Bread is something which she buys daily and she is as good a judge of its qualities as anyone else. She would be an *informed consumer*, able to make rational choices about what is best for her in any given situation. In health care there are many problems relating to information. First, it is a matter of judgement what is wrong with her daughter. Even the doctor cannot be sure and he or she has had years of specialist training and practical experience. Secondly, it is a matter of judgement which treatment will be most effective. Even after the event, we cannot reliably judge success. If the taking of some treatment is followed by a cure, patients will often assume that it was the treatment which cured them, when in fact they might well have recovered anyway. The fact that they know so much less about their condition than the doctor is known as *information asymmetry.*

Instead of making up her own mind and requesting a specific treatment (as in the bread market), Lula is relying on her supplier to advise her on how best to meet her needs. This feature of *supplier as agent* is very important. It means that unless the supplier is informed about the tastes of the customer and represents their interests, the patient's welfare will suffer (or be less than *optimal:* a word which economists use to describe the best possible outcome in a given situation).

It is also hard for Lula to hold her doctor to account for poor performance (e.g., by not going back to him). Lula can probably judge which doctor is most prompt and courteous, for example, but she may not know which diagnosis is more accurate. Some issues of quality are easier to judge than others, and the ones which are hardest to judge (outcomes) are arguably the most important. This is why the medical profession is usually regulated: an independent body with access to more information than patients has the job of ensuring that doctors do not abuse their position and provide a good service. Self-regulation by the medical profession also plays an important role (see Chapter 10 for further discussion of this issue).

Supply

> *Dr Gonk is setting up his clinic in Gombi village. He has taken out a loan to make his house suitable and to purchase some equipment. The repayment costs come to 500 bondis (the local currency) per month. On top of this he has to pay his assistant (300 bondis per month) and cover his costs of supplies, electricity etc. (200 bondis per month). If he charges a flat rate of 5 bondis per consultation and sees an average of 10 patients per day, how much profit will he make (assuming he works a 6-day week)? How could he increase his profit?*

In this example, Dr Gonk will spend 500 + 300 + 200 = 1,000 bondis; he will be paid 10 × 5 × 6 × 4 = 1,200 bondis. He will therefore make a profit of 200 bondis per month, which is in effect his wages (the same rate as his assistant). If he wants to increase his profits, he can adopt one of three strategies:

- Cutting costs (producing the same amount, but more efficiently);
- Increasing productivity (using same inputs to produce more output);
- Increasing his charges.

An example of the first strategy would be, for example, if he decided that it would be cheaper to buy and run a computer than to hire an assistant. This would be what economists call *substitution of factors of production*, when one input becomes relatively cheaper than another, resulting in changed production methods. An example of the second strategy would be if Dr Gonk tried to see more patients per day. Both of these strategies should increase profits in the short run (through decreased costs in the first case; increased revenue in the second), but in the longer term would probably only be effective if the quality of service was not damaged by the changes. As for increasing charges, this would only be possible if Dr Gonk was the only supplier of that type of service in the area (or if he was able to collude with competitors to fix prices).

In a *competitive market*, any shift from the market price by one supplier would lead to loss of all customers. If however he can in some way distinguish his product (its effectiveness, quality or convenience), then he may be able to charge more and still retain his market share. In health care, products have a tendency to be *non-homogenous*. A visit to the government health centre, for example, will not be exactly the same as a visit to Dr Gonk, either in manner or even diagnosis and treatment. This allows Dr Gonk to act in some ways as a monopolist (or only seller) in his particular area. As his product is in competition with similar but different products, this is known by economists as *monopolistic competition*.

Factors influencing demand

Dr Gonk decides to experiment with varying his charges. For the first month, he charges his patients 10 bondi per consultation. 180 patients visit him. Next he charges 15 bondi. 100 patients visit him. Then he drops to 5 bondi, which results in 240 consultations. Finally, he tries charging 3 bondi, and finds himself overwhelmed with 400 patients. Assuming that his costs are the same each month, which fee structure produces the highest revenue for him? Why?

Revenue is calculated as fee times number of consultations. His revenue will therefore be as follows:

3 bondi × 400 = 1,200
5 bondi × 240 = 1,200
10 bondi × 180 = 1,800
15 bondi × 100 = 1,500

If he wants to maximise his profits, he will increase his fees to 10 bondi, but not to 15. If he goes beyond that, the fall in the number of customers will more than offset the increase in fees. This response is known as *price elasticity of demand*. Price elasticity measures by how much demand drops when price increases. (It is usually negative but is generally reported as an absolute value.) Taking the example we have already used, what is the price elasticity of demand at different levels?

$$e = \frac{\text{change in quantity}}{\text{change in price}} \times \frac{\text{original price}}{\text{original quantity}}$$

Price elasticity will be affected by a number of issues. First, is there an alternative good which the customer can buy (a substitute) which is of a similar quality? Without substitutes, price elasticity can be expected to be low as buyers have few options to choose from. Another issue is the nature of the good itself: how essential is it? If it is a luxury, then price elasticity will be high (greater than 1): as prices increase, demand drops dramatically as the good is not essential. If, however, it is a necessity, then price elasticity is likely to be low (less than 1): consumers continue to need and buy it, even as prices rise.

Based on the elasticities we have already calculated, what type of good is a consultation with Dr Gonk? Is this likely to be typical of health care? What are the implications of that?

The response of customers to Dr Gonk's price experiments show the fall in quantity demanded of his product as its price increases. This is known as a demand curve by economists. If the information is available, it can be plotted (see Figure 3.2).

Imagine now that oil is discovered near Gombi, and almost overnight the people of the village become richer as the oil company creates jobs and pours resources into the area (fanciful, perhaps, but we can be optimistic). What would you expect might happen to the demand curve for Dr Gonk's consultations? How would he adjust his price?

Economists try to isolate the effect of different variables on the demand for or supply of a product, although in practice it is not easy to measure their effect, especially when they all occur at once. In this case we might commonly see a shift to the right of the demand curve as income levels rise. This is because people in the area can afford to demand more of the good at the same given price. This is likely to lead to an increase in both price and

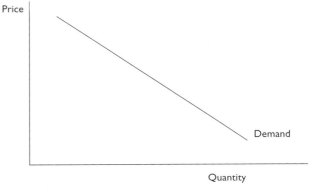

Fig. 3.2   Demand curve

quantity consumed. However, that result will depend on the nature of the good. If the good is a *superior* good, then demand will increase more than proportionately to an increase in income (i.e., income elasticity of demand greater than 1). These are goods which poor people cannot afford. Common examples might be meat or imported foodstuffs. As the income level of a community rises, we would expect to see a disproportionate increase in demand for such goods, whereas *inferior* goods (such as the food that poor people rely on – maybe maize or rice) would suffer a more than proportionate drop in demand. Goods which respond proportionately (i.e., 1 per cent increase in income leads to an increase between 0 and 1 per cent in quantity demanded) are termed *normal* goods.

Note that these categories will vary from place to place: what is a superior good in one place may be normal or inferior elsewhere, depending on the level of development and the expectations of each society. (For example, a car which is a luxury in a poor country may be a necessity in countries like the USA.)

Imagine now that a cheaper rival clinic set up in the village. How would demand for Dr Gonk's services respond? What would be the expected effect if Dr Gonk responded by reducing the drugs prices at his clinic pharmacy?

Demand curves respond not just to changes in income, but to a host of other factors. In the first instance, a *substitute* good has become available at a cheaper price, and this should lead to a leftward shift in the demand for Dr Gonk's services (or a total collapse, if the substitute is identical). A substitute is something which fulfils the same need and can be consumed instead of a given product. By contrast, consultations and prescriptions tend to go together and are therefore *complementary* goods: they are consumed as a package and so a fall in the price of drugs is equivalent to a fall in the price of Dr Gonk's consultation and should stimulate demand for his services.

Supply, demand and equilibrium

Just as demand curves tend to be downward sloping (the lower the price, the higher the quantity demanded), so supply curves tend to slope upwards, as increased prices tempt more suppliers into the market. They too can shift. For example, if the cost of factors of production, such as labour, increase, then the supply curve should shift to the left (other things being equal). Alternatively, if a technological innovation means that the product can be produced more cheaply, then the supply curve should shift to the right.

Where the supply and demand curves meet is known by economists as *equilibrium*. In an unregulated market, this shows the quantity of good which will be sold and the price at which it will be sold. This is not static, however, and will shift over time as supply and demand curves adjust to changing conditions (see Figure 3.3). (Microeconomics is the study of how such markets for specific goods or groups of goods behave.)

> *Let us imagine that the demand and supply curves for paracetamol are represented in Figure 3.3. Mrs Fang, a village drug seller, persuades all of the local drug sellers to increase the price charged for paracetamol to 60 bondis. What will happen?*

The price of 60 bondis intersects with the demand curve to produce a quantity of 75 packets. This is less than the equilibrium quantity because the price is now too high for many people. However, at this attractively high price, suppliers would like to supply 130 (the intersection of the new price and the supply curve). Consequently there will be a build-up of unsold stocks. This in turn will lead to pressure on suppliers to lower the price until it reaches the equilibrium point, at which *markets clear* (i.e., the price at which supply and demand are equal).

> *Next time Mrs Fang decides that they should cut their prices in order to stimulate business. What are the consequences of offering paracetamol at 40 bondis?*

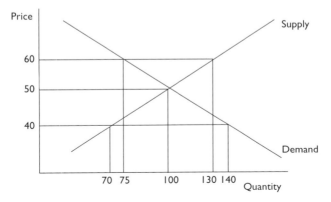

Fig. 3.3   Supply and demand curve

At 40 bondis, the drug is now relatively cheap, and so a high quantity is demanded (140: the intersection of the new price and the demand curve). However, at this price, sellers (represented by the supply curve) are only willing to supply 70 packets. There will therefore be a shortage of the drug relative to demand (a shortfall of 70 packets), which may produce some kind of rationing. For example, only the first customers of the day can buy the drug. Or only the friends of the drugs sellers can buy the drug. Commonly a black market develops. The official price may remain 40 bondis, but paracetamol may be re-sold informally at a price which reflects the higher demand for it. Once again, there will be tendency for the price to converge on 50 bondis, which is what we mean by an equilibrium price.

Not all prices adjust quickly, however. The speed of adjustment will depend on the nature of the good and the market. In labour markets, for example, there are commonly restrictions on price adjustments (such as union-negotiated pay rates, which fix wages for a given period). In this case, quantity is likely to adjust to make up for the price *rigidity*, leading either to involuntary unemployment or a glut of labour. In the longer term, prices should adjust but that depends on the market being allowed to operate flexibly. In other markets, such as agricultural production, quantity may be relatively inflexible in the short term (given the long production time of many crops). If demand drops, suppliers cannot stockpile products which may perish, and so they are obliged to sell at lower prices.

Note too that we can distinguish between the short term response of a market and the longer term. These are relative terms, reflecting how long it takes for suppliers and customers to adapt to new conditions.

Intervention and welfare loss

The government of Ebul has decided that paracetamol is a useful medicine, which should be made as widely available as possible. They have discussed three options. The first is to make it freely available, financed out of general taxes. The problem with that is the expense and the fact that government resources are already inadequate. The second is to regulate, to fix the price at the lower level of 40 bondis. The third option is to subsidise the drug. Which strategy is preferable?

The regulatory strategy would have the same effect as the reduction in drug price discussed earlier. Demand would increase.

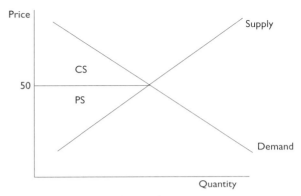

Fig. 3.4 Welfare surplus in the free market

Supply would drop. Rationing and/or black markets would develop to cope with the gap.

Economists analyse this in terms of *consumer surplus, producer surplus* and *welfare gains or losses.* The demand curve represents the amount which consumers are prepared to buy at any given price. In Figure 3.4, if the price is the market-clearing one of 50 bondis, then all of the space above that line but below the demand curve represents extra welfare which consumers have gained by obtaining the product at a lower price than they were willing to pay: consumer surplus (CS). Equally, the space below the line but above the supply curve measures the surplus which producers gain by getting a higher price that they were prepared to accept for those first units (PS).

If the price is dropped to 45 (see Figure 3.5), then the size of that area is reduced by Tb, which measures the *deadweight loss* to society. In this case, the loss falls heavily on producers, whose surplus is reduced to Psb. This should not obscure the fact that there has been an overall loss of welfare.

Let us consider the second strategy, illustrated in Figure 3.6. Let us assume that drug sellers were charging 50 bondis for paracetamol, and are being offered a subsidy. If they operate in a competitive market, this will be passed to customers in the form of a drop in price (say, to 40 bondis). Supply remains at 100 packets and producer surplus remains the same, but consumer surplus increases by the triangle Tc. Alternatively, if sellers have a monopolistic position (e.g., few of them, with a price-fixing arrangement between them), they may retain the subsidy and not reduce prices to consumers. Either way, the consumer or

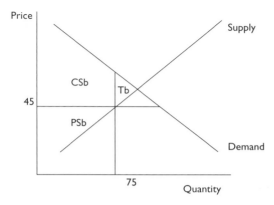

Fig. 3.5   Impact of price regulation on welfare surplus

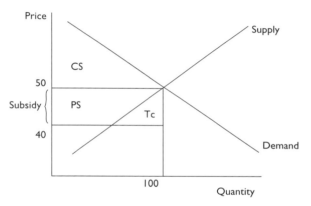

Fig. 3.6   Effect of subsidy on social welfare

producer gain has to be weighed against the social costs of funding the subsidy.

The important point is that all forms of intervention in the markets have their costs. Subsidies cost money to the taxpayer and can be captured by producers. They also distort market signals about which goods are valued by consumers (though there can be good reasons for this: see market failure later in this chapter). Regulation appears to be free, but in reality it causes welfare losses through increased costs for businesses and increased prices for consumers. There are legitimate reasons to intervene in markets, but the justification for and impact of each intervention must be examined carefully, and the least distorting approach used.

Health care and market failure

*There are a number of problems in the health sector in Ebul, including a
shortage of government funds to provide free treatment and poor
management and service delivery in the public sector. A young economist,
Mr Datum, comes up with a radical suggestion. He has learnt that a free
market in a good will produce the best possible outcome for society, so why
not apply this to health? He suggests a total privatisation programme: let
families decide how much to spend on healthcare and from whom to buy
services. Is this, in your opinion, a wise approach? What problems might
you foresee?*

The theory of *free market optimality* is based on the assumption that
a number of conditions apply. These can be grouped into four
sections, relating to:

- perfect competition
- a complete market
- consumers as rational maximisers
- equitable distribution of resources

Let us examine these conditions and see to what extent they
apply to health care markets.

Perfect competition

1 One pre-condition for a perfectly competitive market is that
there should be *free entry* into the market. This means that if
there is excess profit to be made, then new firms can start to
produce and sell that good, bringing profit down to minimum
levels. Consumers are then paying no more than is absolutely
necessary to cover the costs of production, and have more resources available to satisfy other needs.

Free entry is rarely found in health because of the information problems already discussed. If anyone can set up as a
doctor or nurse or pharmacist, or establish a hospital, then
how are patients to be protected from 'quacks' – people who
offer cures but who lack the essential training and skills?
Because of this problem, various types of registration and
licensing exist in most countries to protect the public. A side-
effect is that small local monopolies may develop, with less
pressure to provide a good service as there are few alternatives for customers.

2 It is also assumed that there are many buyers and sellers, so that none can affect prices by their behaviour: all are *price-takers*. If a firm is the only seller of a product, for example, it can choose to reduce the quantity produced and raise the price. This may well produce greater revenue for the firm, but will clearly reduce the welfare of customers. Such *monopoly* power can also be generated if a few firms act in collusion with one another to keep prices high or restrict production (as in a cartel). Some health markets are more competitive than others, in terms of the number of players. In rural areas, in particular, there may only be one supplier of a particular service in that locality, usually because of low income levels.

3 *Perfect knowledge* is another condition, meaning that suppliers have access to the knowledge about how to produce a good, and consumers know what prices are being charged for goods by each supplier and are able to choose the lowest price. As has been noted, products are rarely homogenous in health care.

4 Linked to that notion is *homogeneity of product*. To compare prices assumes that the quality of each good is the same. If this is not the case, or is hard to judge, then competition may not keep prices down.

5 *Equal costs* requires that there is a 'level playing field' between suppliers, so that the most efficient wins business. If one firm gets cheaper credit, or receives some form of government subsidy or protection, then it may be able to undercut more efficient rivals and establish a monopoly.

6 It is also assumed that *factors of production are mobile* – i.e., that land, labour and capital can be deployed flexibly to increase or decrease production levels. If, for example, staff cannot be fired or redeployed, then suppliers decisions about what to produce will be distorted and costs/prices increased.

7 Finally, there should be *constant (or decreasing) returns to scale in production*. What this means is that bigger producers should not face lower costs per unit than small producers. If they do, then there will be a tendency towards monopolies as larger producers undercut and drive smaller producers out of the market.

In secondary or hospital care there is some evidence that *economies of scale or scope* exist – i.e., that larger units or units offering a wider range of services can generate savings through pooled resources or more efficient use of staff. This may be the reason why hospitals tend to face less competition in their area. However, the economies of scale may be exhausted at a relatively low level, after which increased costs of management more than offset savings.

Existence of a complete market

Markets work best when all the costs and benefits of a product are taken into account in the setting of its price. In such a situation, the market can be said to be 'complete' because it incorporates all the relevant information about the product. This is not always the case. For example:

- sometimes when I consume a product, it damages a third party (e.g., passive smoking, when a non-smoker's health is affected by a smoker's behaviour);
- sometimes when I consume a product, it benefits someone else (e.g., getting vaccinated against an infectious disease: this not only protects me, but means that I will not transmit to others);
- sometimes when a product is produced, it damages a third party (e.g., through air pollution, which affects the surrounding area);
- sometimes when a product is produced, it benefits a third party (e.g., planting forests, which also absorb carbon dioxide and provide a shelter for animal species).

Commonly these important attributes are not reflected in the price of the product. In this case they are known as *externalities*. They can relate to consumption or production and can be positive or negative.

Let us consider the example of what would happen if treatment for tuberculosis were provided privately and paid for entirely by patients. In that case (see Figure 3.7), the quantity of treatment purchased would be 200 courses of treatment, at 150 bondis per course. This reflects the private demand curve, incorporating the value placed on treatment by individuals. What is omitted is the wider social benefit of slowing the spread of disease. If social benefit could be measured and plotted, the real demand curve would be further to the right. In this situation, a 'free market' is producing less of tuberculosis treatment than is socially optimal.

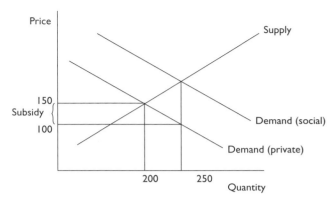

Fig. 3.7   Private and social benefit with a positive externality

One solution might be to provide a subsidy (such as free drugs for tuberculosis treatment), which would increase demand to 250 courses, which happens to coincide with the socially optimal equilibrium level – not that real life policies are quite so neat. The equivalent for a negative externality would be a tax (for example, on alcohol). Another common approach is regulation – e.g., limiting the amount of effluents released into rivers or prohibiting the use of certain substances.

Externalities may also arise where people are affected by the suffering of others (a *caring externality*). One justification for the public financing of health care is that we feel upset or sad to see sick people, who cannot afford treatment, suffering and dying in our midst. Policy makers may also be affected by the positive effects of good health on productivity. Health care may be seen as a *merit good* – one which we would like people to consume more of than they might do, if left to their own devices. Health education material urging people to have dental check-ups, or eye tests, can be seen as examples of public authorities trying to increase private consumption of health care. (Depending on the funding of health care, avoiding future illness may also save money for the public purse. See Box 3.1 for an example.)

The Gamlan district environmental health officer, Mr Splat, has been charged with spraying the mosquito breeding grounds in his district in order to control malaria, a significant local health problem. Under the new private approach, he has to raise funds to pay for this activity from families living in the area. He first visits all the families to find out how much they are prepared to contribute. What do you think their response will be?

Box 3.1   Cigarette smoking

Some of these considerations, and others, are illustrated by the issue of cigarette smoking. If you smoke, you run, on average, a 50% risk of dying prematurely as a result (Jha and Abedian, 1998). In addition, you can harm the health of others around you, who may breathe in your smoke. There is therefore a strong case for discouraging smoking – negative externalities for passive smokers, avoiding suffering for smokers and avoiding the future costs of caring for their illnesses. Common policy measures are taxes on cigarettes, health warnings and health education activity, and out-right bans on smoking in public places or selling of cigarettes to certain people (e.g., young people under a certain age).

Why then do so many people take up and continue to smoke? Is this evidence that they set a low value on health? There are a number of possible explanations.

1. Nicotine is highly addictive.
2. Smokers are often ill-informed about health risks.
3. Present pleasure may be more important than future possible suffering, particularly for poor people with high discount rates.
4. Given the above, price elasticity of demand for cigarettes is likely to be low: increased prices do have some impact on demand, but act more as a generator of revenue for governments.
5. Control measures are often poorly implemented. This is partly through incompetence (the kind view). More cynically, governments can benefit from smoking – first, through revenues generated by taxes; secondly, because smokers tend to die around an age when they would normally switch from being tax-payers to drawing pensions and using health care services intensively; finally, tobacco companies are often generous donors to political parties or highly placed individuals.

To his surprise, Mr Splat finds that no-one is particularly keen to contribute towards his work, although the costs would be low and the benefits to them high – fewer mosquito bites, better health and increased ability to work. Economists call this the *free-rider* problem: each family is hoping that others will pay for a service which they then can benefit from. This is characteristic of activities which are *non-excludable* – i.e., where you cannot limit the benefits to those who have paid for them. Where a good is also *non-rival* (meaning that consumption by one person does not leave less for another), the good is known as a *public good*. Private markets will tend to underproduce public goods and so here, again, some form of intervention is justified. National defence, for example, or health education, are public goods and tend to be publicly funded out of taxpayers' money.

Consumers as rational maximisers

Another important condition for markets to be optimal is that consumers should have full information about the product – not just its price, but its effectiveness, and appropriateness – and be able to use it to plan consumption decisions according to their preferences.

As discussed earlier, the information condition is rarely fulfilled in health care, which is characterised by imperfect information for consumers, asymmetrical information between consumer and supplier, and suppliers acting as agents for patients, with all the possibility for abuse which this raises. The agency relationship also violates the assumption that supply and demand are independent.

There are also issues about how 'rational' consumers are: whether they make choices as individuals (rather than being socially influenced or determined); how consistent their choices are; whether they do try maximise their own welfare; and the extent to which their welfare relates to factors other than their own consumption. These questions are discussed in Appendix 1.

There is, too, a high degree of unpredictability of need, at least in relation to curative care. Health care is a *derived* need: it is not health care that we need, but health, and we are not able to know in advance when ill-health will strike. Consequently, our need for health care is inherently *uncertain*. It is also potentially ruinously expensive. This has implications for the way in which health care is financed: some form of risk pooling or insurance is clearly required.

Equitable distribution of assets

It is not strictly necessary to have an equal initial distribution of assets for free markets which meet all the conditions already described to optimise the outcome. However, given our social nature and 'caring externalities', we are unlikely to be made most happy by a system in which a sizeable part of the population is unable to afford a basic good. This raises the issues of equity (discussed in detail in Chapter 1). This is a particular concern in the health sector because of the correlation between poverty and ill-health (caused by poor housing, diet, education and environmental conditions, as well as possibly more dangerous employment). Equity is an important reason why governments fund and manage activities in the health sector.

Dealing with market failure

Markets have the ability to produce goods efficiently, to channel resources to their most valued use and to maximise social welfare in a general sense. However, there are some integral features of health care, outlined earlier, which mean that unbridled markets will not work well. These are known collectively as *market failure*. They need to be carefully understood so that appropriate intervention can be used (see Table 3.1).

Set against market failure are the hazards of government failure, including poor incentives for quality and efficiency, insensitivity to consumer preferences and self-serving bureaucratic and professional elites. These are addressed particularly by the type of interventions listed in categories 4 and 5 in Table 3.1.

Good health reform programmes aim to combine the best features of bureaucratic systems with the best of market-based ones. This will be discussed later in the book (see Chapter 10). However, it is important to note here that government intervention takes many forms. Some, such as public finance or management of facilities, aims to displace markets. Others, such as regulation of private suppliers, or providing information to customers, or transferring income between social groups, aims to improve the operation of markets. Generally, the question is not *whether* to combine markets with bureaucratic systems but *how*.

Summary

In this chapter we have introduced the economic framework which can be used to analyse health markets. We have seen that the concepts of supply, demand and how these interact are relevant, even in countries where public sector provision is

Table 3.1 Intervening in health markets

Why intervene?	Underlying features of health care markets	Examples of appropriate types of intervention
1. To insure against risk	– Uncertainty of health needs – Importance of health – High cost of many health care goods	– State finance or social insurance and/or – Regulation of private insurance to ensure access
2. To increase access to important 'private' health goods	– Poor income distribution in society – Correlation between ill health and poverty – Caring externalities/altruism	– State finance of health care or – Subsidies for basic health package or – Income transfer through taxation and benefits system
3. To increase consumption of 'goods' and decrease 'bads'	– Existence of public goods/free rider problem – Existence of positive and negative externalities – Health as basic right and merit good	– Subsidies/taxes to increase/decrease level of consumption or production – Free provision of public goods – Health promotion – Regulation of advertising
4. To increase competition amongst suppliers	– Limited resources and unlimited needs in health sector – Need to increase efficiency and quality of services and maximise health gain – Limited number of suppliers and economies of scale or scope	– Encourage active purchasing by consumers and their agents (e.g., health authorities) – Improved incentives for doctors/hospitals – Improved information on performance by doctors/hospitals – Privatisation and/or 'internal markets' in public sector
5. To control overall costs	– Agency relationship – Information problems about product – Tendency for cost escalation	– Maintaining control over finance – Encouraging professional self-regulation – Active purchasing, using information on cost-effectiveness of treatments

dominant. However, the conditions for markets to achieve optimal outcomes are very strenuous (see the checklist in Box 3.2). Health markets have certain inherent features which mean that intervention may be necessary to achieve a better social outcome. Information problems, externalities and uncertainty of needs are inherent in health care markets. Maintaining a competitive environment for suppliers is also a challenge. Health being a basic good, equity is an important goal too. The rest of the book looks at ways of organising the health sector to cope with these issues.

Questions for discussion

1 Take a part of the health market with which you are familiar – for example, the pharmaceutical market in your country – and consider to what extent it meets the conditions in Table 3.2.

Box 3.2   Checklist of conditions for market optimality

Perfect competition
- free entry and exit from market for suppliers
- many sellers and buyers
- homogeneity of product
- perfect knowledge about product qualities and prices
- producers face equal costs
- mobile factors of production
- no economies of scale or scope

Complete market
- market for good exists and is allowed to reach own equilibrium
- no positive or negative externalities of consumption or production
- good is not 'public' (i.e., non-excludable, non-rival)

Consumers as rational maximisers
- supply and demand independent
- consumers aware of own needs and how to satisfy them
- consumers able to plan consumption to maximise own welfare

Equitable distribution of resources
- distribution of resources accords with society's notion of fairness

---

2 Where a specific condition is not met, what are the options for intervention, either to improve or to substitute for the market approach?
3 How do these relate to current controls which are in place in your country? How well do these appear to work?
4 Drawing on lessons from this chapter, can you suggest ways in which this aspect of the health market in your country might be better organised, either by increasing/decreasing or altering the mix of interventions used?

References and further reading

Barr, N. (1993). *Health Care*. Chapter 12 in *The Economics of the Welfare State*. London: Weidenfield and Nicolson.
Donaldson, C. and Gerard, K. (1993). *Markets and Health Care*. Chapter 2 in *Economics of Health Care Financing*. Basingstoke: Macmillan.
Jha, P. and Abedian, I. (1998). The economics of tobacco control. Introduction to *The Economics of Tobacco Control: Towards an optimal policy mix*. South Africa: University of Cape Town.
Le Grand, J., Propper, C. and Robinson, R. (1992). Social objectives and the allocation of resources. From *The Economics of Social Problems*. London: Macmillan.
McGuire, A., Henderson, J. and Mooney, G. (1988). *The Economics of Health Care*. Chapters 3, 8 and 9. London: Routledge.
Rice, T. (1998). *The Economics of Health Reconsidered*. Chicago, IL: Health Administration Press.

PART 2

Financing health care

4

Financing health services (1)

Tim Ensor and Matthew Jowett

Introduction

Obtaining more finance for the health sector is a major pre-occupation for most governments in both low and middle (and even high) income countries. It is increasingly recognised that the state cannot finance all, or even the majority, of health care out of the general government budget. At the same time out of pocket payments have severe efficiency and equity implications. Other options for producing extra funding, including community finance and medical savings accounts, have been tried out in a variety of countries. While these experiments have had some success it must always be recognised that all finance is ultimately derived from the population who, often, have access to very limited income. Any increase in funding for medical care implies a reduction in expenditure on other, both health and non-health related, commodities demanded by the population.

This chapter will cover the following topics:

- current patterns of health sector funding in developing countries
- what constitutes an acceptable and affordable level of finance
- theoretical problems of health insurance – notably adverse risk selection and moral hazard
- recent developing country experience in introducing social insurance.

Further health financing topics are found in Chapter 5.

Current health spending in developing countries

Professor Bluff of the University of Ebulia has been invited by the Provincial Medical Officer of Rungara Province, Dr Fixit, to discuss the financing of health care with his staff. He would really like Professor Bluff to propose that the current government health budget for his area is too small. He is also interested in ways of increasing the level of financing. The provincial accountant, Mr Calculator, who is attending the meeting, has been told he must reduce total provincial spending which is running beyond the agreed annual budget.

Dr Fixit: *Professor Bluff, I wonder if you could explain to my colleagues how the amount we spend on health care in this country compares to other countries. I think we would all agree that the level of funding is far too low for our current health care needs.*

Professor Bluff: How much do developing countries currently spend on health care? At first sight this may appear to be a straightforward question. It is usually quite easy to obtain data on government spending on health care. Some international agencies even publish these data on a regular basis for a large number of different countries. Table 4.1 provides information on spending in a range of low income countries.

Yet these figures hide considerable complexity, under-reporting and inaccuracies. Most statistics held by governments report spending on government-owned, or government-financed institutions. The private sector, which may be substantial in a country, or even dominant, is often largely ignored. Even the reporting of government spending can be incomplete, including expenditures by the Ministry of Health but excluding expenditures made by other government departments, such as the Ministry of Defence on military hospitals.

Another problem area is the comparison of spending across countries, generally expressed in US dollars. Where economies are going through periods of turbulence, structural adjustment or economic transition, or where the government is artificially maintaining the value of the currency through controls, the exchange rate may not provide an accurate guide to the long-run market rate. The consequence is that using current rates will either under or over value actual expenditure.

Even in stable economies without currency controls, conducting a straightforward conversion to a common currency such as the US dollar based on current exchange rates, can produce

Table 4.1 Government health spending in low income countries (1995)

	US$ per capita	Government spending as %GDP
Bangladesh	3	1.2
Lao People's Democratic Republic	3	0.8
Nepal	2	1.2
Zambia	12	2.6
Uganda	4	1.8
Burkina Faso	7	2.3
Haiti	3	1.3
*Average for low income countries =	6	1.4
*Average for middle income countries =	90	2.2
*Average for established market economies =	1,890	6.5

*Each of the average figures are unweighted.

Source: Sector Strategy Paper, Health, Nutrition and Population. World Bank, 1997.

misleading results. The reason is that exchange rates are based on commodities that are traded between countries, and reflect the relative difference in their prices. In contrast much of health care is produced using inputs that are not traded between countries, principally labour. Since labour costs are typically much lower in developing countries, this implies that in the average developing country you can get much more health care for each dollar spent. Attempts to adjust values based on these differences in *purchasing power*, do so by using the cost of a typical basket of commodities consumed by an individual in different countries. Average total health spending in 1995 in low income countries rises three-fold when PPP (purchasing power parity) values are used, although data was only available for 13 countries.

Estimates that include both public and private spending across a wide range of countries have been prepared by the World Bank and the World Health Organisation. The 1993 World Development Report is the most widely quoted source of health expenditure data. More recent estimates for 1995 have been prepared by these agencies, and suggest that private spending accounts for around 59 per cent of total spending in low income countries, a marked increase on the 35 per cent in 1990, although there is substantial variation from region to region (approximately 55 per cent in Africa and 72 per cent in Asia). In

Table 4.2 Private health spending in low income countries (1995)

	US$ per capita
Bangladesh	3
Lao People's Democratic Republic	7
Nepal	8
Zambia	5
Uganda	6
Burkina Faso	7
Haiti	5
*Average for low income countries =	8.1
*Average for middle income countries =	87
*Average for established market economies =	810

*Each of the average figures is unweighted.

Source: Sector Strategy Paper, *Health, Nutrition and Population*. World Bank, 1997.

fact the evidence suggests that government health spending is being increasingly substituted by private spending even where economies are growing (Jowett, 1998). While the statistics published by the World Bank represent the most complete series of world health care financing statistics, many gaps were present in the data. For example, private expenditures for many countries were 'interpolated', a statistical guess based on data in other comparable countries, for over half of the 165 countries surveyed. Further problems were apparent in deciding what constitutes health expenditure.

Surveys of health financing have reinforced how important it is to have a complete and accurate accounting of health finance not only for international comparisons, but also to track the effects of policy over time in one country. The survey approach has attempted to establish clear guidance on some of the 'grey' areas in the accounting of financial flows, and in turn has spurred the development of a consistent National Health Accounts methodology which a growing number of developing countries are introducing (for a description of this methodology and problems faced see Berman, 1997).

What is the correct level of funding?

Dr Fixit: *Even once adjustments are made for purchasing power, it is clear that the poorer nations spend far less than richer ones. It is also clear that there is substantial variation within each group. So how does a country know what is the ideal amount to spend?*

Professor Bluff: There is no simple answer to your question. In addition to arguments based on population changes, health status, medical advance and technological change, and affordability (Appleby, 1992), societal preferences play a large part in determining optimal government spending. Comparisons with other countries are often used to argue for increases or decreases in spending although there are many problems and pitfalls with such comparisons (Jowett, 1998). There is however evidence that the benefits from additional spending on health care diminish at a certain level of spending. At some point they may even become negative. It follows that 'ideal expenditure will be at a level where marginal benefits are equal to marginal costs'. This may not, however, be achievable and funding should first be directed to actions with highest marginal net benefit whatever the sector. In

recent years there has been some attempt to look more closely at
the expenditures required to meet basic health needs in the
context of an essential package of services. This approach is discussed further in Chapter 9. It should be noted, however, that
the information required to make these calculations is generally
lacking.
Another approach is simply to compare spending with health
expenditure in other countries in the same income band.

Mr Calculator: *But surely this assumes that the average spending in
each income group is the 'right' one. How can we be sure?*

Professor Bluff: This is an important objection. Imagine that we
get to the point where spending is similar in each income group.
How will we know whether that amount constitutes an ideal level?
It could be that all countries are in fact wasting money that would
be better spent on other sectors. A middle way is to see the
concept of resource efficiency within and between sectors as a
goal towards which each country should strive, while inter-country
figures provide a crude indicator for immediate comparison.

While the first approach is extremely hard to implement com-
pletely, it does point to some very important methods that both
economists and epidemiologists employ to assess the efficiency of
health sector spending. Of the medical and epidemiological
questions the most fundamental relates to the Hypocratic principle of doing no harm. The second principle is to avoid treatments that do not work. Both require that treatments be
evaluated carefully to assess their effectiveness. Once these questions are answered a further set of economic principles are suggested. The first is to ensure that whatever is done is completed
at least cost (*cost-minimisation analysis*). Second, that each dollar
spent should be used to improve health to the maximum extent
possible (*cost-effectiveness* and *cost utility analysis*). Finally, that any
intervention should benefit society more than it costs and that
the net benefit outweighs the use of the same money in other
sectors (*cost benefit analysis*). These techniques will be described
more fully in Chapter 7.

What are the features of a good health financing
system?

Dr Fixit: *So how should health care be financed?*

Professor Bluff: *Before we try to answer 'how?', we should first address what we expect of the system. Perhaps I could turn that question back to you. What do you consider to be the most important characteristics of the health financing system?*

Dr Fixit: *Well, from the point of view of the community I represent, I would like to be sure that there is sufficient finance to fund the health services we consider to be important. I also expect there to be some reallocation of resources: the rich should pay more than the poor. But as an individual with children and several elderly relatives to support, my primary concern is to ensure that when they are ill they receive quick and effective treatment. I would like to be sure that if I am ill or unable to work for some other reason my family can still obtain medical care.*

Professor Bluff: What is expected of a health care financing system depends upon the perspective from which we are looking. From a community point of view several things are important:

1 Sufficient funding to provide for the health care needs of the community
2 Most societies also place some emphasis on a process of redistribution whereby the rich contribute more than the poor
3 Each person makes a fair contribution
4 The community is able to prevent health care costs using up an excessive proportion of the government budget.

But it is clear from Dr Fixit's comments that the individual, perhaps looking after a family or household, could have other objectives. The individual is concerned that:

1 When the income of the household is low (e.g., when several family members are not working, or during periods of sickness) access to quality health care is assured
2 Funding is available for facilities that are nearby
3 Quality services are offered that meet the family's health needs.

There is clearly overlap in these objectives. The requirements that the rich pay more than the poor, and that individuals contribute when they are healthy in order to benefit when they are sick, are related. But we will see later that it may sometimes prove impossible to meet both these objectives. Another source of possible conflict is the requirement at the community level to control overall expenditure and ensure that total health needs are best met, and the individual imperative to ensure that access to medical care is always available when required. This also brings us back to the terminological distinction between needs, wants and demands encountered in Chapter 3.

We should also recognise that while the way in which finance is obtained is certainly important, so also will be the way in which it is used. The incentives established for institutions such as hospitals are important in determining the pattern of care provided, and hence the allocation of resources. We will examine this question in Chapter 12.

Financing systems that pool the financial consequences of ill health[1]

> **Dr Fixit**:   *I have been wondering whether a system of organised state health sector funding is really required. After all when a motor car which is very old breaks down, I borrow money or dip into my savings to pay for the repair. Is it possible for health care be paid for in the same way?*

Professor Bluff: Most individuals are *risk averse*. This means that if offered the choice between a certain income and an uncertain but equivalent expected income, they prefer the certain option. Assume for example, that each year an individual may either earn $200 (probability:50 per cent), or $100 (probability: 50 per cent). His expected income will be $150. An individual is risk adverse if he prefers a guaranteed income of a little less than $150 (with probability of 100 per cent). The degree of risk aversion is indicated by how much less than $150 he will accept as a guaranteed alternative to the uncertain scenario.

Risk aversion implies that individuals will prefer to pool risk by making a small regular payment into a fund in return for the guarantee that if large expenses occur these will be covered by the fund. This is known as *risk pooling*.

It is indeed possible for individuals to smooth out fluctuations in income by saving. Working people do this all the time. They reduce current consumption in order to save for their retirement or in the event of sickness. There are two problems with this. First there will be some people in the community who will be unable to save even for quite modest medical care bills. Secondly sickness is so uncertain and its financial costs potentially catastrophic, that there is no guarantee that even an individual with

---

1   See Donaldson and Gerard, 1993 for a good general reference which discusses these theoretical issues in some depth.

quite a large income will be able to save enough to pay for them. In the first case it may be sufficient simply to provide some subsidy to the very poor. But the second case requires a rather more general solution to the problem: individual voluntary savings are inadequate. As we will see, however, the principle of saving for health is becoming popular in a number of countries. We shall return to this idea in Chapter 5.

One system of providing risk pooling is to provide cover in a way that pools the risk of financial loss over an individual's life cycle (*inter-temporal* risk pooling – see the discussion of medical savings accounts in Chapter 5). Regular premiums are paid on the basis that when an individual is unwell the insurer will pay for treatment. Such insurance is usually provided on a voluntary basis. As a result an insurer will only attract contributors if the long run benefits outweigh the costs. In the long run the total sum of these premiums are expected to meet the cost of an individual's medical treatment plus the cost of administration. If the insurer is profit-making it should also include an element of profit. The insurer will have to make sure that the expected expenditure on treatment (which are the benefits to the individual of insurance), plus the value of the security provided to a risk averse individual, exceed the premium plus other costs.

There are two main ways of setting a *premium*. One way would be to work out the expected costs of treatment for potential or actual members of the scheme using past medical records of individuals or self-declarations. If the latter is used then some verification, perhaps using a sample of those enrolled, will be required. These service costs are then added to the costs of administering the scheme, the profit margin required and reserve fund to provide for unexpected contingencies. The reserve fund is required because benefits paid out are based on average claims. In any one year however, total claims may be significantly above average and some reserve fund is required. The premium is given as:

$$\text{community premium} = \frac{\text{expected benefits} + \text{administrative cost} + \text{reserve} + \text{profits}}{\text{number insured}}$$

It should be noted that the amount required for this reserve will decline with the number of people enrolled. This is because if there are a very small number in the scheme a very large claim from just one individual might bankrupt the fund. As the number enrolled increase, so the risk is spread out over a large number of people and the proportional risk reserve declines. To obtain the premium level we simply divide the sum of all these costs by the number of people enrolled. This is known as a *community premium* because the same contribution is made by all the insured community.

Dr Fixit: *But I see a problem. I am reasonably healthy and rarely require medical care. My neighbour on the other hand is always going into hospital. If we both enrol in your scheme our costs are shared equally between us. In other words I am subsidising his sickness. Frankly, although you are reducing the uncertainty associated with my future medical care costs, I would rather take the risk and not join the scheme.*

Professor Bluff: You have identified a fundamental problem. A system based on a community contribution runs the risk of losing people like yourself, low risk people who rarely use the health facilities, and retaining only higher risk, higher cost people. This would increase the premium to those remaining – a process known as *adverse risk selection*. Of course the same problem is not present if the system is compulsory since there is then no possibility of leaving the scheme.

You will understand that the problem of adverse risk selection arises because information available to insurer and insured is unequal. If neither you nor your neighbour know your own risk of becoming ill, you would probably both be willing to enrol in the scheme to reduce the uncertainty of future costs. It is because you know that you are lower risk than your neighbour that you would refuse to pay the premium. Likewise your neighbour accepts the premium because he knows he has more to benefit. This information is not available to the insurer and is therefore known as information asymmetry.

The second method of working out an insurance premium is to put some effort into obtaining information on risk and use this to compute an individual premium. This can occur in two ways. The first is for the insurer to try and obtain information on risk status. At a minimum the insurer will find out the person's age, gender and occupation. All of these could provide information on likely use of medical care. It may also require the individual to undergo a medical and seek information on unhealthy lifestyles such as smoking or excessive drinking. A number of studies have suggested that the most important determinant of future use of medical facilities is past use of facilities (Van de Ven, 1997). In practice therefore, obtaining the medical care history of the patient forms the most important part of the risk assessment undertaken by private insurers. Based on this information premiums are adjusted for each patient, a process that is known as *risk* or *experience rating*.

There is however a limit to the amount of information that can be obtained on individuals at modest cost, and some asymmetry of information always remains. A further technique that is used to obtain information is to formulate policies in such a way that they force people to reveal their own risk status. Imagine for example, that you were offered a choice between two policies. The first gives a discount of 50 per cent on the usual premium but covers only 60 per cent of your health care costs. The second offer provides full cover for the full premium. Which one would you choose?

Mr Calculator: *That's easy! I would choose the discounted policy. I realise I will have to pay some of the costs if I am ill but, as I have already said, I hardly ever need medical treatment anyway.*

Professor Bluff: Good! By choosing the first policy you have in effect revealed yourself to be low risk. Your neighbour, on the other hand, may well choose the second policy since he is often ill and would lose out by having to pay part of the costs. In doing this he reveals himself to be high risk. He is also charged a proportionately higher premium – double your premium but less than double the cover. This is know as *self-selection*. In practice insurers may offer a range of policies each designed to attract different risk groups. An insurer, for example, could include low cost paediatric care in a policy in order to attract young low risk families with high potential income.

We have now described two approaches to insurance premium setting. The first relies on risk pooling across the community. We have seen that this works best if the system is compulsory so that low risk individuals cannot opt out. The compulsory nature of the system permit a number of variations.

1 The premium may be calculated in proportion to income rather than as a flat rate contribution.
2 Coverage may be extended on the basis of citizenship rather than contribution. This is only possible if premium collection can be enforced.
3 The insurer can base the development of services on the basis of need rather than individual wants.

The second is the individual risk rated premium. Such an approach arises from the voluntary nature of a system, and is sometimes associated with a for profit commercial approach to insurance. While this is often the case, it is important to realise that risk rating does not primarily arise because a firm wishes to make profits. A private firm could make profits based on a com-·munity premium introduced on a compulsory basis (although a compulsory private scheme may be politically unacceptable). Risk rating arises in order to ensure that both low as well as high risk people enrol in a scheme.

> **Dr Fixit**:   *I am still worried about the costs of treating my neighbour. He seems to see his doctor for the most trivial of illnesses for which his doctor invariably prescribes medicines. At the moment this does not worry me too much as patients must pay for the cost of their own medicines. But all those visits by the patient must be denying some people access to that doctor – there is a limit to the number of hours a person can work and from my own experience a public doctor never works longer that necessary.*

Professor Bluff: This is the second major problem associated with all systems of risk pooling, including insurance and tax funding. Essentially it is a problem of a third party payer: because some other agency incurs the costs of the treatment neither patient not provider have any incentive to economise on the amount of treatment obtained. This problem is known as *moral hazard*. From the point of view of an insurance organisation, methods are required to restrain demand. Two types of control are typically used – demand and supply. It is important to view these controls at both the individual level – as a way of restraining a patient's unnecessary demand – and at the macro level – as a way of controlling national health care spending.

Demand side measures attempt to control a patient's demand through financial penalty in the event of an insurance claim. Some examples are given in Table 4.3. Insurers also use non-financial control techniques to verify that treatment given is appropriate, effective and cost-effective. These techniques are generally known collectively as *managed care* and encompass both financial incentives for providers – such as capitation funding for institutions and individual physician bonuses/penalties – and management of clinical activity – for example utilisation review, physician audit and drug formularies. A review of US managed care is provided in Robinson and Steiner (1998), while lessons

Table 4.3   Financial disincentives for patients used by insurance companies

Co-insurance	– insured pays a percentage of the cost of any treatment.
Deductible	– insured pays a fixed amount of the cost. If costs are more than this amount the insurer pays the rest. These may also be used in designing policies to identify low and high risk.
Pay-out limit	– insurance company pays no more than an established amount.
No-claims bonus	– no (or small number of) claims in a year results in a reduction on the cost of next years policy.

These methods may be combined to restrain demand.

for some developing countries in Latin America are reviewed in Cezar Medici *et al.*, 1997.

Supply side policies are mostly used by the state to control the overall level of expenditure and access to services through limitations on the number of doctors, hospital beds and medical technology using regulatory and bureaucratic controls. The basis of this control is that since much demand is 'supplier induced' restricting supply also controls demand.

Both types of control are sometimes indiscriminate in their implementation and impact. Demand side controls may reduce the access of the ill poor through prices that are unaffordable (see Chapter 5). Supply side controls may penalise people who are unable to wait for treatment.

Table 4.4 illustrates the main types of risk pooling schemes divided up according to three main characteristics. These are: the basis for premium collection; whether contributions are earmarked for health care or go into a general government fund; and whether or not contributions determine entitlements.

At one end of the spectrum is funding through general taxation used in both established market and developing economies (e.g., Sweden, Tanzania). In many countries contributions generally increase with income although this may not be so in poorer countries. Since all revenue goes into a common pot, contributions are not earmarked for health care. Whether taxes are paid or not does not determine entitlement and no proof of payment is required before receiving service. Service entitlement is not

Table 4.4 Characteristics of systems for risk pooling (source of funding)

	General taxation	Earmarked tax	Social insurance	Voluntary community insurance	Private insurance
Are contributions risk, community or income rated?	Income/ Expenditure	Income	Income	Community	Risk
Are contributions earmarked for the health sector?	No	Yes	Yes	Yes	Yes
Do contributions determine entitlement?	No	No	Yes	Yes	Yes

normally specified in detail and use of services is dependent on physical accessibility and physician 'gatekeepers'.

At the other extreme, is private insurance levying risk-rated premiums that determine entitlement, as in the USA and Switzerland. Social insurance contributions are also generally related to income, but all the money is collected for the health sector and contributions determine whether or not someone is entitled to free service at the point of delivery. Entitlement to service is sometimes specified although not normally to the same level of detail as in a private scheme. Usually the scheme is compulsory for a specified population group although there are examples of voluntary schemes. It is very common for health benefits to be offered along with other social benefits such as pensions and unemployment entitlement. This is the social security approach developed from the original Bismark model in Germany, and now common throughout much of Latin America and parts of Asia.

An earmarked tax is somewhere is between taxation and social insurance providing earmarked money from the payroll for the health sector but without guaranteeing any specific entitlement.

Community insurance has similar characteristics to social insurance except that premiums are usually flat rate rather than related to income since individuals are expected to pay voluntarily. The main problem with these schemes is adverse risk selection, i.e., attracting only high-risk, high-use people.

In addition to these main insurance approaches to health there are many examples of schemes that are described as insurance but are really variations on user charge pre-payment schemes – for example, where a user buys a card which entitles him to a specified number of consultations or drugs. When the card is used up he buys another one.

Why tax-based funding is inadequate

Dr Fixit: *For several years I have been told by the national government in Ebulia that the budget cannot be increased. One year low tax collections are blamed, the next it is declining exports or the effect of regional economic recession. I have heard that in neighbouring countries the government is experimenting with different ways of increasing health spending through community insurance. Can you tell me what is the ideal way of obtaining revenue and why tax funding appears to be so inadequate?*

Professor Bluff: We have already examined some of the potential advantages of a compulsory community based system of health insurance. Each of these principles were identified as being important at the beginning of this chapter, along with the requirement that funding be adequate. In principle, they permit contributions to be related to the ability to pay, allow universal coverage and permit the 'insurer', which may simply be a government ministry, to allocate resources according to *need* rather than *want*. Funding from general taxation can be seen as having the further benefit that it requires no costly insurance bureaucracy to be established, and no expensive premium collection and assessment system since it depends on the existing system of general revenue collection. But it is important to examine whether, in practice, these potential advantages can be realised in a specific country context.

The assertion that taxation provides an equitable system of funding is based primarily on the fiscal structure present in a typical industrialised OECD country. In such a country most taxation is obtained from income related sources including profit, personal income, wages and savings. In all these cases contributions tend either to be proportional to income or progressive, taking a larger proportion of income the higher the income. In contrast the amount of taxation coming from regressive sources, where the contribution takes a larger proportion of income the lower the income, is relatively small.

In such conditions, social insurance may, in equity terms, be an inferior alternative since contributions are based on the payroll of firms which tax the incomes of those in waged employment but leave intact income from property or profit which largely accrues to richer members of society (Ludbrook and Maynard, 1988). In contrast in developing countries much government revenue is obtained from sales or import/export taxes. These are easier to introduce since they do not require the same elaborate system for assessment that is required for income taxes, particularly where personal income is derived from numerous and often 'informal' sources. These taxes are by nature regressive. In these circumstances payroll insurance, if feasible, may offer a more equitable system for raising finance. Additionally, the small base for taxation may mean that overall resources are considered inadequate to finance health care.

In addition to these financial weaknesses there are a number of more subtle problems that are attributable to the culture of government bureaucracies and their relationship to society. We argued earlier that community based systems of finance offer the insurer the ability to meet needs rather than wants. In reality it may do neither. Instead it can easily become a self serving institution that exists primarily for the staff working within. In effect the lack of an imperative, forced on a private company, to meet the wants or demands of its client group leads to an institution that is unresponsive to client needs.

A second issue is that funding is frequently seen to benefit large hospitals in urban areas. An extreme, but not isolated, example of this is the main referral hospital in Lesotho which absorbs more than 40 per cent of the total government health budget (Barnum and Kutzin, 1993). Now clearly, because of economies of scale, specialist hospitals must often be sited in one place and the capital city or other urban centre provides access to a concentrated and substantial population. (A tertiary hospital in the middle of a desert would look very odd!) But such facilities are certainly used more by those living nearby who may rely on them for their primary as well as their specialist needs. This raises a problem of equity for more remote areas.

There are some differences between tax-based funding and a payroll-based insurance contribution. One difference is that the payroll contribution is entirely for the health sector. This is popular with the Ministry of Health because it is assured a guaranteed revenue. It is often popular with employees because they know, unlike general taxation, what the contribution will be spent on. A system of social health insurance is usually based on the notion of contribution entitlement – benefits are not paid unless the contribution is paid. This contribution works both ways since schemes are often more explicit about what benefits are covered. For this to be done properly requires an accurate costing of services. Countries with a tax funded universal system have often found this presents an insoluble problem when it is discovered that the historic commitments to 'free care' are in reality unaffordable.

Another possible advantage is that insurance funding may act as a change agent for the reform of the sector. Establishing social medical insurance often involves the creation of a new funding bureaucracy that channels the funds to health sector providers. Unlike the Ministry of Health that is usually directly involved in the management of health facilities, the insurance fund is independent. As a result it may be more willing to bring about change by demanding that providers change patterns of service provision or costs of care. In effect it acts (or has the potential to act) as an independent purchaser (see Chapter 9).

It is also important to observe that even without a full system of health insurance, a payroll contribution can still be earmarked for health care (earmarked tax). In this case, rather than going to an insurance agency, the Ministry of Health receives the appropriate percentage tax as an addition to its budget. The payroll tax introduced by the Romanian government in 1991 to part pay for medicines is one example of an earmarked payroll tax developed to top up existing funding. Sometimes the main advantages envisaged in introducing health insurance may be obtained from an earmarked tax without the administrative cost of creating a new insurance bureaucracy.

The theoretical advantages of social insurance must be offset against its practical functioning. While earmarking may reduce the political uncertainty associated with bargaining between departments for a share of tax revenue, it may render the health sector more vulnerable to economic vicissitudes. The reason is that the funding base for social insurance is much narrower than taxation since it depends on one tax rather than a combination. A downturn in the economy has a direct and significant impact on revenue from payroll taxes as employment rates decline.

Further, even the alleged advantages of social insurance may turn out to be illusory. All systems of social insurance are subsidised to some extent from the budget. This subsidy may be provided explicitly to pay for the non-working population or provided 'lump-sum' in order to sustain the system. Earmarking certain revenues for health may be used by the Ministry of Finance as an excuse to reduce the budget subsidy for the system. As a consequence the net gain may be insignificant.

The potential role of the insurance fund as an independent purchaser may be offset by the reality that most new insurance funds have no such experience in needs assessment or contracting. As a consequence a new bureaucracy is created, with additional administrative costs but with no gain for patients or providers. A survey of new insurance funds in transitional Asian countries found that in most countries they are ill equipped for this new role and continue to rely on the Ministry of Health to influence the management of provision (Ensor, 1997).

Recent experience of social insurance

One of the patterns suggested by Abel-Smith (1992) and others is of an evolving system of pre-payment based entitlement to health care progressing through piecemeal social insurance coverage for the formal sector to a system of 100 per cent coverage. The final development may provide for universal coverage using tax funding as in the UK and Canada, or a system that continue to be based on contribution but that fills all (or almost all) gaps in coverage, as in Germany. Typical stages include:

1 charged services provided by the private sector and public sector with some public subsidy for the poor
2 growth in private insurance and/or social insurance for certain easily targeted groups such as civil servants. Services covered may include both private and public providers
3 increasing insurance of other groups persuaded by higher user charges
4 near universal coverage of the population.

Some countries may attempt to jump this progression but find that a theoretical commitment to 100 per cent coverage does not translate into a practical ability to finance all care from the state budget. The result may be to fall back on other types of funding, both official and unofficial.

Countries can be divided into a number of groups according to the extent to which they have succeeded in extending prepayment for health care to their populations. These groups are not comprehensive but illustrate the diversity of world-wide experience. Most high-income established market economies, with the exception of the United States, now have well developed systems of national health insurance. The principles may vary – e.g., social security versus universal tax funded entitlement – but most cover almost 100 per cent of the population giving access to good quality medical facilities.

Foremost among this group are the South American and Caribbean countries that have adopted en mass systems of social security based on enterprise contributions which may include pension, unemployment and maternity entitlements in addition to health care benefits. Coverage has been extended in the classic way through civil and other public servants, then white and then blue collar industrial workers and later to other urban and rural workers. The most advanced countries in this respect are

Argentina, Brazil and Costa Rica with 75 to 100 per cent coverage followed by countries such as Uruguay and Chile (Mesa-Lago, 1991). Cuba automatically entitles all its citizens to health service provision although it retains a contributory social security approach for other benefits.

With reforms to health finance dating back to the 1980s, Brazil has begun to move towards a system of universal entitlement. Until the 1980s it had a well developed system of employment based cover supported by private schemes for the rich and government provision for the very poor. In the late 1980s Brazil introduced a unified system (Barnum and Kutzin, 1992) whereby public funding sources, from insurance and taxation, are combined and all citizens of Brazil have access to the same providers. Only the private insurance funding remains separate.

The third group are the Newly Industrialising Countries – so called Asian Tigers, such as Taiwan, Korea and Singapore, and Tiger cubs such as Philippines, Thailand and Malaysia. In these countries coverage is being extended to the fast growing urban industrial sector as the economy grows. So, for example, the Korean system of insurance introduced for civil servants in 1977 and nationally in 1989 had achieved 94 per cent coverage by 1994 (Yang, 1996). Similarly, by the mid 1980s coverage of more than 40 per cent had been achieved through payroll insurance in the Philippines (Lieberman, 1996).

The fourth group consists of the large majority of sub-Saharan African countries most of whom do not have widespread insurance schemes. In the few cases where insurance is in place it is provided mainly for civil servants. The exception is Kenya where around 25 per cent of employees are thought to be covered by payroll insurance. In North Africa, Egypt also has a long established social insurance system for the public sector and is currently extending the scheme through the insurance of school children and coverage of the self-employed and rural sector. A number of countries including Ghana, Nigeria and Zimbabwe have conducted feasibility studies for the introduction of national health insurance schemes (Vogel, 1990).

The final group are those economies currently undergoing a process of transformation from centrally planned to market based economies. This may or may not be accompanied by political liberalisation. The group includes the economies of central and eastern Europe and of the Former Soviet Union. It also includes liberalising economies of South East Asia such as

Vietnam and Lao PDR. One of the striking and important features of this group is that most have relied upon health care systems based on public finance and provision with universal access. The exception is China which has never had a universal system although the system of labour and commune insurance meant that, for a time, coverage exceeded 90 per cent of the population. These countries are, in effect, turning back the clock to go from universal to contribution based entitlement.

Within this group of transitional economies there are two distinct sub-groups. One is the highly industrialised economies of Eastern Europe and parts of the Former Soviet Union. This includes countries where insurance development is well advanced, such as the Czech Republic, Hungary, parts of Russia and the Baltic States, and also countries where insurance is still being approved or considered such as Poland. Although much of their industry requires renovation the structure of the workforce is still largely industrial, concentrated in urban areas. This is in contrast to the second sub-group of former centrally planned economies which are still largely agricultural. This includes much of Soviet Central Asia and also the transition economies of South East Asia such as Vietnam and China. Introduction of industrial based social insurance in these countries is harder to achieve.

Table 4.5 illustrates experience of insurance in various regions of the world. A striking feature of this table is the considerable diversity in the coverage of the population that each scheme manages to achieve. Part of this variability appears to be explained by the level of per capita income and partly by the date when the scheme was introduced. Older schemes in richer countries generally have a higher level of coverage than newer schemes in poorer countries.

Dr Fixit: *Surely in a province like Rungara, it is not only income that will be important in determining whether insurance schemes are successful. Much of the population in the province are scattered over a wide area making the identification of those that should contribute difficult and costly. What is more, even in the main town, many people are involved in small informal businesses such as roadside trading and taxi driving. How can the incomes of such people be assessed for the insurance tax? In fact I am not really clear why collection of a health insurance contribution should be any easier than the collection of a tax.*

Table 4.5 Introducing social health insurance in low and middle income countries

Region	Year introduced	Coverage	Per capita income (US $)
Africa			
Key feature:	Gradual introduction for civil servants and formal sector		
Burundi	1984	10–15%	150
Kenya	1960s	25%	260
Namibia	1980s	10%	2,030
Eastern Europe and FSU			
Key feature:	Transition from tax funded to social insurance		
Estonia	1992	94%	2,820
Hungary	1992	High [1]	3,840
Russia	1991	High [1]	1,910
Slovenia	1993	High [1]	7,140
Asia			
Key feature (transitional):	Response to declining level of state funding		
Kazakstan	1995	70–80%	1,110
Vietnam	1993	10%	200
Key feature (other):	Expansion a response to the growth of the economy		
Indonesia	1968	13%	790
Thailand	1990	13%	2,210
South Korea	1977	94%	8,220
Latin America and Carribean			
Key feature:	Introduced from 1920s as part of wider package of pensions, unemployment and other benefits		
El Salavador	1960s	11%	1,480
Argentina	1920s	90%	8,060
Mexico	1930s	42%	4,010
Bolivia	1930s	18%	770
Paraguay	1930s	14%	1,570

Notes: [1] Introduced from a 100% universal tax funded base – coverage thought to be falling as non-working lose effective entitlement.

Professor Bluff: There are three key issues in obtaining an insurance contribution – in fact they apply to most types of taxation. These are:

• identification of those that should contribute,
• assessment of how much they should contribute,
• collection of contributions.

At each stage the government can lose revenue. Some people, such as the people living in the rural areas of your province, may be difficult to identify. Others, such as the informal workers in your city, will earn incomes that are difficult to measure and assess. Still other groups will contribute only part of their assessed contribution – enterprises in financial difficulties, for example, may default on their contributions rather than default on paying wages. Camcho (1991) emphasised that in Latin America it has proved very difficult to increase insurance coverage during a recession because of the problem of bankrupt and near-bankrupt enterprises not paying their contributions on time.

Table 4.6 indicates the groups of the population that are likely to prove most problematic in collecting contributions.

In addition to the transitional state of the economy, other social and geographic factors – we might term them structural conditions – also influence how easy it is to introduce social insurance. Both Shaw and Ainsworth (1996), for sub-Saharan countries, and Ensor and Thompson (1998), for a range of middle and low income countries, point out the likely and observed relationship between the type of industrialisation and distribution of population and the success of social insurance. Both studies ranked countries according to a range of characteristics that make it more or less likely that a system of social insurance will be successful.

The inevitable conclusion is that for a wide range of low and middle income countries social insurance can currently provide coverage for a relatively small proportion of the total population (between 1 and 20 per cent in low income countries where it has been tried). The recognition that social insurance does not provide significant additional funding to general tax-based funding for the majority population in many low and middle income countries has led to a growing interest in other sources of funding for the health sector. These are discussed in Chapter 5.

Table 4.6 Insurance coverage of population sub-groups

	Group	Problems
Employees	Civil servants	No specific problems
	State workers	No specific problems
	Manual and non-manual workers in large enterprises	Collection from near bankrupt enterprises
	Agricultural workers	Identification, assessment and collection
	Employees of small enterprises	Identification and collection
	Casual workers	Identification, assessment and collection
	Military	No specific problems
Self-employed people	Craftspeople	Identification
	Farmers	Identification, assessment and collection
	Owners of small enterprises	Identification, assessment
	Other independent workers	Identification, assessment and collection
Non-working	Pensioners	Assessment
	Children	No specific problems
	Unemployed people	Identification
	Disabled people	Identification, assessment
	Welfare recipients	Assessment
	Students	Assessment
	People in training	Assessment

Source: Normand and Weber, 1994.

Summary

In this chapter we have seen how the need to risk pool between individuals and across time leads to a demand for some form of risk sharing for health care costs. The form this takes depends upon whether the risk sharing evolves in response to individual health care wants and demands or community need.

Market failure in the provision of health insurance was shown to lead to the key problems of adverse selection and moral hazard. Moral hazard is a general problem of funding by a third party and can be reduced through both demand and supply side measures. Adverse selection is a problem of voluntary insurance and leads, without further action, to partial coverage of risk.

The chapter discussed the problems of extending tax and payroll-based systems of risk sharing to the population of developing countries. It highlighted the difficulty in identifying contributors and assessing and collecting contributions.

Questions for discussion

1 Do you think that Abel-Smith's concept of a transformation process from piecemeal to total insurance coverage is valid for your country? What stage is your country at?
2 Consider the problems of identification, assessment and collection of contributions in insurance and tax based systems of health care funding in your own country using Table 4.5 as a guide. For which main groups are these problems most evident? Has the government attempted to improve collections from any of these groups? With what results?

References and further reading

Abel-Smith, B. (1992). Health insurance in developing countries: lessons from experience, *Health Policy and Planning*, 7, 3: 215–226.
Abel-Smith, B. (1994). *An Introduction to Health Policy, Planning and Financing*. Harlow: Longman.
Appleby, J. (1992). *Financing Health Care in the 1990s*, Buckingham: Open University Press.
Barnum, H. and Kutzin, J. (1992). Institutional features of health insurance programs and their effects on developing country health systems, *International Journal of Health Planning and Management*, 7, 51–72.
Barnum, H. and Kutzin, J. (1993). *Public Hospitals in Developing Countries*, Baltimore, MA: Johns Hopkins University Press.

Berman, P. (1997). National health accounts in developing countries: appropriate methods and recent applications, *Health Economics*, 6, 11–30.

Camcho, L. (1996). Financing social security in Latin America: new perspectives in the light of current developments, *International Social Security Review*, 49.

Cezar Medici, A., Londono, J., Coelho, O. and Saxenian, H. (1997). Managed care and managed competition in Latin America and the Carribean, in G. Sheiber (ed.) *Innovations in Health Care Financing: proceedings of a World Bank conference March 10–11, 1997.* Washington, DC: The World Bank.

Conn, C. P. and Walford, V. (1998). *An Introduction to Health Insurance for Low Income Countries*, London: Institute for Health Sector Development.

Donaldson, C. and Gerard, K. (1993). *Economics of Health Care Financing: The Visible Hand*, Basingroke: Macmillan.

Ensor, T. (1997). What role for state health care in Asian Transition Economies?, Guest Editorial, *Health Economics*, 6, 5: 445–454.

Ensor, T. and Thompson, R. (1998). Health Insurance as a catalyst to Change in former Communist Countries, *Health Policy*, 43, 3: 203–218.

Jowett, M. (1998). *Health Resources in WHO.* Evaluation of the Implementation of the Global Strategy for Health for All by 2000: 1979–2000, Geneva: WHO.

Lieberman, S. (1996). Redesigning government's role in health: lessons for Indonesia from neighbouring countries, Indonesia Discussion Paper Series, Number 1. Washington, DC: World Bank.

Ludbrook, A. and Maynard, A. (1988). The funding of the National Health Service: what is the problem and is social insurance the answer, Discussion Paper 39, Centre for Health Economics, University of York.

Mesa-Lago, C. (1991). Social security in Latin America and the Carribean: a comparative assessment, in Ahmad E. Dreze, J. Hills and A. Sen (eds) *Social Security in Developing countries*, Oxford: OUP.

Normand, C. and Weber, A. (1994). *Social Health Insurance.* Geneva: World Health Organisation and International Labour Organisation.

Shaw, R. P. and Ainsworth, M. (1996). Financing health services though user fees and insurance, World Bank Discussion Paper 294, Wasington, DC: World Bank.

Van de Ven, W. (1997). Risk-adjusted capitation payments for catastrophic risks based on multi-year prior costs, *Health Policy*, 39, 123–135.

Vogel, R. (1990). An analysis of three national health insurance proposals in sub-Saharan Africa, *International Journal of Health Planning and Management*, 5, 271–285.

Witter S. and Ensor, T. (1997). *An Introduction to Health Economics for Eastern Europe and Countries of the Former Soviet Union*, Chichester: Wiley.

Yang, B. (1996). The role of health insurance in the growth of the private health sector in Korea, *International Journal of Health Planning and Management*, 11, 231–252.

5

Financing health services (2)

Matthew Jowett and Tim Ensor

Introduction

This chapter follows on from the discussion between Dr Fixit, Mr. Calculator and Professor Bluff in the last chapter. It will cover the following topics:

- user fees
- private insurance
- community financing
- health savings accounts
- informal payments
- official development assistance

User fees

> *Mr Calculator*: *It seems that you are saying it would be difficult, inefficient and possibly inequitable to attempt to increase the amount of health care spending from general taxation. But other systems based on national risk pooling also appear to be inappropriate for much of the population. So are there any other ways of increasing the amount of resources for health care?*

Professor Bluff: The perceived or actual failure of large scale national systems of risk pooling has stimulated the search for alternative methods of finance. During the 1980s the introduction of user charges, that is direct payments by users at the point of service, were favoured as a way to supplement revenues.

Let us have a closer look at the experience of direct user charges for health services. In the late 1980s many governments and donor organisations promoted the introduction of charges in government health facilities for several reasons. The arguments included the following:

1 By introducing user charges, people will stop using health services for unnecessary reasons, bringing demand more in line with actual need.

2 By increasing user fees at higher levels of the system, people will be encouraged to use the primary facilities more, rather than going straight to hospitals and overcrowding them as happens at present.

3 By letting health facilities keep some of the revenue, they should become more responsive to customers needs, particularly where users have a choice of facility, such as in urban areas.

4 By providing instant revenue for health facilities starved of government money, the availability of medicines can be improved, as well as the overall quality of services.

5 If exemptions or reduced charges are implemented in parallel for the poor, then those who can afford to pay will cross-subsidise those who can't, thus improving equity.

The first three reasons address efficiency aspects of the health system, and along with the others are important health policy objectives. Yet user charges have the unattractive feature that they must be paid at the time of illness, which can create problems of access. There may also be a problem of supplier-induced demand, whereby hospitals and health centres try to increase their revenue by prescribing unnecessary services or medicines.

Primarily, user charges are a tool for influencing demand for health services. The concept of price elasticity of demand measures how much the demand for health services changes as a result of changes in their price (see the explanation in Chapter 3). Generally speaking demand for health services is considered to be inelastic, i.e., between 0 and −1, which means that there is relatively little change in demand as the price increases. Clearly however the impact on demand will differ for different subgroups of the population. A study in Burkina Faso found that although overall demand for health services was price inelastic (−0.79), for the poor and the young demand was price elastic: −3.6 for infants, and −1.7 for the lowest income quartile

(Sauerborn *et al.*, 1994). It is also likely that measures of elasticity would vary according to a range of other variables, such as the magnitude of indirect costs and the type of health problem. Much of the research conducted into the effects of introducing user charges focuses on changes in who is using health services and how much they are using. Some of the key studies are summarised in Table 5.1. The evidence, whilst varied, highlights the problems that user charges can create. Whilst exemptions and reductions for the poor may alleviate part of the negative equity effect, it is those with the greatest need for care and with the least money that will be most deterred from using services. Establishing an individual's income is a complex process often requiring a costly administrative bureaucracy, making them difficult to implement. There are however other ways of designing exemptions that target and protect lower income groups. Generally referred to as characteristic targeting, these include exempting people on the basis of where they live (e.g., a known poor area such as a shanty town), what they do (e.g., mining), and what diseases they have (e.g., tuberculosis). Whilst characteristic-based exemptions still mean more work in terms of administration for health facilities, they get over the problem of assessing income.

In addition even those who are willing to pay for health services may have problems in terms of ability to pay. Evidence from several studies have found that expenditures on other essentials such as food and education may be sacrificed, assets such as cattle sold off, or debts incurred by borrowing from money-lenders (Gilson, 1988). Such consequences can in the medium to long term have significant negative effects on health (see Box 5.1).

Another negative consequence of user charges, if not carefully introduced, is a fall in the provision of preventive care. People tend to demand curative rather than preventive services such as immunisations and ante-natal care. As a result much preventive care is delivered to patients who come for treatment for illness or an injury. Where demand for curative care falls some studies have found a subsequent drop in the provision of preventive services such as childhood immunisations. Thus not only are health benefits lost to the individual concerned, but also benefits to the wider community. For these reasons preventive services, and services for children and pregnant women, are commonly exempt from user fees.

Dr Fixit: *Much of what you say about the problems with user charges is true, although I can't see any easier way of raising more money. I think we need to make sure the user charge system works better.*

Professor Bluff: Experience tells us that some of the negative effects on equity can be compensated for by reducing the indirect costs of using health services (e.g., travel and time costs). By retaining a large proportion of the revenue collected (typically 50–100 per cent), and using it to improve the quality of local services, people living in remote areas (often the poor) may decide to use them rather then travelling further afield to hospitals or mission facilities where the quality was previously perceived to be better. In such a case the total cost of obtaining quality care will be reduced. Improvements in perceived quality are just as important as improvements in clinical quality, given its positive influence on demand. This usually involves improving the supply of available medicines, improving the training and attitudes of staff, as well as the state of repair of facilities, and reducing waiting times.

Box 5.1   Access to health services in Vietnam

Studies that measure utilisation as a indicator of access to health services miss out on crucial aspects relating to financing. Access generally has two components, physical access (i.e., distance to a health facility of a given quality), and financial access (payments made in order to obtain services). A study in Vietnam (Ensor and San, 1996) found that the poor generally delayed treatment longer than the rich, made less use of government health facilities, and paid more per episode. Measures of demand such as willingness to pay tell us nothing about ability to pay for services, and several studies have found that sacrifices in expenditure on other essentials such as food and education have been made to finance visits to the doctor.

In addition to time costs, payments made to receive health services can include travel costs, official charges, unofficial payments and payments in kind e.g., for food and bedding. The impact on those seeking demand may involve delays in seeking care, or using self-treatment. Another response may be to sell household assets to raise cash, or to borrow money from family, friends or money-lenders.

Table 5.1 Evidence of the impact of user charges on the utilisation of government facilities

Dimension	Evidence of impact	References
Total utilisation	– Outpatient attendance dropped by 50% in Ghana after 12 months. – Outpatient attendance dropped between 27% and 46% in Kenya. – In Cameroon attendances increased following the introduction of charges, due to subsequent service quality improvements.	Waddington and Enyimayew, 1990 Collins et al., 1996 Litvack and Bodart, 1993
Male/female	– In Kenya, utilisation by men increased from 39% to 51% of total outpatient attendances. – In Ghana the share of services used by men fell following the introduction of fees.	Collins et al., 1996 Waddington and Enyimayew, 1990
Age groups	– In Kenya utilisation increased amongst under 15 year olds (as a, proportion of the total) primarily at the expense of those aged 16–44 years. – In Ghana utilisation became concentrated in the economically active 15–45 years group, whose share increased from 27% to 42%. The main fall was amongst the elderly.	Collins et al., 1996 Waddington and Enyimayew, 1990
Case-mix	– In Swaziland the use of critical services such as STDs, diarrhoeal disease and respiratory infections fell following user charges. – In a review of sub-Saharan Africa, it was feared that those at the greatest risk of ill-health were most likely to be deterred from using government services as a result of fees.	Yoder, 1989 Creese, 1991
Urban and rural	– In Ghana both rural and urban rates of utilisation fell by 50% within 12 months. Four years later urban rates were back at pre-fee levels, whilst rural rates had not changed. – The rural poor face higher indirect costs, and are hence more likely to be deterred from using services as a result of fee introduction.	Waddington and Enyimayew, 1990 Creese and Kutzin, 1994
Income groups	– Higher income groups are less likely to be affected by fees, and more likely to demand 'unnecessary' care. – In Cameroon and Niger, low income groups (often in rural areas) increased utilisation following fees, due to quality improvements.	Dahlgren, 1990 Litvack and Bodart, 1993 Wouters, 1995

It is generally agreed that in order to achieve such quality improvements new systems of management must be introduced. Decentralised management gives facilities more responsibility for running the services they provide, such as having the flexibility to vire budgets (i.e., moving money between budget lines). Whilst support systems and guidelines from higher levels of the system are important to the success of decentralised management, it is also necessary to invest in appropriate skills such as financial management, at lower levels of the system. This itself is something that will take substantial time and money. (See Chapter 11 on decentralisation.)

Finally, once revenue is collected from patients and retained by health facilities, the relationship between the user and the provider changes. Patients have high expectations of service improvements, and want to see those benefits immediately. Given the low salaries of many government health workers much of the extra money is used for salary supplements. Some countries have had negative experiences of money 'disappearing' and for this reason in order to maintain a community's trust in those handling the money, a system of accountability must be put in place. The establishment of village health committees are often used to regulate provider behaviour, such as checking how the revenue is used.

As a general rule charges should be kept low or absent from primary facilities, whilst applying them at hospital facilities tends to have less negative effects. In fact user charges are increasingly seen as part of a broader package of financing, for example as co-payments under a risk-sharing mechanism (see Gilson, 1997 for a more in-depth review). Another alternative system of financing health services is private insurance.

Private insurance

Dr Fixit: *Despite the disadvantages of private insurance, I understand that it is becoming increasingly popular as a way of increasing funding for health services. To what extent could voluntary systems of insurance offer increased coverage of a population in a low or middle income country?*

Professor Bluff: Chapter 4 indicated the differences between a commercial approach to insurance (individual wants-based) and a social approach (community needs-based). In addition, the voluntary nature of enrolment – so that low risks are reluctant to join – combined with the profit motive is likely to lead to higher premiums for the high risk. If these customers are also low income financial equity is hampered. It becomes very difficult to see how any country, particularly low and middle income countries, could finance health care with a system predominantly based on private insurance. But there is a growing interest in private insurance as a way of providing additional funding for non-essential services.

Private insurers are not a homogenous group. In the next section we will examine systems of community insurance which are based on the idea of local populations getting together to pool risk. These are often private in the sense of being non-state managed and sometimes these schemes may be promoted by private companies. But their basis is a long way from the idea of a large company earning profits from health for their shareholders. Individual companies that develop private insurance plans can be constituted in a variety of ways. Some may distribute profits to shareholders. Others may reinvest any surplus into the business while some regard all those insured with the company as 'shareholders' and any profit is redistributed to them through lower premiums. In the UK the largest private insurer, BUPA, is constituted in this last way (provident association).

In established market economies, private insurance is mostly seen as a top-up to state funding of services. In the Netherlands and Germany those on higher incomes may opt out of employer plans into private schemes. In other countries, such as the UK and Australia, no opt out is possible and people buy additional insurance to ensure quicker or more convenient access to hospital for elective treatment.

In low and middle income countries private insurance is generally less developed than in OECD countries. Coverage levels are also extremely variable. Partly this is due to an income gradient – richer countries tend to have higher private insurance coverage than poorer ones. There is little private insurance, for example, across most of sub-Saharan Africa – exceptions being Kenya (11 per cent) and South Africa (16 per cent, mostly white population). But differential coverage it is also due to particular country and regional polices. In much of Latin America, where private funding and provision have strong historic roots, there are well established systems. Coverage in Chile, where coverage is an alternative to the public system, exceeds 27 per cent of the population. In contrast there is very little private insurance across most of Asia: even in fast growing countries such as Singapore and Malaysia levels rarely exceed 3 or 4 per cent. (See Chollet and Lewis for a detailed review of private insurance in low and middle income countries).

> **Dr Fixit**: *My brother is covered by private insurance. Last month he was ill and thought the policy would pay for his treatment. But it turned out that the illness from which he was suffering was excluded from the policy. An acquaintance of mine found out that her policy was useless because the company had gone bankrupt.*

Professor Bluff: Appropriate regulation is an extremely important dimension of the successful development of private insurance. There are a number of aspects that are important.

1 Consumer protection – those purchasing insurance should have an adequate understanding of what the policy does and does not cover. It is important that companies cannot hide behind impenetrable small-print and medical jargon.
2 Financial regulation – companies must adhere to high standards of financial reporting and monitoring to ensure that those insured know that the company is solvent and using contributions for their intended purpose.
3 Entrance and exit of companies – controls may prevent companies that are not large enough to meet obligations to the insured from entering the market. Regulations may be introduced to ensure, for example, that they have a sufficient reserve to pay for unexpectedly large claims. Some support may also be provided by the state to failing companies to ensure that they are able to meet claims obligations, although it is important that the state does not, by default, simply become a subsidiser of private companies.

Accreditation and regulation of insurance companies may be carried out by a number of agencies. Sometimes the Ministry of Health undertakes this function. Where this is the case it is likely that a financial ministry (such as Industry or Finance) will also have a role to ensure that the financial aspects of the regulation are met.

The authorities must also be willing and able to enforce any regulations. It is reported that Brazilian laws on consumer protection, for example, are not enforced sufficiently rigorously. The

Russian authorities are finding it difficult to control the plethora of private companies that provide state mandated and supplemental voluntary insurance. Costs of regulation can be high and may deter the creation of an effective body. It is reported that in Chile, for example, the costs of effective regulation would amount to about 30 per cent of the average premium (Kumaranayake, 1997). The opposite extreme of too much or inappropriate regulation is also possible and may dissuade companies from entering the market (particularly companies that intend to abide by the rules created).

Lessons from private sector regulation might also be applied to state institutions that promise certain benefits to the population. Medical services guaranteed by the state are often provided only partially or not at all. It might be salutary if similar standards of consumer protection applied in the private sector were also enforced on state bodies.

Similar pre-conditions apply to private insurance as those described for social insurance in the previous chapter. Where the population is formalised and industrialised schemes are more likely to develop, particularly if governments permit opt outs from the state system. While opt-outs may be popular for the richer groups of society they can undermine the re-distributive nature of the system without creating significant additional resources. (A similar issue arises with medical saving schemes discussed later.) Private insurance is perhaps most suited to supplementary benefits for those in formal employment or richer income groups.

One other potential role of private insurers are as carriers of state insurance plans. In this case the state pays risk-adjusted premiums on behalf of its citizens to the private company chosen by the individual. This is the foundation of the reforms being introduced in the Netherlands and also the basis of the Russian health insurance system. The main disadvantage is that it increases the need to strengthen the regulation of the system and introduces another layer of bureaucracy – and profit taking – that detracts from the amount that can be spent on patient care. Further information on this complex area can be found in Saltman, 1997.

Community financing

Professor Bluff: *We have learnt a lot about the pros and cons of user charges. National policy makers are particularly concerned about their negative impact on equity, unless part of a broader package of health financing methods, and an overall strengthening of the health management system. Private insurance appears to provide additional funding only for discretionary services for certain income groups. There is, however, renewed interest in the development of voluntary risk-pooling schemes that are organised by the community rather than private companies.*

Community financing schemes are being developed in many developing countries, having been promoted by the Bamako Initiative launched in 1988 by UNICEF and WHO. Community financing is a general term for a wide variety of alternative risk pooling and pre-payment schemes introduced in most regions of the world including South East Asia (e.g., Thailand, Philippines), sub-Saharan Africa (e.g., Democratic Republic of Congo, Niger) and Latin America (e.g., Guatemala). There is considerable heterogeneity in the way these schemes have been implemented. Some general characteristics include:

1 a fixed premium for a limited range of services
2 schemes are usually voluntary
3 services provided are usually those that patients would otherwise have to pay for
4 services are generally easy for patients to evaluate and of high value, e.g., medicines and shorter waiting times
5 revenue rarely covers the full cost of service but provides valuable additional funding for non-staff costs
6 revenue is usually retained by local facilities.

A key issue concerns the setting of premia. The flat rate premium combined with its voluntary nature means that most community schemes contravene the principles of premium setting described in Chapter 3. In theory we would expect that most schemes would suffer from adverse selection with low risk individuals refusing to join. In response a number of methods have been used to enrol the low risk.

1 Attractive benefits to low risk individuals (see Thailand example in Table 5.2)
2 Schemes are subsidised so that no one has to pay the full actuarial cost of services
3 Some schemes have attempted to offer too many benefits and, as a result, have been financially unviable.

In some cases such schemes are a combination of local and national efforts. In the Thai scheme initial momentum came from national government but local schemes were allowed to develop their own rules on operation, benefits offered and premiums collected. Not surprisingly in some areas, where management support and local motivation was high such schemes succeeded; in other areas the schemes failed. Similar experience is suggested in studies of community financing schemes in Africa (Carrin and Vereecke, 1992).

On the basis of existing evidence the worst scheme is one that is conceptualised at the national level but then given to (or forced on) local people to run and ensure that funds revolve. In this case there may not be the experience necessary to run the scheme effectively and when it runs into difficulties little local motivation to keep it going. This may explain the failure of community funding schemes in Indonesia to achieve sustainability. Where the scheme is developed at the national level local communities may be unwilling to contribute fearing that money will simply be appropriated for services in urban specialist facilities. Even if this is not the case the lack of community participation may mean that individuals remain unaware of the scheme. Community schemes must be well understood and sold to the rural population. This is something governments often do not understand, being used to enforcing tax collection. A notable contrast is the recently introduced insurance scheme in Vietnam in that while local pilot projects went to considerable lengths to convince people of the merits of insurance, once the system was imposed at the national level efforts were far less rigorous (Carrin *et al.*, 1993; Ensor, 1995).

Marketing of community insurance might take place in many ways. There is no reason why a policy has to be sold by a hospital or health centre. Much greater penetration can be gained by offering policies for sale through local shops (with a commission for the seller) or attached to other local income generation schemes.

Clearly the benefits of such schemes must be attractive to the community and for this reason many have focused on the supply of drugs. Revolving drug funds, have became particularly popular in sub-Saharan Africa in response to the severe lack of medicines in rural areas. Whilst such schemes can significantly improve the perceived quality of services, they often fail to match the principles of full community involvement stressed by the Bamako Initiative. Research appears to confirm that inclusion at various stages of the development process (e.g., setting scheme objec-

Table 5.2 A selection of community financing schemes

Country	The scheme	Premia	Benefits	References
Guinea Bissau	The 'Abota' scheme was set up in 1980. The primary aim was to improve the local supply of medicines, and improve access to services throughout the year. An initial six months start-up supply of drugs was provided. Initially revenue was too low but, positively, many people joined the scheme. After several years 75 per cent of adults in the village were included. With free referrals the scheme grew to cover 20 per cent of the national population after 10 years. Problems with under-treatment of patients and government's conversion of revenue into foreign currency at the national level complicated the scheme. Stronger regulation and accountability was required to ensure the proper use of funds. The lack of an informal drugs market and the 'localness' of the scheme were seen as major factors in its success.	Villagers were involved in price-setting from the outset through a community committee, with contributions based on what people were willing to pay, rather than service cost. Each year the premium was increased in agreement with the community as benefits became more visible. Annual contributions stood at around a quarter of a chicken (equivalent) per person. Those who hadn't contributed paid a consultation fee greater than the annual contribution.	Free treatment and medicines at the village Health Unit. Children of members were exempt from charges. MoH eventually agreed to accept referrals to higher levels of government health facilities without extra charge.	Chabot and Waddington, 1987 Chabot, Boal and Da Silva, 1991
Democratic Republic of Congo	The hospital pre-payment scheme was launched in rural Bwamanda district in 1986, with the aim of improving access to hospital services, and ensuring its revenue. Evidence shows that admission rates are three times higher for insured over uninsured patients, and that those in high need of hospital care have benefited considerably. Cost recovery	The voluntary, community-rated annual premium was initially set at Z20 with a 20 per cent co-payment, rising with inflation.	80 per cent reduction in insured patients hospital bill.	Moens, 1990 Moens and Carrin, 1992 Criel and Kegels, 1997

Table 5.2 continued

Country	The scheme	Premia	Benefits	References
	rose to 81 per cent of recurrent costs within several years, as membership rose. The scheme is managed by a District Management team which works closely with the local community, and is seen as part of the key to success.			
Philippines	The community health insurance scheme was initially set up by a non-governmental mother and child health project, in La Union Province in 1994. Low income areas were specifically selected. Membership is family not individual based to limit adverse selection. Financial analysis to date has been positive, with adjustments made to the criteria for benefits eligibility (e.g., maternity).	The payment schedule was flexible, on either a monthly, quarterly, bi-annual or annual basis. Premium levels were adjusted for family size. Payment was reduced for members of the national Medicare programme.	A benefit package was drawn up covering approved essential medicines, and both in-patient and out-patient care at the primary level. Hospital benefits were provided by a contracted hospital, with members facing shorter waiting times.	Ron, 1997
Thailand	The Health Card Programme started in 1983, with the aim of promoting primary health care in rural areas. Revenue, which is supplemented by government contributions, is managed by village committees and allocated between primary and secondary level facilities. Currently the scheme has around 1.3 million members. Despite its success continual changes in the schemes design have slowed progress. To attract low risk individuals many local schemes offer low interest loans to members. They are	Initially a one-off payment gave free services with members obliged to use primary services as the first point of contact. Premia design developed over the years. Payments can be made on an individual or family basis, or linked to particular services.	Limited number of free consultations were allowed e.g., eight illness episodes for a family of four, or four episodes for an individual. A ceiling was placed on the costs covered e.g., 2,000 baht per visit. These levels were changed and eventually scrapped as the scheme	Khoman, 1997

Table 5.2 *continued*

Country	The scheme	Premia	Benefits	References
	develop small businesses, generally younger and healthier. One problem cited was that premiums were held in the reserve all year, and lent out to policyholders, with payments to facilities only made at the end of the year. This delay in payment acted as a disincentive to facilities to develop services particularly given that inflation would depreciate the value of income received.			
Guatemala	The ASSABA scheme was set up in rural Guatemala in 1994, to improve access to health care. Service costs and utilisation levels were carefully assessed, although contributions were set on the basis of affordability rather than full cost recovery. Target levels for the utilisation of different services were set. Donor funds were also secured to cover start-up costs. However delays with legal status, administrative staffing, and the definitions of benefits and membership rules slowed down initial progress.	Membership is family-based with premia varying according to family size.	Services at the primary level (health centre and below), including medicines. Both out-patient and in-patient care is provided at a contracted hospital.	Ron, 1997

tives, prices, use of funds, and regulation) is important in the success of community financing schemes. At the same time the decentralisation of responsibility necessitates adequate management skills at the local level, along with support from higher levels. A team evaluating the Bamako Initiative in Africa found health centre staff sitting on bags of money, worried about how to use it. Giving new responsibilities to government staff must be complemented with management support and policy guidelines.

Health savings accounts

Dr Fixit: *I want to go back to a point you raised earlier in your discussion – whether an individual might rely on his own savings rather than population insurance to pay for health care. In Chapter 4 we mentioned that in general such a system is inefficient – since some people will accumulate balances that are never used – and inequitable – since some people will not have saved enough to pay for unexpected illness. Is there no way of mitigating these problems?*

Professor Bluff: What is attractive, to many patients, about the savings approach is that they do not have to give up their own money to faceless individuals or, worse still, a bureaucracy that may or may not use the money wisely. This is particularly important in countries whether the government is not trusted. For policy makers, the central attraction is that patients have incentives to restrain their own consumption – a reduction in the moral hazard problem arising from pooling risk across individuals.

One type of savings system that attempts to reduce the associated problems but hold on to the advantages is medical savings accounts, pioneered in Singapore but also used the USA, China and Malaysia (Kai Hong Phua, 1997; Nichols *et al.*, 1997). Individuals and employers make tax-exempt payments into personal accounts managed by employers, banks or the state. In the event of illness these account are used first to pay for treatment. Back-up insurance is provided, if the balance is exhausted, but carries quite a large *deductible*, a fixed amount that a patient must pay before the policy begins to finance costs. Back-up insurance can be provided by the state, private sector or a combination of the two. Any balance remaining in the account at the end of a year is carried forward into the next. At retirement, or if the balance in the account reaches a certain level, individuals may withdraw funds provided that a minimum remains to pay for future expenses. The balance on death can be transferred to family members so is not 'wasted'. The approach is designed to encourage individual responsibility in health care consumption decisions.

Dr Fixit: *Well individual responsibility is good but I think I can spot a problem. If I had an account I would be extremely careful to avoid needless small health care expenditures such as visits to ambulatory centres for primary care consultations. But this may be detrimental if failure to attend early for a simple treatment leads to more complicated disease. With more complex and costly treatment I will exhaust the savings account anyway and depend on the back-up insurance – with no incentive to restrain treatment.*

Professor Bluff: That is certainly a potential problem. As with ambulatory user charges, savings accounts could lead to a reduction in preventative and early curative treatment. Sometimes this may reduce unnecessary treatment, at other times the delay will compound the severity of developing illness. It is hoped that far-sighted individuals will recognise the value of preventive measures to their future health and savings account.

Another issue is that because some of the resources are kept in individual accounts the state may lose resources contributed by well individuals that could be used for the treatment of the sick. The main empirical question is whether this loss is greater or less than the efficiency gain resulting from a reduction in inappropriate care.

In Singapore medisave accounts contribute around 9 per cent of total funding to a system that is largely funded from the budget and private out of pocket payments. This is in a country where economic growth is high and per capita incomes rival those in established market economies. Around 60 per cent of hospital care is subsidised by the state and the main contribution of medisave has been to the costs of outpatient care. The country is also wealthy enough to afford a 'safety-net' fund for the poor particularly targeted at struggling families. Proportional revenue in poorer countries may well be much lower. Nichols *et al.* (1997) also emphasise that resource mobilisation is likely to develop very slowly in most developing countries, which lack a high degree of formal labour force participation to enable efficient collection of back-up insurance, and the ability to ensure that deductibles charged for care are means tested.

Informal payments

Dr Fixit: *I know from my own experience, and what other staff tell me, that state funding and official user charges only account for part of the* *real spending on health care in state facilities. Significant funding appears to come from individuals who make unofficial payments to health staff. What are the effects of this type of funding?*

Professor Bluff: We had better first define what we mean by informal (or unofficial) payments. A working definition is that they are payments – both monetary or non-monetary – made by an individual to a health care worker that do not form part of the workers tax-deducted formal salary. These payments may be expected or unexpected and may be given for services that are routinely carried out or for an augmented or additional service undertaken by the health care worker. Payments given by patients to health care workers may be non-monetary (gifts) or monetary (tips) and be given in recognition of good service although they might not generally be expected by the agent.

There is indeed growing evidence from a range of low and middle income countries on the prevalence of unofficial payments. In Central Asia a study found that patients contribute at least 30 per cent to state health spending through unofficial payments (Ensor and Savelyeva, 1998). In Bangladesh, Killingsworth *et al.* (1998) found that unofficial payments to staff in hospitals exceeded revenue from official payments (user charges) by a factor of 10. Delcheva *et al.* (1997) found that the informal patient cost of an operation in Bulgaria amounted to more than 80 per cent of average monthly income. A recent study in Poland found that 46 per cent of patients paid for services that are officially free (Chawla, 1998)

Ladbury (1997) found that in near barter economies (such as rural Turkmenistan) patients make substantial non-monetary gifts to practitioners that collectively contribute more than 13 per cent to the actual health care spending. Anecdotal evidence indicates that doctors may refuse treatment if the value of the actual or proposed gift is not enough. Asiime *et al.* (1997) found that payments add between 20 and 37 per cent to the salaries of average rural primary workers in Uganda and more in urban areas.

Dr Fixit: Well this is interesting evidence, but I suspect that there are many different motivations for taking payments. A friend of mine is a specialist at the main city hospital on a salary that is a little bit lower than mine yet lives in a much wealthier part of the city than I can afford and has just purchased a new car. He clearly has an income far larger than his official salary. On the other hand my sister in law works as a doctor in a rural area about 80 kilometres from the city. She tells me that she has not been paid for two months because of problems with the district budget. The only way she survives is because patients give her food and small monetary gifts. Both doctors are receiving unofficial payments yet the size and nature would appear to be quite different.

Professor Bluff: Unofficial payments can certainly take a variety of forms. Some do not go to staff at all but are made, often in kind, to pay for medical supplies to be used during the treatment of the patient. Other payments are taken by staff just to ensure that they achieve a basic minimum salary so that they are able to stay in their employment. Often these are received because of wage arrears or because salaries do not keep up with the cost of living. Yet other payments are extracted from patients because of the monopoly position of the provider – payments to your friend in the city hospital could be an example. There are probably many other forms payments could take. One example is the payments taken by lower grade staff for performing unofficial services for patients (e.g., getting them better accommodation or food). It is quite possible that senior staff might also benefit from this market in return for allowing the practice to continue.

What is clear is that this is a very complex area in which research is very difficult and sometimes even hazardous! Very little is known about their real impact on staff behaviour and formal health sector reforms. This raises a number of issues about how to respond to informal payments.

1 *Effect of penalising acceptance of payments.* If most payments are to medical staff to bring them up to their reservation wage,[1] then attempts to deal harshly with the acceptance of informal income is likely to lead to the better workers (those most able to obtain such payments) leaving the public medical sector. On the other hand if payments are in excess of the reservation wage then management policy to stop payments could be more successful – reducing payments while still retaining staff.

2 *Effect of permitting private practice.* If practitioners are permitted to do some private practice in their spare time then they may tolerate a low official salary in order to build up credibility with private patients. But if policies are introduced to prevent them doing private work while unofficial income in state health facilities is also penalised, then again this may lead to them leaving.

1 This can be thought of as the income they could obtain in other employment less the value of the intrinsic satisfaction they get from working in the public medical sector over other occupations. If the wage sinks to below this point then staff will either leave employment or obtain income from unofficial sources. In economic terms it is represented by the labour supply curve.

3 *Formalising payments.* Policies to formalise unofficial payments could be successful if they provide additional formal income for workers. This would increase the value of the job and could reduce their propensity to obtain unofficial income. But if a patient's main reason for paying workers is to ensure that he gets quality treatment from a named individual, paying a general official payment to a health facility for treatment by an unnamed doctor will not be attractive. Unofficial payments direct to preferred practitioners could persist.

Official development assistance (ODA)

Mr Calculator: *We musn't forget the important contributions we receive from foreign governments, although at times I feel uncomfortable about the conditions that come with the funds, and the extent to which we are dependent on them.*

Professor Bluff: This is another important issue. External support to low income countries for health sector projects has become increasingly important in the last 20 years. In 1980 external assistance amounted to 0.5 per cent of total health expenditures in low income countries, rising to approximately 3 per cent in 1990.

Assistance also tends to come with conditions about how the money is spent, with much aid 'tied' – for example, when recipient governments are obliged to purchase expertise, equipment and other supplies from the donor country. Within the overall flow of ODA to health sectors, almost 50 per cent is currently allocated to the development of infrastructure, with many donor agencies reluctant to fund recurrent costs for any length of time. The other 50 per cent is directed towards specific health programmes, in particular leprosy, onchocerciasis, and sexually transmitted infections such as HIV (Michaud and Murray, 1994).

Whilst capital investments guarantee tangible benefits for foreign governments to justify aid expenditure, they also create substantial recurrent costs which recipient countries may find difficult to fund. This issue of financial sustainability requires a rigorous analysis of future recurrent costs generated by the investment (see Chapter 8). There are indications that many donors are increasingly prepared to fund recurrent costs, providing sector-wide funding (Appendix 2 on health sector reform).

Countries in a state of conflict, or in the immediate aftermath such as Mozambique and Angola, are particularly dependent on external assistance in the health sector. In 1990, external aid accounted for 60 per cent of government health expenditure in Cambodia, and 63 per cent in Nepal. Around 38.5 per cent of total external aid for health went to Africa in 1990 (equal to US$2.45 per capita). In Asia, meanwhile, aid comprised 60 per cent of total government expenditure. Such dependence creates uncertainties concerning future health sector funding.

Summary

Recognising the difficulty in raising sufficient funding from nationally implemented risk pooling, this chapter has explored options for additional funding in developing countries. User charges are seen to offer some potential for additional funding which, while not being significant in national terms, could offer individual facilities valuable additional income to fund mainly recurrent costs. The problems of reduced access for certain groups can be reduced through appropriate exemption mechanisms. Exemption mechanisms can be expensive to design and implement, reducing the net revenue obtained from charging.

Private insurance poses severe problems of access, both for low income and high risk groups. It is therefore not suitable as a main source of funding, but is likely to grow as a supplementary source, particularly for higher income groups and for services which have been excluded from state funding (e.g., through the implementation of 'essential packages', see Chapter 9).

Community insurance schemes are becoming increasingly popular in developing countries. As with user charges the revenue can be valuable at the local and facility level, and the emphasis on cross subsidy can avoid some of the problems of equity encountered with user charges. The crucial problem is enrolling the low risk in a voluntary scheme that does not risk rate. Ways round this problem may render the scheme unsustainable.

Medical savings accounts offer some advantage in encouraging individual responsibility. They also have equity implications and are perhaps most suited to countries experiencing significant economic growth.

While informal payments do not constitute an alternative funding source, their prevalence does indicate the size of the funding gap between what is officially covered and what can be afforded. External aid provides a critical source of health financing in many countries. Such dependency tends to increase uncertainty about the future flow of funds into the health sector.

Questions for discussion

1 The Minister for Health has asked you to make recommendations concerning the introduction of user charges for government health services. What would be your priority areas of investigation and how would you go about it? Think about:
   • the popular acceptability of charging for health services
   • how much to charge and for which aspects of health services?
   • how to ensure the improved uptake of priority services?

2 In 1996 a government in Asia introduced a voluntary system of insurance to cover 80 per cent of the cost of outpatient pharmaceuticals. The scheme attempted to enrol employees by collecting a payroll contribution fixed as a proportion of wages for employees and a flat rate contribution for the self-employed. Within one year the scheme had enrolled 60 per cent of employees in large enterprises and about 10 per cent of the self-employed. The scheme was hailed as a success but closer analysis suggested there were difficulties.
   • Based on what you know about the operation of insurance systems what would be the main advantages of such a scheme?
   • What are likely to be the main disadvantages?
   • How might the weaknesses of the scheme be remedied?

3 Do you think medical savings accounts would be a popular health finance strategy in your country ? What are the equity and efficiency implications of their introduction?

References and further reading

Abel-Smith, B. (1994). *An Introduction to Health Policy, Planning and Financing*. Harlow: Longman.
Asiime, D., McPake, B., Mwesigye, F., Ofumbi, M., Ortenblad, L., Streefland, P. and Turinde, A. (1997). The private-sector activities of public-sector health workers in Uganda, in S. Bennett, B. McPake and A. Mills *Private Health Providers in Developing Countries*. London: Zed Books.
Carrin, G., Sergent, F. and Murray, M. (1993). *Towards a Framework for Health Insurance Development in Hai Phong, Vietnam*. Macroeconomic Health and Development Series, 12. Geneva: WHO.
Carrin, G., and Vereecke, M. (eds) (1992). *Strategies for Health Care Finance in Developing Countries with a Focus on Community Financing Sub-Saharan Africa*. Basingstoke: Macmillan.
Chawla, M., Berman, P. and Kawiorsha, D. (1998). Financing health services in Poland: new evidence on private expenditures, *Health Economics*, 7(4) 337–346.

Chabot, J., Boal, M. and Da Silva, A. (1991). National community health insurance at village level: the case from Guinea-Bissau, *Health Policy and Planning*, 6(1).

Chabot, J. and Waddington, C. (1987). Primary Health Care is not cheap: a case study from Guinea Bissau, *International Journal of Health Services*, 17(3): 387–409.

Chollet, D. J. and Lewis, M. (1997). Private insurance: principles and practice, in G. Sheiber (ed.) *Innovations in Health Care Financing: proceedings of a World Bank conference March 10–11, 1997*. Washington, DC: The World Bank.

Collins, D., Quick, J., Musau, S. N., Kraushaar, D., Hussein, I. M. (1996). The fall and rise of cost-sharing in Kenya: the impact of phased implementation, *Health Policy and Planning*, 11(1): 53–63.

Creese, A. (1991). User charges for health care: A review of recent experience, *Health Policy and Planning*, 6: 309–319.

Creese, A., and Kutzin, J. (1994). Lessons from cost-recovery in health. Paper presented for the workshop on The Social and Economic Effects of Alternative Methods of Financing Education and Health Services in Developing Countries, Institute of Development Studies, University of Sussex, Brighton.

Criel, B., and Kegels, G. (1997). A health insurance scheme for hospital care in Bwamanda District, Zaire: lessons and questions after 10 years of functioning, *Tropical Medicine and International Health*, 2(7): 654–72.

Dahlgren, G. (1990). Strategies for health financing in Kenya – the difficult birth of a new policy, *Scandinavian Journal of Social Medicine*, Supplement No. 46: 67–81.

Delcheva, E., Balabanova, D. and McKee, M. (1997). Under-the-counter payments for health care: evidence from Bulgaria, *Health Policy*, 42, 89–100.

Ensor, T. (1995). Introducing health insurance in Vietnam, *Health Policy and Planning*, 10(2).

Ensor, T. and San, Pham Bich (1996). Access and payment for health care: the poor of northern Vietnam, *International Journal of Health Planning and Management*, 11: 69–83.

Ensor, T. and Savelyeva, L. (1998). Informal payments for health care in the Former Soviet Union: some evidence from Kazakhstan and an emerging research agenda, *Health Policy and Planning*, 13, 1; 41–49.

Gilson, L. (1997). The lessons of user fee experience in Africa, *Health Policy and Planning*, 12(4): 273–285.

Gilson, L. (1988). *Government Health Care Charges: Is Equity being Abandoned?* London: London School of Hygiene and Tropical Medicine. EPC Publication 15.

Goodman, H. and Waddington, C. (1993). *Financing Health Care*, Oxfam Practical Health Guide no. 8. Oxford: Oxfam.

Kai Hong Pua (1997). Medical savings accounts and health care financing in Singapore in G. Sheiber (ed.) Innovations in *Health Care Financing: proceedings of a World Bank conference March 10–11, 1997*. Washington, DC: The World Bank.

Killingsworth, J., Hossain, N., Rahman, A., Begum, T., Hedrick-Wong, Y. and Thomas, S. D. (1999). Unofficial fees at health care facilities in developing countries: price, equity and institutional issues, *Health Policy and Planning* (forthcoming).

Khoman S. (1997). Rural Health Care Financing in Thailand in G. Sheiber (ed.). *Innovations in Health Care Financing: Proceedings from a World Bank Conference, March 10–11, 1997*. Washington, DC: The World Bank.

Kumaranayake, L. (1997). The role of regulation: influencing private sector activity within health sector reform, *Journal of International Development*, 9, 4: 641–649.

Ladbury, S. (1997). *Turkmenistan health project social assessment study.* Report to World Bank/ Government of Turkmenistan.

Litvack, J., and Bodart, C. (1993). User fees plus quality equals improved access to health care: results of a field experiment in Cameroon, *Social Science and Medicine*, 37(3): 369–83.

Michaud, C. and Murray, C. J. L. (1994). External assistance to the health sector in developing countries: a detailed analysis, 1972–90. *Bulletin of the WHO*, 72(4) 639–651.

Moens F. (1990). How Replicable is the Bwamanda Prepayment Plan. Paper presented at the International Conference 'Economics of Health Insurance in Low and Middle Income Countries', Belgium.

Moens, F. and Carrin, G. (1992). Prepayment for Hospital Care in the Bwamanda Health Zone (Zaire), in G. Carrin and M. Vereecke (eds) *Strategies for Health Care Finance in Developing Countries with a Focus on Community Financing Sub-Saharan Africa;* 157–170. Basingstoke: Macmillan.

Nichols, L., Prescott, N. and Kai Hong Phua (1997). Medical savings accounts in developing countries in G. Sheiber (ed.) *Innovations in Health Care Financing: proceedings of a World Bank conference March 10–11, 1997*. Washington, DC: The World Bank.

Ron, A. (1997). Community Health Insurance Schemes: Experience in Guatemala and the Philippines. Paper presented at the International Conference 'Economics of Health Insurance in Low and Middle Income Countries', Belgium.

Saltman, R. (1997). Applying planned market logic to developing countries' health systems: an initial exploration, Forum on Health Sector Reform, World Health Organisation.

Sauerborn, R., Nongtara, A. and Latimer, E. (1994). The elasticity of demand for health care in Burkina Faso, *Health Policy and Planning*, 9(2).

Robinson, R. and Steiner, A. (1998). *Managed health care*, Buckingham: Open University Press.

Waddington, C. and Enyimayew, K. (1990). A Price to Pay, Part 2: The Impact of User Charges in the Volta Region of Ghana, *International Journal of Health Planning and Management*, 5: 287–312.

World Bank (1980). Health Sector Policy Paper. Washington, DC: World Bank.

World Bank (1993). *Investing in Health: World Development Report 1993*, Oxford, Oxford University Press.

Wouters, A. (1995). Improving quality through cost-recovery in Niger, *Health Policy and Planning*, 10(3): 257–270.

Yoder, R. (1989). Are people willing and able to pay for health services? *Social Science and Medicine*, 29: 35–42.

PART 3

Allocating resources for health and health care

6

The use of cost information

Sophie Witter

Introduction

Information on the costs of health care is required for many different purposes. We need to predict costs in order to plan services while staying within budget. We need to analyse costs to compare efficiency between different facilities. We sometimes need to allocate costs to different programmes in order to set prices (for customers, insurance funds, or for use in contracting). We also need to understand costs in order to prioritise between different health care interventions.

Cost information is a vital managerial tool, but it usually has to be interpreted together with other information. For example, to prioritise between different programmes requires information not just on costs but also on benefits. Similarly, assessing efficiency by looking at costs alone would be misleading: the quality of the activities and outcomes must be compared too (see Chapter 13 for further discussion of how to do this). Costs are often the start of the process of investigation, but they are rarely the end.

This chapter starts by introducing the most relevant general cost concepts. The first section focuses on the direct costs of health care. That is, the costs incurred by a particular programme or service in a specific period. This could thus be described as a narrow costing approach.

In the second half, the focus is on a much broader range of costs. The analysis of costs for economic evaluation focuses not only on the direct costs incurred by a facility or programme, but also the indirect costs borne by individuals and society as a whole. This links with the next chapter on the measurement of health benefits (Chapter 8). It will cover the following topics:

- the difference between fixed, variable and semi-variable costs
- the use of marginal and average costs

- the distinction between capital and recurrent costs
- how to allocate costs between programmes
- issues in assessing costs for economic evaluation
- the meaning of opportunity costs
- use of shadow prices
- use of discounting, and where this is appropriate
- allowing for uncertainty

Cost concepts and definitions

Mrs Darling is manager of the district hospital in Gamlan. She faces an increase in demand for admissions without getting any increase in the hospital's budget. Mrs Darling approaches the Regional Health Team asking for more money. They in turn request figures about how much it costs to increase the number of patients treated. Mrs Darling starts by listing her three main cost categories: staff; consumables (drugs, food, laundry, etc.); rent, maintenance and utilities.

She then puts together the estimates in Table 6.1 for the cost implications (in bontlis) of increasing the number of patients seen each day from the current level of 20 to 50.

What is the difference between the three categories in terms of how they respond to increased activity? How are marginal and average costs calculated, and what do they tell us?

The first cost category (rent, maintenance, etc.) does not increase over the range shown here (increasing from 20 to 40 patients). These types of costs, which do not relate to volume (or output, in business terms), are called *fixed costs*. At the other end of the spectrum are the costs, which relate directly to the number of people treated – i.e., the drugs and supplies category. These

Table 6.1   Hospital cost estimates

Activity levels	Heating, rent, lighting and maintenance	Staff costs	Materials: drugs, food and laundry	Total cost	Average cost	Marginal cost
20	50	80	200	330	16.5	0
30	50	80	220	350	11.6	2
40	50	100	240	390	9.75	4
50	50	100	260	410	15.8	2

are known as *variable costs*. Staffing costs tend to fall into an intermediate category – they do not rise immediately, but once the increase in volume reaches a certain level (an extra 5 patients, in this example), an extra person has to be hired, increasing the staffing costs. They are therefore termed *semi-variable costs*. Added together, they produce the *total costs* of production.

If we plot these on a graph (see Figure 6.1), the fixed cost curve is horizontal, the variable rises smoothly, and the semi-variable rises in a stepped fashion. The total cost curve reflects their combined behaviour, and rises but in a slightly stepped pattern.

Average cost is the total cost, divided by the total number of activity. It tells you how much it costs to see each person. This is very useful for budgeting purposes. However, if we are taking a decision about whether or not to expand or by how much, the *marginal cost* can be more useful. This tells us how much costs increase if you increase your activities by 1. This will depend at what level you start and the extent to which spare capacity exists. When there is spare capacity, then marginal costs will be determined by variable costs alone. In Figure 6.1, for example, the marginal cost is 10 bondis (except when crossing a threshold at which a new member of staff will be required). These threshold points, at which costs suddenly leap up, are masked by the average figures (see Figure 6.2). They decline gently as numbers increase, rising only slightly as new staff are taken on. Marginal

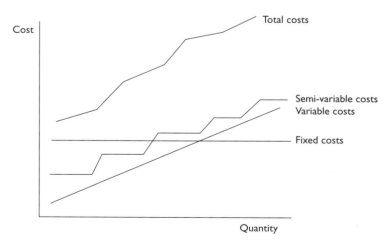

Fig. 6.1   Total, fixed and variable costs

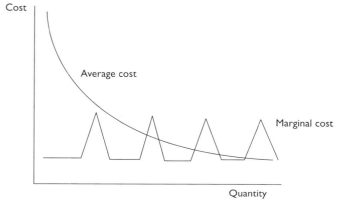

Fig. 6.2   Average and marginal costs

costs show the implications of specific increases or decreases more clearly.

The inclusion of costs within a specific category (e.g., variable, semi-variable, and fixed) should reflect the technical and physical constraints, or indeed flexibility, of an institution to alter the cost structure of their services. Sometimes, for example, staffing numbers are fixed by bureaucratic rules, so that whether activity increases or decreases, the staff will remain the same. In this case, they should of course be considered as fixed costs, as opposed to semi-variable. On the other hand, there may be flexibility about building space, with the ability to hire or shut down spaces as volume of patients vary. In this case, rent/heating/maintenance will fall into the semi-variable category.

The variability of different costs in relation to volume is often also an indicator of how quickly supply can respond to changes in demand or the general environment. For example, if more patients attend clinic today than were expected, the only adjustment which can be made instantly will be an increase in supplies of drugs, etc. used. Over the medium term, however, more staff can be hired to cope with increases in demand, while buildings and land may well be increased in the longer term (though these are pragmatic distinctions again, and will depend on labour market conditions, etc. in the locality).

Similarly, the shape of the cost curves will vary by product. Average costs may get smaller the larger the number of units produced; in other cases, average costs start to rise after a certain level as management, for example, gets more complicated (diseconomies of scale, in effect).

Using her projections of cost, can Mrs Darling tell what the optimal level of activity is for her hospital? How should she going about determining output?

If average costs fall until a certain point and then start to rise, it is tempting to think that the optimal level of activity will be at the lowest point in the average cost curve. However, costs are only one side of the story. The other side is revenue or benefits. These have to be taken into account when deciding on optimal levels of activity or output.

Assuming that the hospital charges the same price for all units produced of a given good, the minimum which it would accept as price is the marginal cost of producing the last unit. In a competitive market, this also represents the maximum, which it could obtain. According to economic theory, then, optimal output will be the level at which marginal cost and marginal revenue curves intersect. This intersection will also give you the price of the product. (See Figure 6.3).

In health care, goods are commonly unpriced and information about benefits is harder to come by. However, the principle remains the same: the point at which marginal cost and benefit curves intersect – if this information can be calculated – gives you the level of optimal activity. Any more and the costs outweigh the benefits. Any less and there remain gains to be made by increasing activity levels.

If Mrs Darling is setting up her budget for the next five years, what other categories of cost might she need to distinguish between?

Budgets are concerned with financial flows: what amounts of money are needed and when they are needed. Some costs are

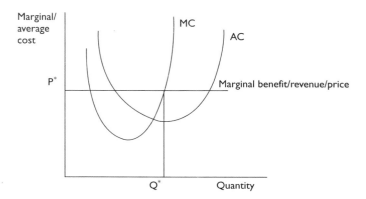

Fig. 6.3   Marginal costs, average costs and marginal benefits

Table 6.2   Different types of costs: family planning mobiliser

Cost categories	Recurrent	Capital
Fixed	– bicycle maintenance – salary	– bicycle – training
Semi-variable	– travel allowances	– log books
Variable	– pills – injections – condoms	

paid regularly – every week or month or year. These are known as *recurrent costs*. They usually include supplies, staff costs and support costs such as rent and heating. By contrast, some items are only purchased every few years. These are known as *capital costs*. They tend to be large items, such as cars, buildings and equipment – anything which has a lifetime longer than a year. They should be separated in budgets as they are incurred only irregularly. It should be noted though that capital items create recurrent costs, such as fuel and maintenance for cars, repairs for buildings and replacement parts for equipment.

While recurrent costs can be either fixed, variable or semi-variable, capital costs tend to be either fixed or semi-variable. See the example in Table 6.2 of the costs incurred by a family planning mobiliser working at village level.

Allocating costs between programmes

We often need to allocate shared costs to a particular programme. For example a number of village health centres may share an ambulance. The costs of maintaining and renewing the vehicle will need to be shared between the facilities. This can be done in a number of ways, but should accurately reflect the resource use of each of the centres. Some items are easier to allocate than others. Supplies are usually straightforward, for example, as drugs, slides, etc. are specific to malaria control activities and can be counted directly. For other items, the dimensions indicated in Table 6.3 are used to allocate costs.

If clinical staff are seeing malaria patients mixed in with other patients in a general clinic, how can we tell the proportion of time spent on malaria?

Table 6.3   Allocating the cost of different inputs

Input	Dimension determining cost
Vehicles	Distance travelled/time used
Equipment	Time used
Building space	Space used/time used
Staff	Time worked
Supplies	Volume/weight used
Vehicle operation and maintenance	Distance travelled/time used
Building operation and maintenance	Time used/space used
Other inputs	Miscellaneous

- We could ask staff to keep records for a sample period and then generalise from that, although there might be seasonal distortions in the pattern of disease being presented at any one time.
- We could ask them to provide estimates based on their impressions, which might however be inaccurate.
- We could track them and keep our own records for a period, although this would be very time consuming.

Let us assume that we come up with an estimate of 10 per cent of clinical staff time spent on malaria activities. This might also serve as a weighting factor for other costs that are hard to attribute, such as building and building maintenance costs.

In more complex units, like hospitals, a *step-down costing system* can be used to allocate support and overhead costs, such as administration, to direct patient care activities.

- The first stage is to attribute all fixed costs, such as heating, lighting, etc. to a department (e.g., administration, X-ray department, kitchen, accident and emergency unit), according to some measure of resource use, for example, space utilised by the department.
- Next, overhead department costs (e.g., administration) are allocated to support, paraclinic and direct patient departments.
- Finally, paraclinic costs (e.g., the laboratory services) and support costs (e.g., cleaning or cooking) are allocated to patient care departments, according to some criterion such as number of tests or number of patients admitted.
- This gives a total expenditure by department, which can be used to calculate *costs per patient treated* or *cost per bed day*.

The calculation of accurate costs can be time-consuming, particularly if information is not readily available. For more detailed information on costing services see Shepard *et al.* (1997).

Assessing costs for economic evaluation

Costing in economic evaluation has a much broader definition than the financial or accounting costs which we consider when we are calculating budgets or looking at cash-flow issues as described earlier. Economic evaluation tries to answer the question: 'what is the best possible use of resources, from society's perspective?' It therefore tries to collect information on all opportunity costs for all relevant groups (see Box 6.1 for a definition of this

---

Box 6.1   Opportunity cost: what does it mean?

Economists often talk about the 'opportunity cost' of a particular activity. By this they mean the next best use to which the resources could have been put, if they had not been consumed in this activity. This measures how much is 'given up' by carrying out the activity (and therefore its real cost).

Let us take the example of Lula visiting the district health centre. What are the real costs to her? First, there is the value of the time she spends. What would she have been doing if she had not been attending? She might have been working, and the value of that production lost is one opportunity cost. Or she might have been taking care of her children. That, too, is valuable, even though it may not have a direct value in money terms. It has value because she enjoys it, and both she and the children gain from their interaction. It also has value in the sense that there is a cost to replacing her – for example, she may owe the neighbour a favour for looking after them while she is away. These costs tend to be ignored because they may not involve actual transfers of money. Nevertheless they are real to the patients and influence decisions about which services to use. In addition, there may be a small direct financial cost: the cost of travel, a small gift to the doctor, and of buying some drugs in the market after the visit. These resources could have been used for food or some other desirable commodity. Again, this alternative use measures the opportunity costs of the visit.

term). However, compromises are made in practice if data is really unavailable.

> *The government research team has come to town. Under investigation is the malaria control programme, which is co-ordinated by the District Public Health Officer, Mr Do-Good. How much value for money does it provide, they want to know. First of all they ask him to provide them with information on all of the costs of the programme. Which ones is he likely to remember and which costs is he likely to forget? How easy will it be for him to find the information?*

Mr Do-Good is likely to focus on the costs that are most immediate to him, which will be the costs to the health service in the district. These will include the types of costs in Table 6.4.

Mr Do-Good would be proud of this list: he has not only remembered to include the capital items, but has also remembered all three aspects of the programme.

However, these categories of cost should also be considered:

1 Higher level service costs (e.g., management support or training by other levels within the MoH, where this relates specifically to the programme).
2 Costs incurred by other organisations (e.g., mobilisation by village associations, or support by staff of another ministry).

Table 6.4   Malaria control programme costs

Programme component	Capital	Recurrent
Prevention	Vehicles	– Staff time – Travel expenses – Sprays – Provision of bednets – Vehicle maintenance
Screening	Equipment	– Supplies (slides, etc.) – Lab staff time – Rent – Heating – Building maintenance
Treatment	Equipment	– Medicines – Clinical staff time – Rent – Heating – Building maintenance

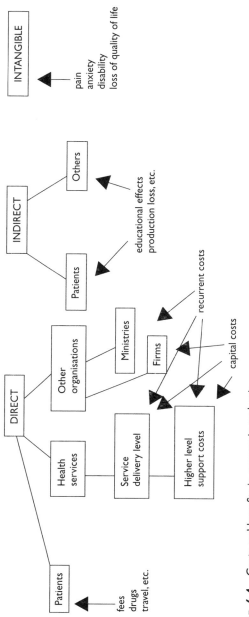

Fig. 6.4 Costs and benefits in economic evaluation

3 Costs incurred by patients and their families (e.g., costs of buying bednets, or having them sprayed, or travelling to the clinic, or buying drugs). Remember too that 'gifts' or informal payments are just as real to the patients as formal user fees.

All the categories listed so far are *direct costs*. These are costs where actual sums of money are handed over in payment. However, there are two more types of costs which should be included if the evaluation is to be comprehensive (see Figure 6.4):

4 *Indirect costs.* These are real costs that are incurred as a result of the treatment even though no money is paid over. For example, when a sick person travels for screening, perhaps with a relative, both of them lose time that would otherwise have been used productively. Similarly, if volunteers help to carry out some part of the programme, their time is valuable and should be attributed a monetary value, even though they are not paid. The question to ask in giving a value to that time is: what would the value have been of the best alternative use that they would have made of it?

5 *Intangible costs.* These are non-financial costs such as anxiety, pain or depression, which are attributable to the programme.

Direct costs to the health service are time-consuming to collect, but do not pose any theoretical problems. It will sometimes be impossible to collect cost information from all areas, in which case samples must be used which are large enough and representative enough to be reliable. Where possible, expenditure figures should be used, rather than budgets, as budgets are commonly not adhered to in practice. Staffing costs should include not just salaries but any other payments in cash and kind, such as free meals or free access to services. Estimates for supplies should include wastage but exclude stocks which are available for future use.

Indirect costs and patient costs are a bit more complicated, as surveys must be carried out and some proxy used to value inputs like time (or opportunity cost – see Box 6.1). Commonly the local hourly wage rate is used as an indicator of the value of time, although this is only appropriate if the patients would otherwise have been working. If they are predominantly unemployed or retired, or are able to substitute in other family members without a knock-on loss of production, then indirect costs may be low or non-existent. For a programme which targets an average cross-section of the population, a standard weighting can be applied based on the national figures for labour force participation.

Intangibles are even harder to estimate and value. We will discuss how this might be done in the chapter on benefits (Chapter 7). However, note here that it is only relevant to include intangible costs *caused by the programme itself* – pain and disability caused by the disease would have existed anyway and is not a programme cost. Similarly, it would be wrong to include an estimate for production loss, under indirect costs, by those attending a clinic where their condition prevents them from working anyway.

Sometimes cost information cannot be obtained directly, but has to be constructed – for example, by using disease treatment protocols and the average price of drugs to calculate drugs expenditure. In such cases, allowance should be made for likely wastage, loss, theft or inefficiency, which may substantially increase real costs (Jha *et al.*, 1998 gives a good example). The aim is to produce a realistic estimate of costs, not an ideal one.

One short-cut which is legitimate in collecting cost information for evaluation is to omit counting common costs – i.e., costs which are shared by all the options under consideration. If these are identical, then they will not influence the final decision about which option is relatively more cost effective.

There is also a type of payment which would be included in financial or accounting costs *but* omitted from economic ones. These are known as *transfer payments*. These are sums of money which are not spent, but rather passed from one group of the population to the other. For example, sickness benefits or social security payments are not included as costs of a programme as they are still available to be spent by the group to whom they have been paid.

Although we have emphasised the need to include patient and social costs, it can be helpful for decision-makers to present these separately from health service costs. This brings out more clearly different perspectives on the merits of different arrangements. For example, if outreach services are planned they may increase health service costs, but greatly decrease patient costs and be more cost-effective overall.

Shadow pricing

*Mr Datum, a health economist from the Ministry, comes to assist
Mr Do-Good in his costing work. 'These prices do not reflect the real value
of some of these goods', he tells Do-Good. 'You should use shadow prices.'
What on earth does he mean?*

Shadow prices are very confusing to non-economists. The price, which you pay for something in the local market, is the real price, and that is that. Or is it? What economists argue is that there may be high taxes, or agreements over wages, or overvalued exchange rates which 'distort' markets. In this situation, a good can have a price that is out of line with its 'real' value in international markets. In other words, the price is not consistent with the opportunity cost to society.

For budgeting purposes, local market prices are always appropriate, as these are the prices which will in fact be paid. However, for carrying out an economic evaluation, we try to assess the real value of goods to society by constructing a shadow price.

- For example, if an imported good has been subject to high import duties and a fixed exchange rate, we may take its price in international markets as a shadow price.
- For foreign exchange, black market rates may be closer to the real value of a currency than the official rate.
- Labour markets can also be distorted. For example, urban wage rates may be maintained at an artificially high level by wage agreements, while a pool of unemployed labour from rural areas exists. In this situation, we might take the rural wages as a shadow price for labour in the city (because the rural rates reflect the real levels of supply and demand for labour in that economy). On the other hand, wages for skilled workers may be artificially depressed by wage agreements, which do not reflect the real scarcity of such skills locally. In that case, a shadow price above the market price would be appropriate (perhaps taken from a neighbouring economy, with similar conditions but a more flexible labour market).

As many developing countries have liberalised their economies, the use of shadow pricing has become less necessary. However, evaluators still need to consider the extent to which markets are distorted. If they are very distorted, the next question is the overall value of that input in the project. The larger its contribution to the costs, the more time should be spent in calculating shadow prices. If small, the effort may not be justified.

Discounting and allowing for differences in time

If we have to spend $1 this year, and $1 in a year's time, are the sums equivalent (leaving aside inflation)? How do we adjust for the difference in timing of costs (or benefits)?

If you offer someone $1 today and $1 in a year's time, they will generally prefer to have it today. This is known as *time preference* and in theory it can be measured. You could, for example, reduce the current offer until the other person is undecided about taking that reduced sum now or $1 next year. If this took place at 95 cents, then that would suggest a discount rate of 5 per cent per year. For that person, every extra year away that the cost or benefit falls will reduce its present value by 5 per cent.

We need to know what the social rate of time preference is in order to decide on the best use of resources. If a project is estimated to produce $300 million in health benefits in 10 years' time, and an alternative project would produce $250 in five years' time, which one should we invest in (assuming a discount rate of 5 per cent)?

$$\text{Present value} \ = \ \frac{\text{future value}}{(1 + r)^n}$$

where r = discount rate and n = number of years

$$\frac{300}{(1.05)^{10}} \ = \ 167 \qquad \frac{250}{(1.05)^5} \ = \ 186$$

The answer then is that the latter project would be more worthwhile. Because discounting does significantly affect estimates of costs and benefits, there is some controversy about which discount rates should be used. (There is also a debate about whether and on what basis discounting should apply to health benefits. This is quite a complex area and so is omitted here. See Olsen, 1993, for further reading on this topic.) Western studies tend to use 5–6 per cent, while the World Bank often uses a higher rate of around 10 per cent to reflect the increased urgency of needs in many developing countries. Local bank interest rates could be used, as long as these are not fixed by government and allowance is made for inflation. For example, if bank interest rates are around 15 per cent per year and inflation is running at around 10 per cent, then the real interest rate (and implied discount rate) is 5 per cent. The difference between the rate paid by government treasury bills and inflation may also be a guide.

Discount rates are also used for capital items, whose future replacement cost is generally discounted and divided over the period of its lifetime. (In the absence of better estimates, buildings are often assumed to last 20 years, cars 10 and medical equipment 5.) This process, known as *annualisation*, allows capital items to be incorporated with recurrent costs in annual budgets. Alternatively, where a rental market for a good exists, rental rates can be used to provide an estimated annual cost of a capital good.

The reverse of discounting is known as *compounding*. This can be used to calculate the effect of compound interest rates over a number of years on a present sum, or to allow for the effects of future inflation. The future value of $1 today, will be $1 $(1+r)^n$ (where r is the rate of interest or inflation and n is the number of years).

Where an item was purchased in the past and an estimate of its replacement cost is required, allowances must be made for inflation. General retail price indexes are usually available from the Ministry of Finance which can be applied to the original price to obtain an estimate of its current value (assuming that no market price can be found at present for the exact same good).

Allowing for uncertainty

> *In the example given earlier, the discount rate of 5 per cent was taken as given. But there may be some uncertainty about whether this is the real discount rate. How can we deal with that uncertainty? Does it shed doubt on the results?*

In economic evaluations a number of parameters have to be estimated and this has given rise to what is known as *sensitivity analysis*. This proceeds by:

1 identifying uncertain parameters
2 drawing up the most realistic range of values for them
3 inserting these into the final calculation of costs and benefits
4 considering the effect of changing the values on the final outcome.

Where the final outcome is significantly altered *and* the value of the variable is genuinely uncertain, the conclusion will be shown to be weak by such sensitivity analysis. However, commonly it reinforces the conclusion by showing that within the probable range of values, the final outcome remains largely the same. Another possible use of sensitivity analysis is to highlight the parameters which it is worth returning to to make more accurate estimates.

In this example, what are the probable alternate values for the discount rate? It is unlikely to fall below, say, 3 per cent, or to rise above 10 per cent. If we insert these two into the calculation, the results are as follows in Table 6.5.

Table 6.5   Sensitivity analysis on discount rates

Discount rate	3%	5%	10%
	Present value in millions ($)		
Option A (300 in 10 years)	217	167	116
Option B (250 in 5 years)	215	186	155
Conclusion: preferred option	A preferred, but narrowly	B preferred	B preferred

These results reinforce the conclusion as B is preferred over almost the whole range of probable discount rates.

In some cases, uncertain parameters may be linked. In that case it is worth simulating them changing value together in a variety of scenarios, so that their combined effect on the outcome is seen.

Summary

This chapter has introduced a number of important concepts relating to costs, which will be useful in several contexts. The distinction between fixed, variable and semi-variable costs and between average and marginal costs is particularly useful in planning services. Capital and recurrent costs, meanwhile, are particularly important for budgeting purposes. Distinguishing financial from economic costs is relevant when it comes to economic evaluation or appraisal, where the broader economic costs are estimated. The idea of opportunity costs is generally useful for analysing health markets: it highlights the point that choices by doctors or patients have costs, even where these costs are not expressed in direct financial form.

Many of the distinctions and techniques in this chapter will also be relevant to the next chapter on measuring benefits in health. (Taken together, these chapters provide the tools for carrying out or analysing an economic evaluation.) If we are attributing monetary values to health gains, we would also need to distinguish between direct benefits (money saved in health service costs or costs to patients and society), indirect benefits (production gains) and intangible gains (relief of pain; improved mobility; improved mental health, etc.). The use of discounting and sensitivity analysis is equally relevant to benefits as to costs, and under the same conditions (i.e., if benefits occur in the future, and if estimates relating to them are subject to some uncertainty).

Questions for discussion

1 You have been asked to cost the existing family planning pro-gramme in your district. Your results will be compared with another district where services are organised differently. Assuming the two approaches achieve similar results, which one has fewer opportunity costs?

   • Start by outlining the categories of data which would need to be collected. Make sure that you have not forgotten any important types of costs. If you think that some are not rele-vant, be clear and open about why they have been excluded.
   • How would you collect the data? For what time period? From which sources?
   • Would any costs need to be adjusted to obtain their real value?
   • How would you deal with any allocation issues?
   • Do you need to apply discounting?
   • Are you uncertain about any of your values? How might you allow for that?

References and further reading

Creese, A. and Parker, D., (eds) (1994). *Cost Analysis in Primary Health Care: A Training Manual for Programme Managers.* Geneva: WHO.

Hanson, K. and Gilson, L. (1996). *Cost, Resource Use and Financing Methodology for District Health Services: A Practical Manual.* New York: UNICEF.

Jha, P., Bangoura, O. and Ranson, K. (1998). The cost-effectiveness of forty health interventions in Guinea, *Health Policy and Planning* 13(3), 249–262.

Olsen, J. A. (1993). On what basis should health be discounted? *Journal of Health Economics,* 12.

Phillips, M., Mills, A. and Dye, C. (1993). *Guidelines for Cost-effectiveness Analysis of Vector Control.* Geneva: WHO.

Shepard, D. S., Hodgkin, D. and Antony, Y. (1997). *Analysis of Hospital Costs in Developing Countries: A Manual for Managers.* Geneva: WHO.

World Health Organisation (1979). *Expanded Programme on Immunization: Costing Guidelines.* Geneva: WHO.

World Health Organisation (1988). *Estimating Costs for Cost-effectiveness Analysis: Guidelines for Managers of Diarrhoeal Disease Control Programmes.* Geneva: WHO.

7

Measuring health benefits

Sophie Witter

Introduction

> *Dr Do-Good, the public health officer in Gamlan, has a limited annual budget with which to attack what he sees as the major public health problems in the district. He already has some estimates of the cost of different programmes. Relying on what he believes to be economic principles, he goes about drawing up his priorities by selecting the programmes which are the cheapest. Is that the right approach?*

It is commonly thought that economics is about money and that the job of economists is to cut costs and save money. However, that is a misperception. The job of an economist is to maximise benefits for a given investment. So while cost is one side of the equation, the other, very important one, is benefits. This chapter will look at how they can be measured and compared with one another.

The chapter will cover the following topics:

- how to establish medical effectiveness for a programme
- different measures for cost-effectiveness analysis (CEA)
- giving a utility value to health benefits: cost-utility analysis (CUA)
- giving a monetary value to health benefits: cost-benefit analysis (CBA)
- using economic evaluation data to prioritise between different interventions

Medical effectiveness

The first stage in assessing benefits is to establish whether interventions work, and how well they work. This is known as medical efficacy or effectiveness (see distinction in Box 7.1). There is a

---

Box 7.1   Efficacy vs effectiveness

If a drug is tested in laboratory conditions, then the results will show the *efficacy* of the drug: how well it controls the disease which it is intended to combat, when used under ideal conditions.

In the 'real world', however, other factors may affect the results. Doctors may give varying degrees of guidance on how to use the drug, for example, and patients may not fully understand or comply with their guidance. If a drug is tested in the normal circumstances in which it will be used, then the results should reflect such issues as how 'user-friendly' a product is. The results in this situation are referred to as *effectiveness*. This measure is clearly more realistic and will be used in this chapter. However, it may also be subject to more variance from place to place than efficacy.

---

growing recognition in the West that there are big variations in practice and that many of the treatments which doctors have used have been untested and this has led to a movement towards *evidence-based medicine*.

The *randomised control trial* (RCT) is the ideal vehicle for establishing the effectiveness of an intervention. It attempts to control a variety of biases by:

- comparing treatment and control groups
- randomly allocating patients between the two, so that patient characteristics do not influence outcomes
- assessors of results are unaware of which group the patients belong to, so that their expectations of the outcome do not influence results.

RCTs are routinely used for new drug trials in the West. However, they are complicated and expensive to carry out and so are rarely used in developing countries. Many of the Western results may be valid though, depending on the treatment and how it is delivered locally. The Cochrane Database of Systematic Reviews is one of the main sources of information, containing reviews of studies and protocols for treatment of many disease groups. (For details of how to access it, see 'Useful resources' section in Appendix 4.) Alternatively, results from controlled studies in the region may be used, as long as conditions influencing effectiveness are thought to be similar.

Note also that effectiveness depends on patient characteristics and so estimates of benefits may have to distinguish between different groups – for example, between early sufferers who can be successfully treated with a drug and very advanced cases, where it may be less effective.

Cost-effectiveness analysis

Following on from the collection of cost information, Dr Do-good wants to compare two different strategies for preventing the spread of malaria, which is endemic in the district, to see which one offers the best value for money. One option is to spray mosquito sites with insecticides. Another is to provide impregnated bednets for households. What measure of benefit should he use to compare them? What information does he need to calculate it?

Both approaches aim to prevent illness and death from malaria. One measure which could be used to compare them is *number of cases averted.* This is an intermediate indicator, though, as it does not quantify the benefits of the programme, in terms of how much illness or death was avoided. Leaving aside the illness aspect, we could compare them in terms of the *number of deaths averted.* Another option is to consider the number of *life years gained.* This requires data on survival rates and the likelihood of complications. As the disease being prevented is the same, we may assume that the survival patterns would be similar; thus deaths averted may be the most simple and appropriate measure.

To calculate the cost per death averted, Dr Do-Good needs the following information:

- annual programme cost (see Chapter 6)
- efficacy of treatment (cure/prevention rate, for people treated)
- number treated
- the probability of contracting the disease (prior to treatment, in that area)
- case fatality rate (if contracted, how many die, on average)

$$\text{Cost per death averted} = \frac{\text{cost}}{\text{efficacy} \times \text{no. treated} \times \text{prob. contracting} \times \text{CFR}}$$

The question of onward transmission should also be considered. If you treat for tuberculosis, for example, it is estimated that you

Table 7.1   Cost-effectiveness data

	Spraying breeding sites	Impregnated bednets
1 Annual programme cost	$10,000	$4,000
2 Efficacy of treatment	15%	85%
3 Number treated	10,000	1,000
4 Probability of contracting the disease	80%	80%
5 Case fatality rate	5%	5%
6 Deaths averted (2 × 3 × 4 × 5)	64	34
7 Cost per death averted (1/6)	$156	$118

are preventing the transmission to a further 10 people, and these are important benefits. In the case of malaria control, some impact on transmission would also be expected, but this is omitted for simplicity here.

Consider the data in Table 7.1. Which option comes out as more cost-effective?

In this case, the high efficacy of the bednet approach more than compensates for the relatively lower coverage of that programme.

There are a few important points to note about using cost-effectiveness ratios like these.

1 You must compare programmes whose aims can be captured by a single index, such as life years gained or deaths averted. If other factors, such as quality of life, are important health outcomes, then cost-utility analysis (CUA) (utility is an economic term, meaning, broadly, welfare, or happiness) may be more appropriate. If productivity increases are a significant benefit, then cost-benefit (CBA) may be better. These are discussed later.

2 The comparison is only as strong as the questions asked and the data obtained. If you have ignored an important alternative or if, say, evidence is not available on the effectiveness of an intervention, or the full costs of implementing it, then the comparison will be flawed. One common weakness of studies is the short time frame adopted, which may leave out important consequences, or fail to allow for variations over time.

3 The final cost-effectiveness ratio tells you how one option compares with another. It does not tell you whether the strategy is worth pursuing in an absolute sense. Nor does it help you to prioritise in relation to other health activities with different

goals (such as easing pain, prolonging life, increasing mobility etc.) For that, CBA or CUA is useful.

4 Even if you get a clear result at the current level of activity, you would still require marginal information on costs and benefits in order to determine the right degree of expansion of the programme. Collecting that data can be difficult. Educated guesses sometimes have to be made instead. For example, if coverage is currently concentrated in urban areas, it can probably be assumed that costs will increase steeply with expansion.

5 Cost-effectiveness ratios (CER) have to be used with care. One option may be dominant because it is both more effective and cheaper, and in this case it will clearly emerge as the method of choice. However, sometimes the choice will be between the option with the best CER, and one which is more effective but also costs more. Although the latter's CER may be higher, it might still be the best choice if (a) high coverage is a high priority; (b) it is affordable and (c) it is still efficient relative to other possible uses of the funds.

6 We have simplified the epidemiology here. Bednets, for example, have been found to be very effective in reducing child mortality from a number of diseases (not just malaria), but there is some uncertainty about whether those gains persist (i.e., whether the children succumb, but at a later age). In other situations, the possibility may exist of eradicating a disease in a particular area, which would naturally increase the potential benefits enormously. All these should be modelled in reality.

7 Different measures of effectiveness are appropriate in other situations. For example, if you are evaluating different strategies for treating a disease, then 'cost per case cured' may be most useful. Note that this is different from cases treated, which is an indicator of activity, rather than outcome. Outcome measures are more useful, as they link directly to the goals of a programme. However, they usually require more data to calculate (in this example, you would need to know the success rate, as well as the numbers treated).

Cost utility analysis (CUA)

Dr Do-Good is unhappy with his analysis so far. He wants to be able to take into account the reduction in sickness which malaria prevention

*should produce, as well as reduced mortality. How can he combine them?
What are the advantages and problems of this method?*

Dr Do-Good now needs to collect information on the incidence
of sickness from malaria in the district and to get some estimate
of its impact. This latter task can be done in broadly two ways.
The first is to ask doctors to judge the degree of disability produced by the illness and how long it lasts. The second approach is
to interview patients on the impact of malaria on their quality of
life. The aim of either of these approaches is to construct a
weighting factor so that disability effects can be incorporated
with life years gained.

Let us assume that the earlier data stands, and in addition, he
puts together the following estimates:

- *average number of life years gained per death averted* (discounted at
  3 per cent): 40. This is because most of the patients who die of
  malaria are children. Some go on to die of other childhood diseases, while those who survive will have life expectancies of
  around 60 years. The average is therefore high. (There is a
  debate about which life expectancy to use: the local, average international or highest national average. The World Development
  Report (1993) used Japanese life expectancy of 81 for males and
  82.5 for females, but this can be challenged on grounds of
  realism in the local context. See Williams, 1999, for a critique of
  their methodology.)
- *case morbidity rate* in the district: 20 per cent. Because malaria is
  endemic, adults develop immunity after repeated infection.
- *average length of illness episodes*: 1 month. This might be lower if
  people sought treatment more quickly, but there are problems
  with diagnosis by health staff and affordability of drugs for
  the patients. This figure includes recurrences of the symptoms
  after an initial infection, which is a feature of malarial
  diseases.
- *degree of disability during illness*: 80 per cent. This might be based
  on some survey of patients or doctors. It reflects the fact that
  those who do fall ill are unable to work and feel extremely
  unwell for the duration of the episode.

Using this information, we can compare cost per discounted
disability-adjusted life years (DALYs) gained in the malaria
control programme. DALYs were first developed for the World
Development Report of 1993 to allow a comparison of the causes
of death and disability globally. If linked with costs, they can be

used to make recommendations about prioritising health expenditure. This approach is discussed further in Chapter 9.

DALYs gained = deaths averted × discounted average number of life years lost by 1 death, plus: case morbidity rate × probability of contracting disease × numbers treated × efficacy × length weighting × disability weighting.

For the spraying option, the calculation is as follows:

$$\frac{10,000}{64 \times 40 + [0.2 \times 0.8 \times 10,000 \times 0.15 \times 0.083 \times 0.8]}$$

$$= \frac{10,000}{2,560 + 16}$$

= just under \$4 per DALY gained

This compares with the following for the bednets:

$$\frac{4,000}{34 \times 40 + [0.2 \times 0.8 \times 1,000 \times 0.85 \times 0.083 \times 0.8]}$$

$$= \frac{4,000}{1,360 + 9}$$

= just under \$3 per DALY gained. This option remains the more cost-effective one, then, once disability is taken into account.

A number of points should be made about cost-utility analysis.

1 In this case the morbidity effects are relatively minor in comparison with mortality. However, for some diseases, such as polio, long-term disability is the main problem, rather than death. The choice of method of calculation should reflect the nature of the burden of disease.

2 The advantage of a measure like DALYs is that that malaria figures can now be compared with the cost per DALY of any other interventions. This helps to define relative priorities, although a measure of absolute worth is still lacking. The opportunity costs of resources and level of available funding will have to be considered alongside cost per DALY estimates to reach a decision about the desirability of a programme.

3 For simplicity in the earlier example, we have assumed that a DALY is worth the same, no matter at what age it is gained. However, some societies may consider certain periods of life to be more valuable than others. The World Development Report

(1993) for example, weighted DALYs by age, rising from 0 at birth to 1.5 at age 25, and then gradually declining to 0.4 by age 90. Future DALYs were also discounted at the relatively low rate of 3 per cent. Both age weightings and discount rates should be tested in the local context.

4 If time and money permits, a more sophisticated approach can be taken to morbidity, by constructing patient quality of life indices. These can use a number of dimensions, such as pain, mobility, ability to look after yourself, etc. Patients can, for example, be asked to rank disease states according to these different criteria, between a score of 1 for perfect health and 0 for death (or negative scores for states worse than death). These are then amalgamated with estimates of the probability of being in those states and for how long. These can be added to years lost through death to produce a Quality-Adjusted Life Year (QALY).

There is considerable debate among health economists about techniques for measuring patient preferences, the reliability of QALYs, and the issues of whose values should be counted. The reader is referred to the articles by Williams (1996, 1999) for further discussion of QALYs.

Cost-benefit analysis (CBA)

Mr Datum, the health economist, now arrives on the scene. He want to know not just which malaria control strategy is more cost-effective, but whether either is worth doing at all. 'Compare like with like', he says, 'place a monetary value on the benefits, and then compare them with the costs involved. That's how we do it in other sectors'. What are the different benefits likely to be in this case, and how would you value them? Discuss the results.

CBA seeks to value all benefits of a health programme in money terms. As with costs (see Chapter 6), there are three types of benefits of most health programmes:

1 *Direct*: i.e., savings in future costs of prevention/ treatment/ control, which would be incurred by the health service *or* patients *or* society at large
2 *Indirect*: i.e., production losses which would have occurred as a result of death, or incapacity, or reduced productivity, including through interrupted education, which have now been avoided

3 *Intangible*: i.e., pain, anxiety, or other reduction in quality of life, either of patients or their relatives and friends, which has now been avoided.

The calculations become increasingly complicated as we work our way down the list.

First work out:

• the number of cases prevented: number treated × effectiveness × probability of getting the disease

Multiply this by:

• the average cost of treatment, both for the health services and patients and others

This gives you the direct costs of treatment of that disease which are saved by the intervention. Some interventions may more than repay their costs even before we consider the intangible (health) benefits. Some, like voluntary testing and counselling for HIV in pregnant women, offer scope for variety of benefits, such as prevention of transmission from mother to child, prevention or treatment of STDs, early access to medical care for HIV positive women, opportunity for counselling on sexual behaviour, and reassurance to the patient. Estimating and valuing all these is a complicated but important task.

However, note that in some cases overall costs to the health service may be increased by programmes which prolong life, leading to other future demands for health services. This is one of the paradoxes of increased efficiency in the health sector – it can cost more money!

To this is added productive gains:

• number of deaths averted × expected average life span × average yearly earnings

plus:

• number of disabled life years avoided × estimated financial losses which would have been incurred per year.

This approach is known as *the human capital approach*. It is rarely used now in this 'pure' form. One problem arises in relation to unemployed people or people (especially women) whose work is unpaid or underpaid: does this mean that they are not worth curing or keeping healthy? Or is the life of a poor person worth less than a person earning more money? Another question is whether production is considered gross or net. If we deduct the consumption of individuals from their production, we may end up with the unacceptable conclusion that some people are worth more to society dead than alive.

The fundamental problem with the human capital approach is its assumption that health exists to permit individuals to work and that increasing aggregate wealth is the main social goal. If we challenge that, and replace aggregate wealth with aggregate happiness, then health becomes inherently valuable and value of health interventions will have to come from estimates of how much health is valued by individuals, rather than how much production it facilitates.

Table 7.2 lists some of the methods used to attribute monetary value to health states. This approach focuses on measuring our third category of benefits – intangibles – as the main reason why we invest in health programmes.

These techniques are still being tested, at present, and a number of problems have arisen.

1 Decision-makers valuations are notoriously changeable, depending on the political pressures and media interest in the case. Moreover, there is some circularity of argument in using their judgements to influence a calculation which is, in itself, supposed to be informing public decision making!

2 As for direct surveys of the public, these are open to problems of bias, poor understanding by the interviewee of the nature of the condition and the information with which they are being presented, and inconsistency because of the sheer difficulty of attaching monetary values to normally unvalued goods.

3 Values will also be influenced by the income of interviewees and the health market conditions which they face (i.e., how much it costs to be ill in that area). This makes it hard to transfer estimates from one region or country to another.

4 Behavioural approaches are even more unreliable because of the different factors which are reflected in wages, for example, or life insurance premia. Wages will related to the supply of appropriate labour and the cost of living in the area, for example, as well as how dangerous the work is. As for insurance premia, these usually reflect how much money is required to support the family in the event of a breadwinner dying, rather than the inherent value of their life.

Table 7.2 Methods for attributing a monetary value to health states

Whose judgement?	How it is elicited	Example
Policy-makers/public figures	Explicit/stated preference	e.g., court orders: how much is paid in compensation for injuries?
	Implicit in decisions/revealed preference	e.g., legislation on road safety: how much is spent on it?
Individuals (patients or general public)	Direct survey/stated preference	*willingness to pay (WTP) surveys* e.g., 'contingent valuation': how much would you pay to avoid X condition? e.g., 'conjoint analysis': ranking scenarios with different attributes to ascertain preferences and WTP
	Implicit in behaviour/revealed preference	e.g., wage premia for risky job, or life insurance payments

If cost-benefit is calculated then an estimate of *net social benefit* (NSB) can be produced, as is commonly done with investments in 'productive' sectors (where it is known as net project worth or NPW). This is done by deducting discounted costs from discounted benefits. A positive result (i.e., NSB>0) indicates a project which in absolute terms is worth investing in. If budgets are limited (as they usually are), interventions would need to be ranked in order of size of NSB.

A major strength of this approach is that it can encompass all benefits, including ones which fall outside the health sector. CEA and CUA focus exclusively on health outcomes for patients, so that their feelings about the process and the impact of the intervention on others (e.g., their families) is ignored.

One option (for those struggling with the methodological problems of finding out WTP) is to combine CBA with cost-effectiveness or utility techniques. Health gains can be left in natural units on the right side of the equation, while future health costs avoided and estimated production gains are deducted from the costs on the left hand side.

> Cost:benefit ratio = costs of the programme − costs averted − production gained: health gained (in DALYs, QALYs, or other measure, such as deaths averted)

This has the disadvantage that an absolute figure for NPV is not produced.

Economic evaluation as a tool for decision making

After considerable effort, Dr Do-Good has come up with the results of his CUA: an estimate of just under $4 per DALY gained by spraying with insecticide, as against $3 per DALY by using impregnated bednets. He presents the figures proudly to the Regional Health Team, together with the recommendation that the budget for malaria control should be used entirely on provision of impregnated bednets from now on. Is this the correct conclusion? What other information should be taken into account in making final decisions about which services to fund?

Carrying out an economic evaluation is not just about producing a final figure for the cost-effectiveness of a particular strategy. That figure is very powerful in showing in that situation how much health benefit can be obtained for a given investment, relative to other possible strategies. However, the discussion of results should also include a consideration of the following issues:

1 *Marginal cost and benefit information* (or, if hard information is lacking, speculation). This will relate to the epidemiology of the disease in the local area, geographical characteristics, existing service infrastructure, etc. A strategy may be more cost-effective at the current level, but expansion of the programme might alter that, if new sufferers are living in remote areas, unserved by health centres, or thinly distributed. If coverage is already high, then increasing it beyond the current level may be disproportionately expensive (this is known in economics as *diminishing returns*). Alternatively, if a service is cut, will savings be realized (for example, if many of the costs are fixed)?

2 *Affordability.* There is no point recommending the expansion of a service if the money is simply not available to fund it. If a programme is to be funded from public money, then the question should be asked at a general level: how much will it cost to provide the service in this area (eligible population, or proportion of them likely to attend, multiplied by estimated cost per person, taking into account efficiency of services and projected input costs), compared with the resources available (e.g., in the relevant budget, adjusted for likely future changes). If, on the other hand, the service is to be paid for by users, the question is how the likely price of the service compares with household disposable income or current expenditure on health. There is no absolute measure of affordability, but these figures can give an rough indication.

3 *Flexibility.* Recommendations should take into account the degree of flexibility which health service managers have over resource use and transfer. If budgets are fixed, then managers will be unable to act on cost effectiveness information. Existing services tend to be regarded as fixed, so cost effectiveness information may only influence the development of new services. This is less than ideal, but may be better than a situation where all decisions are taken without considering cost and benefit information.

4 *Health service capacity and attitudes.* The impact of the recommendation on health service structures and processes should be considered, as this is likely to influence whether or how it

will be adopted. Are the necessary human and physical resources available? Will it cause job cuts? If so, how will these be handled? How will staff react to the new procedures? What are the implications for other services, etc?

5 *Patient attitudes.* These should be incorporated into the discussion of costs and benefits in the main body of the evaluation. For example, in the case of bednets, it is likely that families receive benefits from bednets beyond the prevention of malaria. They reduce the nuisance of mosquito bites and tend to reduce infestation by other insects, such as bed-bugs, head lice and fleas. These will enhance the benefits and also influence decisions about funding and affordability, as families may well be willing to cover some or all of the costs of the nets and/or the recurrent costs of impregnating them with insecticide every 6–12 months. If, on the other hand, local awareness of the connection between mosquito bites and malaria is low, then costs for promotion will be increased. Issues of acceptability of services to patients are also important as these will influence utilisation and hence the extent to which benefits are realized.

6 *Connecting different options.* A simple recommendation to increase or decrease a service may be less useful than presenting the implications of a decision on a range of connected services. For example, spraying mosquito habitats and promoting the use of impregnated bednets may be complementary, rather than substitutes for one another. In that case, how much of each should be carried out, and where? How will these affect the malaria treatment programme? Different scenarios can be costed and presented.

7 *Are the results generalisable?* Economic evaluations are costly to carry out. It is therefore important for decision makers in other areas to know if they can rely on cost and benefit estimates from the original study, or if they have to carry out their own study. How far are conditions likely to be similar in other areas? Evaluators should consider this question in general, and compare their results with any comparable studies to see if results are similar or different (and why).

8 *Opportunity costs.* What activity will not be funded if this programme is funded? Alternatively, what additional services can be provided if we cut back this programme? These questions show the real value of resources in the form of alternative services gained or foregone. They also have the advantage of

realism: would the money saved be retained by the unit, or the health budget, for example? Would staff be free to reallocate it? If not, the gains might be theoretical rather than real.

Summary

Different types of evaluation

Economic evaluation covers a range of techniques, some fairly simple, others more complicated.

- At its simplest, it compares two or more options that achieve the same effect, to find which one can be carried out using fewest resources. For example, if we continue to use malaria as an illustration, we might wish to find out which option is cheaper: organising communal days for periodic reimpregnation of bednets, or distributing individual kits for home use. This is called a *cost minimisation study.*
- A slightly more complex comparison might be made between different strategies with differing degrees of effectiveness, but which can be compared using a single natural measure, such as number of cases cured. The example used here was habitat spraying versus impregnated bednets, and the number of deaths from malaria prevented by each. This is known as a *cost-effectiveness study.*
- It may be that the alternatives under consideration have implications for quality of life as well as morbidity. These can be incorporated in a compound measure, like a DALY or QALY, so that direct comparisons between the options can be made. In our example, days of illness from malaria were included in the estimated benefits of spraying and bednets. This is known as a *cost-utility study.*
- Another option, where the range of benefits is very diverse, or where cost savings or production gains are a major feature of the impact of the programme, is to attribute a monetary value to the benefits of each programme. For example, what is the total value of benefits from the use of bednets, in comparison with provision of clean water to the village? If we can value the direct costs to patients and health services, the indirect costs, such as time saved collecting water, and the other attributes,

such as getting a better night's sleep without being bitten by mosquitoes, then an objective comparison can be made. This is known as *cost benefit analysis*. It produces a relative ranking of options as well as an absolute estimate of whether a project is worth funding (if net project value is positive). However, valuation techniques are time consuming and still subject to methodological debate.

Methodology

Whatever the type of economic evaluation, certain broad principles apply (adapted from Drummond and Maynard, 1993).

1 The study question perspective and design should be clearly stated. What is the question being studied? Why (what is the policy interest in it)? Whose costs and benefits are to be included?

2 The study should involve a comparison of at least two options. For a new programme, the 'do nothing' option should be considered. The least costly and most commonly used options should also be included, as a general rule.

3 The effectiveness of the interventions should be established, preferably by randomised controlled study.

4 All relevant costs and benefits should be identified and appropriately valued. This is the most time consuming part. Commonly important costs or benefits are overlooked. Valuation techniques can be quite complicated or require data which is hard to obtain. However, the validity of the conclusions rests on this part of the process.

5 The study should be of a sufficient size to assess significant differences between alternatives. Statistical techniques will reveal what the sample size should be in each case, depending on the magnitude of expected differences between the outcomes.

6 The marginal costs and benefits should be valued. This is important to inform decision makers, who rarely face an all-or-nothing decision, but rather the option of expansion or reduction of services.

7 Future costs and benefits should be appropriately discounted if these occur at different points in time. This was discussed in Chapter 6.

8 Detailed sensitivity analysis should be conducted. Again, this was discussed under costs, and applies to any uncertain para-

meters, be they on the costs or the benefits side. This helps to determine how reliable the final result is.

9 Finally, the results should include a discussion of relevant factors for decision-makers, such as affordability within existing budgets, acceptability (both for staff and patients) and implications for other parts of the health sector.

When to carry one out

Economic evaluation can inform choices and play an important role in the decision-making process, though as the analysis above makes clear, it has to be considered alongside a range of other information. Moreover, economic evaluation itself takes up time and resources, and may be more or less useful in different circumstances. As a general rule, it will be worth undertaking one when:

1 Decision makers minds are genuinely open, as between a number of options, and there is flexibility to move resources between them; and

2 The resources implications are potentially large.

Using existing studies

More commonly, decision makers will rely on the results of economic evaluations conducted at other times and in other places. Some caution should be applied to their use.

• The context in which they occurred may have been quite different, with different patterns of costs and benefits.
• The study methodology also needs to be closely examined to see if it was sound (as laid out in the earlier questions).
• Relative prices may have changed, or new technologies been introduced.
• The scale of the programme may have been very different from the one under current consideration.
• The values embodied in measures of quality of life or disability weights may differ from one society to the next.

With critical interpretation, however, existing studies can yield valuable information to debates about which services to fund and how to implement them.

Questions for discussion

1 Find a published economic evaluation, preferably relating to a programme area with which you are familiar. Apply the nine questions listed in the final section of this chapter to the article. You may find a lot to criticize in some studies. Sometimes researchers appear to have failed to consider some important aspect or failed to use techniques correctly; at other times they faced problems of data and had to make pragmatic decisions, which have been explained to the reader. You as the reader have to decide whether such omissions or shortcuts render the results invalid.

2 Consider a programme which you have been involved in. Could economic evaluation assist with the decisions which have to be made about it? Design a study methodology, outlining the questions to be asked; how to collect cost data; where to find evidence of effectiveness; how to measure benefits etc. What problems do you predict, and how might you deal with them?

References and further reading

Drummond, M. and Maynard, A., (eds) (1993). *Purchasing and Providing Cost Effective Health Care*. London: Livingstone.

Drummond, M., O'Brien, B., Stoddart, G. and Torrance, G. (1997). *Methods for the Economic Evaluation of Health Care Programmes* (2nd edn). Oxford: Oxford University Press.

Evans, D. and Hurley, S. (1995). The application of economic evaluation techniques in the health sector: the state of the art, *Journal of International Development*, 7(3), 299–574.

Jefferson, T., Demicheli, V. And Mugford, M. (1996). *Elementary Economic Evaluation in Health Care*. London: BMJ.

Mooney, G. (1977). *The Valuation of Human Life*. New York, NY: Macmillan.

Ryan, M. and Hughes, J. (1997). Using conjoint analysis to assess women's preferences for miscarriage management, *Health Economics*, 6.

Williams, A. (1996). Qalys and ethics: a health economist's perspective, *Social Science and Medicine*, 43, 12.

Williams, A. (1999). Calculating the global burden of disease: time for a strategic reappraisal. *Health Economics*, 8, 1.

World Development Report (1993). *Investing in Health*, Washington, DC: World Bank.

8

Financial and economic appraisal of health care projects

Tim Ensor

Introduction

Chapters 6 and 7 have discussed the economic evaluation of individual treatments and investments. In this chapter we present a general framework for considering the overall net worth of a health care project or programme. The techniques presented here are suitable for the analysis of projects funded from the health budget or through a donor loan or grant from an agency such as the World Bank. The general technique is to:

1 measure the direct financial costs and savings to the health sector
2 measure the fiscal impact of the project (how the net added costs can be funded)
3 consider more broadly the overall community (economic) impact of the project.

The justification for this ordering is that there is little point in developing a project that is likely to have substantial net benefit to the community if the government has inadequate resources to fund it and ensure its sustainability.

> **Dr Fixit**: *A foreign government has recently offered to build two new district hospitals and renovate the main provincial hospital in my province. The Ministry of Health is extremely keen and the Minister is already planning an elaborate opening ceremony at the main provincial hospital with the Ambassador. But in the province we are not so sure if this is a good investment.*

It is certainly true that that occupancy rates are high – over 100 per cent in two of the facilities. At the same time, however, use of the local health centres are extremely low. On average, each cater for a population of about 6,000 yet many see fewer than ten patients a day. Patients bypass this facility in order to use the better equipped district hospitals. We are concerned that building better hospitals will simply reinforce this pattern and, incidentally, rather contradict the government's stated objective of building up primary care services (agreed with WHO last year).

We have made an alternative proposal to the foreign government. We have recommended that they spend money on equipment instead of buildings. This could be distributed between hospitals and, most importantly, health centres. I am also concerned that we might not be able to maintain the investment once made. My colleagues, however, have said that any gift made to the health sector must be beneficial for our people, even if not quite what we would ideally spend money on given a free choice.

Professor Bluff: This a complex issue, as it requires consideration of a wide range of costs and benefits both financial and non-financial. What is required is a framework for project appraisal in the health sector. This builds upon many of the concepts introduced in previous chapters.

When considering the financial implications of a project or new investment it is useful to consider the costs over a reasonably long period – from 10 to 20 years. The reason for taking such a perspective is that many of the costs, for example equipment, will not arise for maybe 10 years. To ensure sustainability we should attempt to ensure not just that the equipment is used effectively but also that we are able to replace it when required. Of course some investments, notably many buildings, will have a useful life much longer than 10 or even 20 years. But any costs incurred more than about 20 years into the future will be heavily discounted and, with the growth of the economy, the costs when viewed today should be quite small.

Financial analysis: impact on health sector costs

The first stage of the financial analysis is to list both the direct (health sector) costs and financial savings of a particular investment. Each of these is then estimated over a 10–20 year accounting period. The purpose of this is to check that the direct savings outweigh the costs to the health service.

On the cost side we should include:

- Equipment costs – an allowance for maintenance and replacement of new equipment, training for users
- Building costs – maintenance of new buildings and eventual replacement
- Vehicles – maintenance and spare parts, replacement, fuel, drivers
- Training costs and staff allowances.

Equipment

The costs of replacing and maintaining equipment are important but easily overlooked. An example will serve to illustrate the issue. Assume that the foreign government has approved your plan to provide packs of medical equipment to be given to rural health centres. Recurrent costs can be worked out in the following way.

1 Begin by listing all the main items. A typical list might include multiple provision of basic medical equipment – stethoscope, sphygmomanometer, thermometers, test tubes and syringes, single larger items such as steriliser and microscope, medical furniture such as a stretcher and general items such as fridge and instrument tables.

2 The next stage is to estimate the average replacement rate for each item over the relevant period. This will depend on the item. Small glass items might have to be replaced every year or two, basic medical items such as stethoscope might last for 4–5 years while equipment could last 10–15 years or more (remember we are concerned about useful life; some items may actually be kept far longer).

3 Include the annual cost of maintenance for each item based on 'rules of thumb' obtained in consultation with an engineer or medical equipment specialist. This can be quite high, perhaps around 10 per cent on average, and more for complex items.

4 Calculate the cost of replacing items based on the individual replacement times over the project period. Using a spreadsheet makes this task quite straightforward.

Figure 8.1 shows the replacement cost profile for a typical package of equipment containing basic primary care items

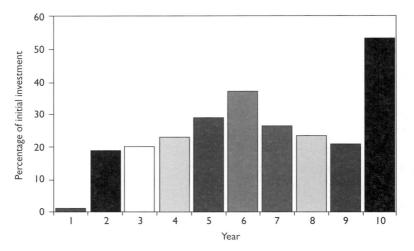

Fig. 8.1   Replacement cost profile for basic equipment package (10 years)

costing about \$6,500 for a population of 5,000 people.[1] Note that by the fifth year of the project replacements and maintenance have doubled the (un-discounted) cost of the original investment.

Buildings

Building maintenance, relative to the initial investment, will be quite low if constructed well. Help from an architect will be required to estimate these costs and will depend on working conditions and, to some extent, use. Estimates used in typical analyses range from $\frac{1}{30}$ to $\frac{1}{40}$ of the total cost per year.

Vehicles

The issues are similar to equipment although the number of different items is likely to be less which makes working out replacement rates easier. The replacement rates will depend on working conditions such as terrain and temperature. An allowance for

---

1   The scenarios presented in this chapter, as in other chapters, are fictitious. The figures are, however, based on similar analyses carried out by the authors in Central Asia and Africa.
Note: the bars indicate the annual replacement cost as a proportion of the initial total investment. These expenditures are in *addition* to the initial investment costs.

fuel should be included. To some extent, new vehicles could sub-stitute for older vehicles so fuel costs may not rise much although, inevitably, new vehicles will get used more because they are in better working order.

Training costs and staff allowances

Costs may be incurred in obtaining new equipment, particularly electro-medical specialist equipment, for re-retraining existing staff in their use. In addition it may be necessary to increase the salaries of existing staff or employ people with higher qualifications.

Medicines

Medicines are often provided as part of a joint government-donor financed project. Once again the important point is that the service should continue beyond the funding and that there-fore the future recurrent costs are incorporated into the regular funding of the health sector.

Let us assume that the foreign government has now been con-vinced to purchase basic primary care equipment and medicines (3 year supply) packages, worth $5,000 each, for all 150 health centres in the province (see Table 8.1). Hospital equipment and medicines worth $45,000 will be provided for all 7 district hospi-tals while $110,000 of equipment will be provided to the main provincial hospital. The annual provincial health budget for the current year (1999) is the dollar equivalent of $4.38 m. With a total province population of 1.25 million this is about $3.5 per capita.

We can now examine the total recurrent cost burden of the donated equipment (Table 8.2). Replacement and maintenance of equipment are based on the profile indicated in Figure 8.1 and maintenance of 10 per cent per year. Vehicles are assumed to last for five years while medicines are provided for a three year period after which they must be absorbed by the local budget. It is assumed that the budget grows at a rate equivalent to the growth of the economy (1.5 per cent per year in real terms).[2]

---

2 All figures are in real (i.e., without including provision for inflation) terms. Figures could be adjusted up to take account of expected inflation and also antici-pated movement of the exchange rate.

Table 8.1 Equipment donated by foreign government (cost in US$)

	Number of units	Medical equipment	Medicines*	Vehicles	Total per facility	Total
Health centres	150	3,500	1,500	–	5,000	750,000
District hospitals	7	30,000	7,500	7,500	45,000	315,000
Provincial hospitals	1	80,800	14,200	15,000	110,000	110,000
Total for all facilities		815,800	291,700	67,500		1,175,000

Note: *Medicines (3 years supply of certain essential drugs and anaesthetics)

Table 8.2 Recurrent costs of investment (US $)

Year	Medical equipment	Medicines	Vehicles	Staff incentives and training	Total
1999	–	–	–	12,000	12,000
2000	7,698	–	13,500	1,500	22,698
2001	151,841	–	13,500	1,500	166,841
2002	161,964	97,233	13,500	1,500	274,197
2003	206,180	97,233	13,500	1,500	318,413
2004	208,890	97,233	13,500	1,500	321,124
2005	296,013	97,233	13,500	1,500	408,247
2006	209,013	97,233	13,500	1,500	321,246
2007–2018	2,131,093	1,166,800	162,000	18,000	3,477,893
Sum	3,372,692	1,652,967	256,500	40,500	5,322,658
Present value	2,162,029	1,096,215	163,152	28,693	3,190,103

Note: present value calculations are based on a 5% discount rate.

The resulting total over the 20 year period is what is required to maintain the investment. The bottom line is that the annual costs of the investment average more than 8 per cent of the budget per year. Of course if the predictions about the size of the economy are inaccurate then the percentage could be above or below this figure.[3]

A related consideration, that may increase costs, is if the initial investment 'gifts' are in some way tied to future purchases from the donor nation. The provision of specialised equipment, for example, may require the country to purchase technical help or spare parts from the donor country in the future. This has no effect on costs if the equipment offers good value for money as judged, perhaps, through success in international competitive tenders. But if other manufacturers offer a better deal in terms of after sales support and spare parts, the costs to the receiving country are increased accordingly. This point is particularly important for very expensive items such as large diagnostic scanning equipment (Computerised tomography, magnetic resonance imaging, etc.) where the costs of spare parts and technical advice can exceed the initial investment in a very short time.

> **Dr Fixit**: *The costs are, as feared, large. But are you not forgetting that the investments could reduce other costs. I am thinking particularly of reduced costs of hospitalisation as a result of improved primary care.*

Professor Bluff: It is certainly true that some costs can be expected to fall. Some examples include:

1 Buildings – new buildings might replace older buildings that were expensive to heat or air-condition. Simple projections of fuel efficiency savings can be obtained by multiplying the total area (square metres) affected by the changes by the expected percentage saving per square metre multiplied by current fuel expenditure.
2 Reduced time in hospital – improved primary care could reduce the amount of time a patient stays in hospital. The main saving would be in terms of reduced variable costs such as food and some medicines.

---

3   It is worth pointing out that a recent study (Jowett, 1998) found that public per capita dollar health expenditure fell by more than 40 per cent between 1990 and 1995 in low income countries. Spending fell in 12 out of 17 countries for which data were available for both years.

3 Improved health centre treatment could reduce the number of self-referrals to hospitals for primary outpatient care. Using an expensive secondary or tertiary care hospital mainly as a large primary care centre is an expensive option that few countries can afford.

4 Over a 10–20 year period the structure of expenditures will change as the total population, and numbers in different age groups, change. This factor can be accommodated in a simple way by allowing the number of patients, and associated expenditures, to grow at the same rate as the population. A more complex formulation is to break the population into key age groups (a minimum would be children under 5, elderly, adult males and women of reproductive age), obtain age related utilisation data and project total utilisation and expenditures on the basis of a change in the population structure.

It is also important that we consider the possibility that improving facilities could increase recurrent spending both appropriate and less appropriate. Better hospital equipment might attract more patients who bypass the primary care level of the system. A primary care network that has an improved ability to identify and diagnose disease may 'find' more illness that requires treatment at an appropriate facility. Improved medical transport can dramatically increase the number of patients that require help in reaching a facility. All add to recurrent and even capital costs if it leads to equipment wearing out more quickly.

These issues show the need for investments, even those provided through donations, to be planned together with changes in the organisational structure of the health care system. The possibility of more self-referrals could be tackled by introducing a more closely regulated referral system and gatekeeper role of primary care. Non-emergency self referrals could be penalised through significant co-payments although even this solution has its own dangers. Chinese hospitals, for example, generate much revenue from wealthy patients who are only too willing to pay quite high charges for the privilege of being diagnosed on the latest scanning equipment. Hospitals over-invest in such technology just to generate income (Ensor, 1997).

In the context of the example, assume that the main demand impact on costs is the increase in use of health centres. This is expected to reduce hospital use by around 10 per cent but only if health centres can be motivated to provide the medical care made possible by the provision of better equipment and supplies.

Organisational changes required may include:

• co-payments in hospitals for self-referrals
• increased incentives for health centre staff to treat patients rather than referring on to hospital.

The latter incentive might be paid to workers on the basis of the number of treatments provided for certain illnesses that have previously been treated mainly in hospital. In addition, some retraining may be required to upgrade the skills of health centre workers so that they can provide effective treatment for a wider range of illness.

The impact on current budget expenditure can be analysed by decomposing total expenditures into the level and type of input (Table 8.3). In some countries this decomposition may need to be estimated, especially when dividing expenditures between levels of facility.

The next stage is to place project expenditures in each category. It can never be assumed that expenditure will stay constant even in real terms. One reason is that some of the items may have been under financed in the past – actual expenditures are, therefore, less than costs. A second is that population structure and requirements change. Perhaps the easiest way is to base projections on reasonably simple rules, such as average utilisation by each group, using a spreadsheet (see Table 8.4).

In Table 8.4 expenditures in each category were projected using the following rules.

• The health budget is assumed to increase at 1.5 per cent per year. This provides additional resources for the health sector which can contribute partly towards the extra recurrent costs of the investment and partly to the general increase in existing health sector costs. When projecting the health budget, information on the expected growth of the economy will required from macroeconomists and Ministry of Finance. Sometimes different groups – e.g., IMF compared to Ministry of Finance – may disagree about the rate of growth and general state of the economy. The analyst may wish to experiment with a range of growth rates to measure the impact of different states of the economy on the project.
• One such existing health sector cost is staffing. We assume that salaries increase at the same rate as average wages. But if some further bonus is to be paid as incentive for staff then salaries might be increased at a faster rate to begin with. In the example

Table 8.3   Provincial budget expenditures by level and item (US $)

	Number of units	Staff (%)	Running costs (%)	Medical supplies (%)	Food (%)	Maintenance (%)	Other (%)	Total	Distribution* (%)
Health centres	150	74	15	10		1	0	1,093,750	25
District hospitals	7	53	16	15	9	2	5	1,968,750	45
Provincial hospitals	1	49	21	18	8	3	1	1,312,500	30
Total for all facilities		2,495,938	754,688	640,938	282,188	89,688	111,563	179,156,250	

Note: *75% spending on hospitals in low income countries is a high proportion although comparable to figures found in countries such as India, Lesotho and Somalia (see Barnum and Kutzin, 1993). The proportion is reduced if spending on public health and vertical programmes are included.

Table 8.4 Projected expenditures, available budget and the resource gap (US$)

Year	Total recurrent costs of investment (1)	Budget available (2)	Projected budget expenditures (3)	Resources available (4)	Net financial gap (5)
1999	12,000	4,375,000	4,375,000	–	–12,000
2000	22,698	4,440,625	4,429,498	11,127	–11,571
2001	166,841	4,507,234	4,484,747	22,488	–144,353
2002	274,197	4,574,843	4,540,757	34,086	–240,112
2003	318,413	4,643,466	4,597,541	45,924	–272,489
2004	321,124	4,713,118	4,655,110	58,007	–263,116
2005	408,247	4,783,814	4,722,799	61,015	–347,232
2006	321,246	4,855,571	4,791,391	64,181	–257,065
2007–2018	3,477,893	64,272,372	62,398,317	1,874,055	–1,603,837
Sum	5,322,658	101,166,044	98,995,161	2,170,883	–3,151,775
Present value (6)	3,190,103	61,548,064	60,457,271	1,090,793	–2,099,309

Notes
(1) Recurrent costs of investment including replacement and maintenance of equipment and vehicles, provision of drugs and training of staff.
(2) Current real budget increased each year at the same rate as economic growth.
(3) Projected expenditures based on assumptions about costs described.
(4) Funding available for recurrent investment costs – difference between expenditures and real budget.
(5) Gap in financing left once funding available (4) is deducted from total recurrent costs (1).
(6) Net present value of column based on 5 per cent rate of discount.

we assume that salaries are increased by an additional 1 per cent per year for the first ten years. In practice much of this increase might be paid to health centre staff.

• Providing more treatment at the health centre level may enable staffing in hospitals to be reduced particularly the outpatient staff who are, at present, providing primary level services. We assume that hospital level staff are reduced by 5 per cent over 10 years.

• In some countries health facilities accumulate debts to electricity or other fuel suppliers. Projecting future costs should take these into consideration and make provision for true costs of this item. In the example no such debts have accumulated and we assume that running costs – electricity, stationery, telephones, etc. – remain constant in real terms.

• Medical supplies and food may fall with shorter stays in hospital. We assume that expenditure falls by 1 per cent a year over a 5 year period based on the reduction in provincial hospitalisations. In later years this is offset by an increase in expenditure arising from the projected growth in population (1 per cent per annum).

• In many countries maintenance is often the first budget line to be cut when budgets are tight. The low expenditure shown in Table 8.3 reflects past reductions. The example assumes that expenditure is increased by 50 per cent over a 10 year period to reflect the under expenditure and backlog of work to be undertaken on existing buildings.

These effects only concern the direct health sector impact. We may also wish to consider wider financial impacts on the government sector. For example, reducing health sector staffing has an implication for overall levels of unemployment. Even if the country wide impact is relatively small, where health facilities are concentrated in certain areas the effect could be much more significant and potentially impacting on labour market policy.

The result is a projection of expenditure based on the existing supply of health care and a projection of the budget based on the economic growth rate. The gap between these two series represents the additional recurrent costs that can be used to pay for the costs of the new medical equipment. This is represented by column (5) as a substantial deficit based on a 1.5 per cent annual projected growth in the budget. Growth would have to increase to around 2.5 per cent in order to reduce this deficit to zero.

Recurrent costs ratio

There is a close similarity between the replacement and maintenance costs reported here and recurrent cost ratios that are sometimes used to estimate the recurrent cost burden of investments. These ratios express the total annual recurrent cost of an investment as a proportion of the purchase cost of the initial investment. Barnum and Kutzin (1993) summarise cost ratios for new investments in nine different countries finding ratios ranging from 11 to 40 per cent. The average recurrent cost ratio in the example, not untypical of other similar financial analyses, produced an average ratio of 22 per cent. But this ratio only reflects the additional or incremental recurrent costs to be incurred. It assumes, for example, that the staff currently in post will continue to operate most equipment. If total recurrent costs are considered then the ratio would probably be between 30 and 40 per cent.

It is important to realise that the recurrent cost ratio varies considerably between types of investment. Additionally the divergence between the incremental and total ratio differs. New buildings, for example, have a relatively low incremental ratio – only around 2.5 per cent per year to maintain them. If they replace existing old buildings the net recurrent financial impact could even be positive – fuel and maintenance savings compare with the old building may offset the costs of maintaining the new investment. An efficient new building may even permit some staff reductions. But if the building is adding to the existing stock then recurrent costs – including running costs, staffing and medical supplies – all contribute to a recurrent cost ratio which may exceed 30 per cent. These differences reinforce the need to look at the detail of investment-recurrent costs and to rely on rule of thumb estimates only as a basis for provisional estimates of the burden.

Fiscal impact: paying for the added net costs

The next stage of the analysis is to consider how any excess costs can be funded within the government budget or from other sources.

In the example Table 8.4 indicates that even once budget growth money is taken into consideration there is still a gap between expenditures and revenues. The possibilities to fund this gap include:

1 additional budget resources for the health sector
2 reallocations within the sector as a result of efficiency improvement or policy decision to prioritise specific areas of the sector
3 additional sources of earmarked health sector revenue
4 reduce the level of investment
5 change the nature of investment.

First, the government as a whole might find additional resources for the health sector. In a growing economy this may be possible despite other demands on a limited budget. Indeed, as suggested in Chapter 2, there is empirical evidence to suggest that the proportion spent on health increases as the economy grows. Where the economy is stagnant or declining this is unlikely to be possible. Where the economy is undergoing structural change an increase may also be difficult. In China, for example, the state budget as a proportion of GDP declined, and then remained constant in absolute terms, during the 1980s and 1990s despite growth of more than 10 per cent per annum in the economy as a whole. This is largely due to the changing structure of employment from easily taxed state employment to small private firms. Similar trends are apparent in other countries.

Second, resources might be reallocated within the health sector. So, for example, one way of paying for higher primary level recurrent costs is to re-direct money from hospitals. But this is difficult to do in practice. There are many political objections to closing or reducing hospital expenditures. There are also practical medical objections: current inpatient treatment may rely on relatively old and perhaps unreliable equipment that mean any treatment provided takes longer than would be the case at a more modern facility. Also in order to reduce hospital use patients must be confident that health centres are really improved. It could take some time to convince them by which time the financing for primary care could be exhausted.

Thirdly, the health sector might raise revenue through user co-payments or earmarked insurance. A justification for this is that patients that are benefiting from investments in an area will be willing to pay for improved services. If quality improves the overall price may still fall if waiting times at health centres, or distance costs to hospitals, fall.

Sometimes, donors will themselves make funds available for recurrent costs. This can be a good way of reducing the short term impact of investment and ensuring that the project starts off well.

But such funding could give a government unrealistic expectations of the affordability of an investment. Recurrent funding provided on a declining basis with a strong agreement by the government to an increasing contribution may be important in ensuring sustainability.

But the scope for user charges to raise significant revenue without damaging access are, particularly in rural areas, quite limited (see Chapter 5). Also a user charge strategy usually begins with charges for higher level, national and possibly provincial, facilities. Charges for district and health centre facilities may conflict with the overall objectives of reform. Once again, it is important that methods for closing the financial gap are considered together with overall health sector policies.

In order to reduce self-referrals, user co-payments for self-referrals might be used. It is likely, however, that the revenue generated will be quite low since fees are to deter treatment and will be set at a level sufficient to achieve this for most patients.

A fourth option is that the overall investment and accompanying recurrent costs, could be reduced. This may even mean that 'gifts' are turned down or simply stockpiled and not used (which may be politically easier). In the example, the total investment would have to be reduced by about 60 per cent per cent to ensure that recurrent costs can be covered from within the budget.

Finally, the type of investments might be changed since some capital spending carry higher recurrent costs than others. Durable items based on simple technology will require less maintenance and less frequent replacement than more complex electrical-medical equipment. But it is not correct to assume that basic medical equipment for primary centres are necessarily low cost. Small items, such as thermometers and stethoscopes, that wear out quite quickly, can be very costly if purchased on a scale sufficient to equip all basic health facilities (such as the 150 health centres in the example). Although the costs of equipping new buildings facilities can add significantly to annual costs, if they are built to substitute or renovate existing buildings their annual cost is quite low compared to their value.

A good financial and fiscal impact analysis should not only assess the costs and savings and estimated resource gap (if any). It should also provide a list of options for reducing the gap showing the size of, for example, potential co-payments or reduction in investment required to bring about fiscal balance.

Dr Fixit: *OK, I can now see how we might attempt to make a project sustainable. Indeed, given all the costs associated with the equipment, I am not sure that it makes sense to accept the gift. Does this mean that I was wrong to ask the government to invest in equipment rather than buildings?*

Professor Bluff: Not necessarily. You are probably right in arguing that building larger facilities will simply induce patients to come to the hospitals rather than existing health centres. Indeed the effect could be to provide a justification to increase the recurrent expenditure share on hospitals at the expense of the under-used health centres. Why spend on facilities that are not used?

But targeted investment in facilities, even hospital facilities, designed within the context of an overall reform strategy could promote rather than detract from the objective of building up primary care. Investment money could be used, for example, to support a smaller but better equipped specialist provincial hospital while at the same time improving primary care in health centres or smaller hospitals. Investments might be released on condition that targets for re-directing simpler cases to district hospitals or health centres are met. It may actually prove to be cost effective to invest quite substantially in hospital facilities as a way of releasing recurrent resources for use at lower levels. Similarly, if some investments are used to improve the living conditions of a provincial hospital people may be more prepared to pay charges for a hospital stay. Again this could release resources for lower levels.

It is salutary to realise that this pattern of financing strategic investment in hospitals in order to help the reallocation of recurrent funding to primary care is exactly opposite to the practice in many countries. In these countries donors often provide funding for primary care through investments in the health centre network often tied to an essential package of services, while governments spend most of their recurrent budget on hospitals. Although local circumstances vary, in general this is a recipe for an unsustainable public health system.

In fact to answer the question properly, we should investigate not just the financial impact of each of the projects, but the overall economic impact on the community as a whole. The fundamental question is will the project put back into the community more than it costs? In order to answer this question fully we need to use cost-benefit analysis and value all the costs and benefits in money terms (see Chapter 8). We might also use cost-effectiveness or cost-utility analysis to compare the project with another use of the same resources – for example the option to spend the money on investment in buildings. The analysis should embody distributional issues since what is being considered is society welfare which may include a concept of distributive justice.

Once we have carried out the economic analysis then further issues may have to be faced. It may be that the high equipment investment option turns out to be more expensive in terms of net recurrent costs but offers more to the community in terms of financial and health benefits. If it turns out that the project is unsustainable financially but offers positive net economic benefits, then it is a controversial question whether the project should be carried out. Some would argue that the project is worth doing if benefits during the project exceed costs even if afterwards the project collapses. Others might say that confidence in the sustainability of projects is an important long term objective and that projects that constantly fail once donor funds lapse encourage donor dependency culture and declining community confidence in the programmes provided.

Economic analysis: do the community benefits exceed costs?

Dr Fixit: *So what additional information do I require in order to carry out an economic analysis?*

Professor Bluff: We have so far considered the direct financial costs and savings to the health sector. To produce an economic analysis we must quantify the wider community impact. The additional community benefits can be divided into two main groups: those associated with the costs of treatment and those associated with the outcomes of treatment.

Those associated with the costs of treatment include, for example, reductions in the time it takes to wait for treatment at a health centre. Also changes in travel time or transport costs associated with going to a different facility for treatment.

Cost of treatment may also include a change in the time a patient must spend in hospital and away from work undergoing inpatient treatment. A reduction might be obtained if, for example, equipment was obtained to enable shorter stays for surgery through less invasive surgical procedures. More mundanely, improving medical supplies might mean that operations are not delayed so that, for example, patients are not kept unnecessarily in hospital because of a lack of anaesthetics.

In the example, the crucial changes are likely to be the reduction in financial costs of obtaining quality treatment associated with going to health centres rather than hospitals for primary care. Also some reduction in days spent in hospital caused by delays in treatment.

Benefits associated with improvements in treatment outcome and health status are obtained in a number of ways. Improving health centre care not only speeds up treatment but may also ensure that emergency treatment, which if delayed would lead to death or more serious injury, can be provided immediately. Better preventive care at this level can also prevent much illness. Quicker services that reduce the financial costs to patients also have a secondary health related benefit that more patients can be treated with the same number of hospital beds or staff.

Quantifying the health-related benefits of a health project is an extremely difficult and inexact task. There are two central difficulties: first, in specifying the range of possible health benefits that might accrue, and second, in valuing the benefits. The first issue is related to the second since the simpler the range of benefits the easier will be the task of deciding the most appropriate outcome indicator to use for valuation.

Where a project is aimed at one particular disease the range of benefits is narrow and setting targets for the reduction of the disease in the project area is relatively straightforward. What is required are data on the disease incidence-prevalence in the first year of the project and an estimate for the last year of analysis with and without the project. The difference is important since the disease may well fall (or rise) as a result of factors outside the scope of the project. Valuation of these benefits requires a decision on the most suitable unit to use. If reducing the disease mainly leads to mortality reductions then the number of life years is a suitable unit. Cost per life years could then be compared to other life saving interventions. Cost per DALY or QALY would provide a wider valuation that also encompasses disability reductions or quality of life improvements.

If a monetary value is required then a valuation of lives saved will be required. A human capital approach would value life years at their expected (shadow) annual wage rate. A fuller method-ological discussion of the problems involved is provided in Chapter 7.

Rather than affect one or two indicators it is probably more usual for projects to have a range of health benefits. This is par-ticularly the case where the project is involved in health sector restructuring through strategic investments in different levels of care – as in this example. In this case a full economic analysis of the different impact of the project will extremely difficult. An al-ternative strategy, rather than attempting to quantify all benefits, is instead to build up a general picture on expected benefits. This should indicate whether the project is likely to benefit the com-munity. This could be done in the following way.

First, quantify the financial benefits associated with treatment costs. These are compared to the net financial burden to the community including the value of the initial investment. This will be an interesting exercise even if the investment is a 'gift', since it will indicate whether the investment is sufficiently valuable for the government itself to commit resources even if foreign donor resources are not available.

In the example we assume that the number of bed days in the provincial hospital is reduced by 5 per cent. Initially the total number of bed-days is 562,000 (corresponding to an admission rate in the population of 5 per cent and length of stay of 9 days). Assuming the annual wage is \$350 per annum and people work around 220 days a year the total saving is given as:

$$\frac{350}{220} \times 562,000 \times 5\% = \$44,705 \text{ per annum.}$$

For simplicity we assume that the opportunity cost of time is equal to the average wage. Given that many sick people will dis-proportionately fall into the non-working groups, some adjust-ment for this less than average wage cost of time might be incorporated in practice.

In the case of distance, and confining our attention to the provincial hospital, assume that there are 50,000 primary care consultations per year. Presenting patients are distributed accord-ing to Table 8.5 which also shows the costs incurred. Reducing the number of patients treated at the hospital rather than health centre yields a saving of \$78,450 per annum.

Further complexity may arise in practice. Increasing access to primary care to those in distant communities may lead to more

Table 8.5   Distribution of provincial hospital primary out-patients and costs by geographic distance from hospital

Kilometres	Average cost per patient ($) (1)	Distribution of primary care outpatient consultations (%) (2)	Expected percentage reduction (3)	Expected saving to patients (%) (4)
> 50	5	16	100	40,000
10 – 50	3.5	12	80	16,800
5 – 10	2	22	70	15,400
< 5	0.5	50	50	6,250
Total		50,000		$78,450

Notes:
(1) Average cost including transport and waiting time of outpatient visit in provincial hospital (assume that these costs are above what would be incurred at the local health centre).
(2) Percentage distribution, and total, outpatients.
(3) Expected reduction (over 5 years) in outpatients as a consequence of improved health centre services.
(4) Savings to patients from improved access to health services for primary care.

disease being revealed and more referrals to the hospital. As a consequence the figures on total changes in patient numbers at hospital may need to be adjusted.

Of course neither of the changes can be introduced immediately. For the purposes of the example we assume that it takes 5 years to realise all the savings suggested. Other financial benefits are also likely, such as changes in use of district hospitals. The total net present value of the benefits illustrated is $1,204,855.

There may be economic dis-benefits (costs of the project). In the example, it is assumed that all people who no longer attend hospitals for primary care can be treated effectively and at lower cost at health centres. But in some cases access may be reduced if hospital outpatient treatment is penalised (through charges) and the nearest health centre is situated farther away. Other costs may also be present and must be offset against the benefits.

Second, work out the remaining economic gap. In the earlier example, the investment value (if the equipment were not donated) is $1,175,000 and present value of recurrent costs are $3,190,103. Part of this gap is covered by the direct financial benefits to the community ($1,204,855). This leaves a gap of

$3,160,248. For the total economic net benefit to be positive, the value of health benefits must exceed this gap.

Sometimes it may be apparent that even without health benefits that the net impact is positive and the project can be justified on health sector treatment costs alone. Even then, however, it is still important to give a qualitative idea of the benefits that are expected from the project even if it is not possible to quantify them. This is because project appraisal should not only show whether benefits are greater or less than costs. It should also demonstrate that the project is better than others at delivering improved health. It may turn out, for example, that health benefits justify the investment in equipment but increased net benefit could be obtained by investing more of the funding in new buildings, staff training or other items.

Third, further assessment of the health benefits of a project could concentrate on quantifying the most significant benefits while also providing general information of other benefits. It should also provide general information on the main population sub-groups to benefit. This will be useful when taking distributional issues into consideration (see later in this chapter).

One way of concentrating on the most important benefits would be to look at some general indicator that is expected to improve as a result of the project. For example, if much of the project is expected to enhance maternal and child health the infant and maternal mortality rates may be good outcome indicators of health status. Many projects improving primary health care through health centres might be expected to bring disproportionate benefit to these groups. While perhaps not much affected in the short term, over 10–20 years a significant impact could be observed. If these or similar indicators are chosen the important measure, as with more specific measures, will be to project the net project impact taking into consideration the natural evolution of the indicator over the period. The difference in mortality could then be used to project the number of life years saved as a consequence of the project. These could then be used as a basis of a cost-per-life-year calculation or, more controversially, a monetary valuation of the lives saved following a human capital approach.

The economic analysis of the health benefits of a project, or investment, is hampered by substantial identification and measurement issues. Partial analysis can be achieved by first estimating the financial impact on patient access to health services and then describing the general benefits that can be expected. A complete numerical assessment of all benefits is unlikely to be feasible. Any such calculation should, as with any economic appraisal, be accompanied by sensitivity analysis to show the impact of changing assumptions on the final result.

Other issues

Shadow prices

It is important to use relevant shadow prices for inputs where market prices do not properly reflect their social opportunity cost. In our example at least two shadow prices may be required. First, some of the benefits of the project are valued in terms of reduced time costs to patients. These are valued at the average wage rate but a local assessment will be required to obtain the actual opportunity cost of labour. Second, a different exchange rate may be required for the conversion of some costs since the market rate could over-price the cost of, for example, locally available expertise used for (some) equipment maintenance since it is largely a non-traded item.

A fuller discussion of this topic can be found in texts on project appraisal methods in developing countries (for example Brent, 1998) and in Chapter 6.

Issues of distribution

Up to now we have implicitly assumed that costs and benefits are valued in the same way no matter who suffers or benefits. Yet most project appraisal methodologies allow for the fact that impacts on certain groups should be valued more highly. One of the most common ways of doing this is to ascribe different weights to different groups. Those whom society wishes to benefit more highly than others are giving a higher weighting. Typically low income groups might be given a higher weighting than high income groups. The approach adopted by many standard approaches (see Brent, 1998) is to assume that all individuals have a similar welfare function but that as consumption increases the additional welfare obtained declines (the assumption of diminishing marginal welfare or utility). Weights can be derived for different levels of consumption relative to the average consumption (individual expenditure). Low consumption individuals receive a higher weight than high consumption individuals. If information were available on the pattern of beneficiaries these weights could be used to adjust the net economic impacts.

Unfortunately such detailed information on the income of beneficiaries is not usually available. Instead a rough weighting could be done based on the general characteristics of the population known to be affected. So, for example, if it is known that rural areas are generally poorer than urban areas then project appraisal would favour projects that benefit rural populations. In the context of our example, we might wish to weight the reduction in costs for those living far away from the hospital more heavily than those living nearer on the grounds that they are likely to be worse off than those living close to the hospital.

A final issue is that ideally we should evaluate different options for spending resources from an economic and financial point of view and then compare the results – a full economic evaluation. The problem is that, unlike the economic evaluation of individual interventions, the evaluation of a large project with many different components is a complex task. It is very difficult to carry out the analysis for many different options. Even if difficult, we may still be able to go some way towards a comparison. We might take the options of equipment or buildings expenditure and compare their financial and economic costs using the methodology of this and previous chapters. Evaluation is a complex but critical task. A wrong investment decision could lead to lower net benefits and/or a project that is not sustainable. It is, therefore, important that any project devote sufficient resources to this evaluation.

Summary

In this chapter we have presented a general framework for considering the costs and benefits of a project both in terms of health sector costs and cash flow and in terms of the wider (economic) impact on the community.

The key ideas presented are:

- Even if a project is likely to bring positive net economic benefit, financial balance must be assured to ensure sustainability
- Investments can have large and variable recurrent costs – it may sometimes be better to refuse investments, even those that are 'free', if the recurrent costs are shown to be unaffordable
- A full economic assessment of health projects is hampered by the problem of accurate identification and valuation of outcomes. However, health sector and financial costs to patients

may be sufficient to justify a project. If they are not a partial economic analysis should at least indicate the main types of benefits expected.

Questions for discussion

1 Obtain information on the capital and recurrent costs of one recent investment made in the health sector in your country. What is the ratio of new recurrent costs to investment? How does this compare to total recurrent costs?
2 Attempt to quantify the net financial benefits to the community of the investment. Include time and other costs of treatment.
3 List the main health benefits of the investment. How might these be quantified and what problems would there being in attempting to do so ?
4 Given that most reforms have an important political economy dimension, what obstacles do you think there would be to the proposals put forward?

References and further reading

There are few references that deal with the specific application of project appraisal analysis to the health sector. References are to general discussions of project appraisal and to discussions of the recurrent cost burden of health sector investments.

Abel-Smith, B. and Creese, A. (1989). *Recurrent Costs in the Health Sector*, Geneva: WHO.

Barnum, H. and Kutzin, J. (1993). *Public hospitals in developing countries*, Baltimore, MA: Johns Hopkins University Press.

Brent, R. J. (1998). *Cost-benefit Analysis for Developing Countries*, Aldershot: Edward Elgar.

Ensor, T. (1997). What role for state health care in Asian Transition Economies?, *Health Economics*, Guest Editorial, 6, 5: 445–454.

Jowett, M. (1998). Health resources in *Evaluation of the Implementation of the Global Strategy for Health for All by 2000: 1979–2000*. Geneva: WHO.

Peters, D. and Chao, S. (1998). The sector-wide approach in health: What is it? Where is it leading? *International Journal of Health Planning and Management,* 13: 177–190.

Stout, S., Evans, A., Nassin, J. and Roney, L. (1997). Evaluating health projects: lessons from the literature. World Bank Discussion Paper no. 356. Washington, DC: World Bank.

World Bank (1996). *Handbook on Economic Analysis of Investment Operations*, Operations Policy Department, Washington, DC: World Bank.

9

Setting priorities in health care

Sophie Witter

Introduction

This chapter looks at a broad range of issues around how resources are used in the health sector. Its focus is allocative
efficiency: putting resources to use in ways which maximise
health or other social goals. This builds on the economic evaluation approach described in the last three chapters, but moves on
to how that information is used. Who should be consulted on priorities for services? How can their different inputs be combined
to produce plans for services? How are resources allocated
between regions, as well as programmes? And where resources
are inadequate to fund the full range of cost-effective services,
how are rationing decisions taken?

   This chapter will cover the following topics:

- priority setting: whose priorities?
- the users' perspective on needs and services
- the doctor's perspective
- the role of 'commissioner' or 'purchaser'
- allocating funds between regions
- rationing of services: the 'essential package' debate
- making decisions on new capital investments

Priority setting: whose priorities?

*Mrs Foresight, a planner in the Ministry of Health, has been asked to
draw up the national priorities for health care. Her work will feed into the
government's planning process and help set the health budget for the next*

year. How should she go about this task? Who should she consult? What different aspects should she consider?

There are many different groups whose views on health care matter. For example:

- individuals and families
- community organisations
- health staff
- district and regional health administrators
- national level policy makers, in the Ministry of Health and other ministries.

Each influences the setting of priorities in health in different ways, and each is likely to have a different perspective on health services. For example,

- families will often focus on the *process* of health care delivery, such as price, quality, accessibility, and acceptability
- health staff and Ministries of Finance are often more concerned with *inputs*, such as number of staff or beds available
- higher level planners and administrators may want information on *outcomes* or patterns of *need*
- the distribution of health and health care, i.e., *equity*, is important for politicians and community organisations in particular.

Priority setting therefore takes place at different levels of the system and in different ways. There is no one correct way of setting priorities, as priorities are subjective and relative. Priority setting involves finding a balance between different objectives and different viewpoints. We will not deal with all aspects (see further reading section for some recommended texts on this topic), but will concentrate on topics of particular importance to health economists.

The users' perspective

Demand for health services by individuals and families is affected by a great many factors, including

1 their objective need, in terms of the illness suffered or susceptibility to a disease
2 their perception of illness, what causes it, what treatment is appropriate
3 the accessibility of services, in geographical terms
4 the affordability of services (ability to pay for services)

5 the acceptability of services: whether the manner of service delivery encourages or discourages the potential patients.

How can planners find out about these important areas?

Epidemiological data is the most obvious source for information on objective health needs. Data related to mortality, such as life expectancy, crude death rates, maternal or infant mortality are important aggregate indicators of need. Where these vary significantly between areas with similar characteristics, differences in services may be at least partly responsible.

The limitation of these data is that while it gives us an idea of what diseases people die of (some of which might not be influenced by medical services), they do not provide a picture of the burden of illness with which people live. For this we need data on morbidity. Which diseases have the highest prevalence rates (i.e., most cases occurring at any given point in time; usually quoted per 1,000 population)? What is their incidence rate (i.e., number of new cases occurring each year, per 1,000 population)? Sometimes this information can be broken down into different rates by age and sex group. These needs should be considered in the light of the availability of effective treatments (see Chapter 7).

Note however that most statistics on morbidity are dependent on records kept at health facilities. This leads to an inherent bias that those areas with a higher concentration of facilities will record more illness just because access by patients is easier. As a result, an area with fewer facilities could record little illness but actually be one of the areas with the highest levels of disease. Periodic household surveys, such as demographic and health surveys, may be a less biased source of information.

Qualitative survey methods can be used to elicit information on a number of important areas, including perceptions of health and health services. These usually take the form of focus group discussions with community members or open-ended surveys of individuals. (See Mays and Pope, 1996 for guidance on how to conduct qualitative research.) Household data is very important as it provides information on the whole population. By contrast, information collected in health centres only records the views or behaviour of people who are already using the services (i.e., it cannot address the issue of *unmet need:* why others may not be doing so).

Patients will not use services unless they perceive their own need and are convinced that an effective remedy is available at the health centre. Stimulating demand for preventive services is particularly important, given the lack of immediate need by patients. Moreover, patients are commonly deterred from using public facilities by the discourteous manner of staff, lack of privacy and other issues of perceived service quality. It is crucial that staff understand the priorities of their customers and respect these. Just because a service is 'free' (in terms of fees) does not mean that quality does not matter. There is evidence from developing countries that people will travel further and/or pay for services if they perceive a difference in quality (see discussion of user fees in Chapter 5). Given the fundamental importance of good health, this is understandable.

Access (in physical terms) is most commonly measured in terms of distance to health facilities or the size of the catchment population which is served by a health post or hospital. The relevant issue for economists are the costs of getting to health care, so terrain and transport networks will be equally relevant in determining time taken and costs incurred.

Affordability can be measured by collecting information from patients or households on expenditure on health care and income. Of particular interest is the proportion of disposable income which is spent on health care. Problems of affordability are signalled by families spending a high proportion of their income on health, by decisions not to use health care for reasons of cost, and by health expenditure-related indebtedness. A common equity issue also relates to choice of facility: typically, richer families will use higher level services than poorer ones, and this may result in differential quality of care. (See equity checklist in Chapter 1.)

Utilisation rates may highlight strong or weak demand. For example, if utilisation of family planning services is considerably higher in one district than in its neighbour, that should raise some questions. Are the differences attributable to different wants or needs? If not, then some aspect of service delivery is responsible.

Utilisation of services of other providers can also give important information. For example, families may prefer to use traditional birth attendants rather than health centre midwives for deliveries. A household survey could suggest the reasons why. Some positive lessons for the public sector might emerge. (See Chapter 10 for further details on the relationship between public and private providers).

Low *coverage rates* for such programmes as Expanded Programme in Immunisation (EPI) or antenatal care are similarly indicative of problems. These portray the proportion of the estimated target population which has been reached. Problems of service delivery, accessibility, affordability and acceptability are common causes of low coverage rates.

High *drop out rates* can also be a signal of problems, usually related to the acceptability, convenience or affordability of services. Let us take tuberculosis treatment as an example. Completion rates for treatment are often very low (in the range of 50 per cent). There are a number of reasons for this, some of which can be addressed directly by planners.

• The traditional treatment takes a long time, and requires repeated visits to the clinic for medication and check-ups. This is time-consuming and costly for the patient (even if services are free – see Chapter 6 for the different costs faced). Once they begin to feel better, their motivation to continue treatment will be reduced. This can be tackled by changing drug regimes to shorter course drugs. Another approach is to involve community health staff and/or family members in administering drugs and encouraging completion of treatment by the patient (commonly known as the DOTs approach – directly observed therapy).

• Other problems can be more intractable. The low status of women, in some areas, can be a barrier to treatment, if their in-laws are unwilling to incur the cost and time involved in completing a long course of treatment. In this case it is not so much the user's perspective that counts as much as the perspective of the dominant family members.

The philosophy of primary health care (PHC) emphasises the involvement not just of individuals but also *the community* in setting priorities and promoting health. The extent to which this is likely to be effective will depend on how much 'community' exists in a given area and how well it is organised. In Vietnam, for example, where families have only recently been freed from decades of collectivised production, there is resistance towards collective activities or sharing of assets at the local level (Witter, 1992). There is also the tricky question of how representative existing community organisations are. It is almost a tautology to say that where local residents share a common perspective and have created a body to represent them, that body can have a valuable input into what services are provided, where and how. However, a 'community organisation' can equally be a group of self-selecting, self-serving local elite. (See Zakus and Lysack, 1998, for a review of community participation in practice.)

Leaving aside that important judgement about representativeness, should community organisations be consulted, or should they be given the power to actually determine local services? Very few examples exist of handing over complete control, but communities have been consulted in a variety of ways. For example:

• Ask a representative group to prioritise between different services. This can be combined with the epidemiological information and cost-effectiveness data (see Chapters 6 and 7) to produce some kind of local ranking. An important issue is what information the group is given during its debate and how the questions are phrased, which is likely to influence their decisions. Another issue is how the ranking is used.
• Give the group the choice of which services to cut or keep in a constrained budget situation. This has the advantage of realism and prevents the from giving all services a high importance (which they often would: nobody finds it easy to cut services).
• Consult a user group on a particular service. This is often a very effective way of finding out why a certain group does not use that service (i.e., of dealing with questions of service delivery rather than overall priority setting).

The medical staff perspective

Another group of people with an interest in and knowledge of health service issues are of course the front-line medical staff. This includes doctors, assistant doctors, nurses, pharmacists, midwives, dentists: anyone delivering direct care to patients. They play a key role in priority setting in that they currently ration health care (i.e., decide who will be treated and who not) in any situation where demand outstrips supply (as occurs in almost all health services, particularly when treatment is free at the point of delivery).

Their role as agents of the patient has been discussed in general in Chapter 3, where it was pointed out that they are imperfect agents, as they can never be fully informed about the patients preferences and values, as well as their objective health needs. This last point comes as a surprise to many, who have been led to believe that doctors are akin to gods, knowing everything. In fact, variance of medical practice between regions with similar health needs suggests a number of observations about the way in which doctors work.

• Diagnosis is a matter of judgement, relating to the doctor's training, their experience, interpersonal skills and equipment.

- Many treatments are of unproven effectiveness. Hence the current concern in the West with 'evidence based medicine' and the development of treatment protocols to disseminate 'best practice' amongst clinicians

- As well as being the patient's agent, they are their own agent and factors like convenience and profit play a role. For example, if payments systems are changed so that doctors are paid per patient visit instead of on a salary basis, there is strong evidence that the number of visits by patients will increase (supply induced demand – see Chapter 12 for further discussion). Neglecting their public duties in order to encourage attendance at a fee-paying afternoon private clinic is another example of the doctor as profit-maximiser. Doctors also respond to the ability of pay of the patients themselves. In Chile, the proportion of births done by caesarian section was found to be linked with the proportion of women covered by private insurance (Murray and Serani Pradenas, 1997).

- Doctors only see those patients that come to see them, and while they can be expected to be well aware of those people's general health needs, they often lack a broader perspective. Their duty is towards individuals, rather than allocating re-sources to maximise the health of the community as a whole.

- In particular, doctors have little awareness of costs (other than their own). They are therefore unable to allocate resources ac-cording to cost-effectiveness criteria, unless involved in some specific way in the purchasing process (as described hereafter and in Chapter 12).

This is not to imply that doctors should not be setting priorities. Indeed it is unavoidable that they should do so to some extent. However, their most important contribution should be to provide effective treatment based on an accurate recognition of the needs of individual patients. For this reason, much effort has been put in recent years into developing protocols for disease management together with clinicians to promote 'good practice' (i.e., both effective and cost effective practice). The natural loca-tion for prioritising between different needs and different groups lies elsewhere.

The role of 'commissioner'

The term 'purchaser' or 'commissioner' has been much used in recent health reforms in the West. In the UK, for example, the government in the late 1980s tried to improve efficiency and quality in the publicly funded and managed National Health Service by breaking it into providers – self-governing organisations that provide services (such as hospital and general practitioners) – and purchasers – the health authorities and some new fund-holding GPs (primary care doctors), which were responsible for deciding which services to buy from which provider. Instead of being vertically integrated in a bureaucratic organisation with historic budgets, providers were supposed to compete for contracts from purchasers. This is known as a *quasi-market*. It has some market-like features, like the need for providers to 'win' business. On the other hand, these organisations continue to operate within the public sector, funded almost entirely by taxpayers' money and heavily regulated by the government (see Chapter 10 for further details).

One idea behind this 'purchaser-provider split' is that the purchaser will concern itself with allocative efficiency (directing resources to their most productive use: see Chapter 1), while providers worry about technical efficiency (how to produce specific health goods using least resources).

Even without the development of a quasi-market with contracts, etc., the notion of commissioner is useful. If individual patients are in a weak position to judge the quality of services, for the reasons discussed in Chapter 3, then it makes sense for a 'superclient' to be developed to buy services on their behalf. This commissioner can fulfil a number of important strategic functions (see Box 9.1).

The process described in Box 9.1 is idealised. Most regional health authorities or similar bodies in a position to operate as purchasers will not have the ability, mandate or will to do everything described. However, the ideal is valuable. There should be some part of each health system that is thinking, not just about operational issues such as staff and drugs and payment, but about health outcomes and how the health system can be most effective at improving these, within the fixed constraints (usually money, but also central government policies) which it faces.

One important question is whether organisations in developing countries which are potential purchasers have any mechanisms by which they can bring about change, other than exhortation. Some financial sanction or reward is probably necessary – for example, the ability to make additional money available for a particular programme, or productivity payments to

---

Box 9.1   Stages in purchasing or commissioning health services for a population

1 Assess population health needs.
2 Assess availability of effective prevention or treatments to meet those needs.
3 Using data on cost-effectiveness of treatments, health needs and available financial resources, decide what is the most appropriate mix of services.
4 Consult the public on its values and priorities.
5 Combine these to produce health objectives and priorities.
6 Monitor the performance of providers and the existing pattern of services to see what sorts of change might be introduced.
7 Negotiate with other parts of the health system to make changes, with the possible use of sanctions to back it up.
8 Feed information from this process back into the next round of reviewing and negotiating.

---

staff for outstanding performance, or the ability to move or sack staff who are not performing well. This implies a degree of independence at the local level which is commonly lacking. This important issue will be discussed further in Chapter 11 on decentralisation.

Geographical resource allocation

Mr Slick from the World Bank is visiting the Ministry of Health in Ebul. He asks the ministry staff what formula they use for allocating resources to the regions. There is some surprise at this question. What can he mean? Every year the budgets are set for each region based on last year's budget, adjusted upwards for inflation but often downwards too for shortfalls in the central allocation to health? What alternative approach is there?

The theory of resource allocation (of recurrent funds) to the regions and districts is as follows:

- Money, and other resources such as staff, should be allocated according to need (rather than according to current service provision, which is commonly the case)

- The process should be simple, using data which is available, regularly updated and reliable
- Calculations should be objective and transparent so that no one feels they are being unfairly treated
- It should avoid creating 'perverse incentives' (for example, if utilisation of facilities is used as an indicator of need, then people may be kept in hospital or clinic for unnecessarily long periods).

In practice, how do we calculate need?

1 The first measure which is commonly used is *population size*, which gives some indication of the need for services. Any formula using population data must anticipate changes in population size over the period, due to birth rates, death rates or migration. If data is available, this can be adjusted for a number of other factors, such as:

2 *Age and sex profiles* of the population. Weightings could be developed locally to reflect the different usage rates of different age groups. For example, typically women of 25–40 use services more than men; young children and old people also tend to have higher levels of need than mature adults.

3 *Morbidity proxies.* Age-weighted population accounts for only part of the total need for health care. Among people of the same age group the experience of ill health can vary enormously. It is therefore desirable to introduce a further adjustment that takes account of these differences.

One option is to use a proxy for morbidity, such as the standardised mortality rate (SMRs). These are calculated for each region, by comparing the observed deaths in each age and sex group with the expected deaths (the national average for that group, multiplied by the number in that region in that group). A high ratio would result in a higher allocation of funds to reflect the higher health needs of the population in that area (though the increase is usually less than proportionate, to reflect the extent to which increased need may be more appropriately addressed outside the health budget).

In developing countries, other proxies (such as infant mortality rates,) might be used, depending on what data is available.

These aim to incorporate predicable variations in health needs. Unpredictable occurrences, such as natural disasters or major epidemics, might of course require additional assistance from national emergency funds.

4 *Social deprivation indicators.* Given that there is commonly a correlation between poverty and health needs, some weight

should be given to indicators such as regional income levels, where these can be measured, or unemployment rates. Deprivation proxies will be very context-specific. For example, in some countries (like Kyrgyzstan) the mountainous areas are generally poorer than the lowlands, and here altitude is used as a simple indicator of socio-economic status.

5 *Cost of providing services.* If costs vary considerably between regions, then some allowance can be made for this, too. In Zambia, for example, population density was used as a proxy for costs, with high density districts given a weighting of 80 per cent and low density 120 per cent (Kamanga, 1996) to reflect the increased transportation costs, etc. An index of fuel prices was also used to reflect local cost differences in inputs.

If indicators are calculated as an index, then they can be applied directly to the population data. Indicators such as altitude must be converted into a scale and given a weight, relative to the other factors which are being taken into account.

There are a number of other issues to be considered in establishing resource allocation formulae.

1 *How to introduce it.* If the introduction of this new system of allocating resources will dramatically change the current payments to the regions, then it is probably better to allow time for them to adjust by giving advanced warning and phasing in the new system over a few years.

2 *Cross boundary flows.* Commonly residents of one area use services in another and in theory this should be taken into account in the resource allocation process. In particular, the capital city will often provide tertiary care for cases referred (or self-referring) from elsewhere. Some increased allowance should be made for this, although not as much as traditional budgets have usually suggested.

3 *Allowing for other sources of funds.* One of the main problems for developing countries in trying to achieve a fair and rational allocation of resources is that many channels of funding are beyond their control. In particular, some regions will have a much greater capacity to raise money from private sources, in the form of fees or insurance premia, than others. If successful local revenue generation is penalised by the withdrawal of equivalent public funds, then that would deter local fundraising and/or lead to its concealment. The only option may be to increase the deprivation weighting in the original formula to account for wide differences in the economic status of different parts of the country.

A second channel which commonly operates outside government control is donor funding. For example, a major donor may decide to fund a programme in some regions, but not others. Should the government in some way compensate the regions which have been left out? That would not be practical. Governments should enter into negotiations with donors to ensure that aid money is distributed according to need and that overall flows fit with government resource allocation policies.

In countries with a large and disproportionately funded private sector, such as South Africa (see Doherty and Van Den Heever, 1998), the resource allocation formula should take some account of the proportion of the population who are members of private insurance schemes. Whether they should be fully or partially discounted from public allocations is debatable.

4 *Varying capacities.* A separate concern relates to differing levels of infrastructure and staff capacity between regions. For example, one province may have a dense network of facilities and well trained staff. Should they not get more money than a province which has few facilities and poorly trained staff, but an equivalent population? Can the first province not spend the money better?

This is a common situation. In theory the answer is that resource allocation is based on need, and that other (development) funds should be used to bring the physical and human resource capacity of the second province up to the level of the first. However, some problems are chronic, and where resources are constrained it is practical to relate at least some part of the funds to ability to use them well. Ideally this would be carried out as a temporary measure, and accompanied by an 'action plan' to upgrade the second province.

Resource allocation is one of the main tools for achieving equity in provision of health services between different regions (though there are many more, as outlined in Chapter 1). It may seem complicated, but formulae can be kept quite simple. Often just adjusting for population brings a big change from traditional financing patterns. The main requirement is that data is available and reliable (i.e., not easy to invent or falsify). The shift to a needs-based formula can also be an opportunity to debate the allocation of resources between levels of services and to reinforce the role and financing of primary health care (as was the case in the Zambian example: Kamanga, 1996). The alternative to needs-based allocation is to base funding on past investments (such as infrastructure or past budgets), which reinforce inequalities, or on *ad hoc* political decisions, which are at best arbitrary.

Rationing health care and 'essential packages'

Rationing implies the need to limit the amount of treatment available or to deny certain treatments to certain people. Any public health system which claims to provide a universal service finds it difficult to do this, or at least to publicly admit that it is doing it. However, all health services ration. Even relatively prosperous Western countries are unable to provide all the health services which their population think they need or would like. The US, for example, rations by ability to pay insurance premia, and also by cost cutting measures within its publicly funded programmes. The UK has traditionally rationed by putting 'non-urgent' cases on waiting lists, especially for elective surgery.

These are implicit ways of rationing (i.e., rationing without having to say that you are rationing, which is politically more agreeable – See Fig. 9.1). However, recent debate in the West has focused on the need for explicit rationing, given the ageing of

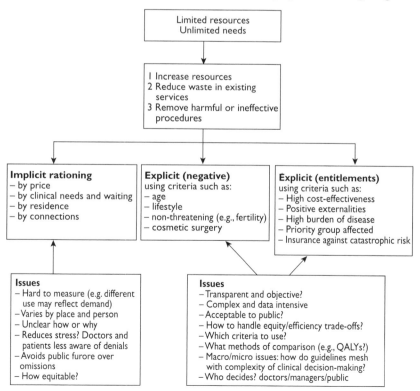

Fig. 9.1 Rationing in health care

populations and the growth in medical technology and expensive new drugs. (See Maxwell, 1995 and Ham, 1997, for discussion of rationing debates in the West.) By and large, explicit rationing has taken the form of 'negative' lists – i.e., defining the services which will *not* be provided by publically financed systems. Common criteria for exclusion include:

- non-effectiveness of procedure
- 'private' nature of the procedure (e.g., plastic surgery for cosmetic reasons; sex change operation; in some cases, infertility treatment)
- in some cases, more controversially, individual characteristics are used – for example, if a smoker is unlikely to benefit from the intervention, or discrimination on grounds of age.

In developing countries the rationing debate is even more acute. Public finances do not suffice to provide a free and universal service. As well as improving fund raising mechanisms (see Chapters 4 and 5) and improving the management of resources (see Chapter 13) health managers have to ration services.

The current situation in many developing countries is that public funds provide a limited subsidy to general health services. As this is insufficient, patients top up via formal or informal payments, go elsewhere or fail to be treated at all. This type of rationing is far from ideal. Public funds are neither targeted to those in most financial need (many richer people receive free services they could have paid for, whilst poor families are unable to afford the drugs etc. to get treatment) nor focused on the most cost-effective treatments. Given the problems of targeting by income group (see Chapter 5) the debate has turned to whether it is feasible to target by cost-effectiveness criteria instead.

The idea of a *basic* (or *essential*) *package* of services which should be available to all was promoted by the World Bank in its 1993 World Development Report. If funds are insufficient for all health care services, it argued, then resources should be directed from interventions which yield low DALY (disability adjusted life years – see Chapter 7) gains per dollar spent to those with high gain. The report looked at the worldwide burden of disease in terms of DALYs, and the cost of common interventions to prevent or cure these conditions. Out of this approach, it developed an essential public health package. This is a 'positive list', stating which services *will* be provided. They included the following highly cost-effective items:

- immunisation (EPI Plus)

- school-based health services
- health promotion and selective services for nutrition and family planning
- alcohol and smoking reduction programmes
- regulation, information and limited investments in the household environment
- AIDS prevention

It also suggested that a minimum clinical package in each country should include five groups of interventions:

1 pregnancy-related care
2 family planning services
3 TB control
4 control of STDs
5 care for serious childhood illnesses, such as diarrheoa, acute respiratory infection (ARI), measles, malaria and malnutrition

The cost of the public health component was estimated at $4.2 per person per year for low income countries, and the clinical package at $7.8, bringing the total to $12. The equivalent for middle income countries was $21.5 per person per year, for both elements (all 1993 prices).

It was suggested that as resources for health care increased, countries could include more items in their public health package. At the other end of the spectrum, services such as heart surgery, some cancer treatments, intensive care for premature babies and expensive drug therapies for HIV are unlikely to ever be cost-effective enough to be financed by the state.

For health economists, the idea of shifting resources from activities which yield relatively low gain for a given investment to more cost effective activities is definitely appealing. However, we have to bear a few important points in mind.

Local information and priorities. While the idea of prioritising is important, the information on burden of disease and the cost of interventions should be collected and analysed locally. Global data provided by the World Bank is illustrative, but should never be followed rigidly without considering its relevance to the local level. The essential package is unlikely to be the same in any two places. Different regions or districts will have different disease patterns and should be encouraged to develop local priorities.

Shortcuts can be taken – for example, when calculating DALYs, local morbidity and mortality data can be combined with regional weightings (Murray and Lopez, 1994) to produce an estimate of DALYs lost due to different disease groupings. If disease profiles are very different, though, from neighbouring countries, then this method may be misleading. Similarly, international cost estimates can be used as a crude basis for calculations, but may need to be adjusted for variations in efficiency of diagnosis and provision, quality of care, levels of coverage etc.

For details of how to calculate cost per DALY, see Chapter 7 and the World Bank website (Appendix 4).

Resource shortfalls. Even the very limited package already outlined is beyond the spending power of the poorest countries, where public finance on health per person per year at the time of the report was about $6 (i.e., half of the minimum required). The issues raised in Chapters 4 and 5 about additional sources of funding still apply therefore. There may also be trade-offs between the range of services included and the coverage of the population which is achieved. Ideally, public funds should be targeted at those who cannot afford basic services, with the better off paying. However, such targeting is hard to achieve, and the basic package may be more politically acceptable if it is free for all.

The health system perspective. By concentrating on specific interventions, it is argued by many, the 'basic package' proponents reduce the overall sustainability of the health system (Rifkin and Walt, 1986). This debate has been raging, between those ('idealists') who want to see PHC operating in its entirety, and those ('pessimists', or maybe 'realists') who believe that in the present economic climate, developing country health systems should concentrate on being really effective in a number of important interventions.

The pendulum swings to and fro on this '*comprehensive-selective PHC*' debate. The late 80s was a time of focusing on targets, such as reaching 80 per cent coverage for immunisation against the six major childhood killer diseases. The 1990s has talked more about integrating the vertical programmes which were built up to meet those targets into national health systems. Some worried that the approach promoted by the WDR heralded a return to vertical programming and centralised control.

This need not be the case, if priority setting is carried at the regional or district level, with guidance from higher level staff. Services should also be bundled together according to risk factors to minimise costs to the patient as well as the health services. For example, the 'integrated management of the sick child' combines the treatment of diarrhoeal diseases and acute respiratory infections (ARI) for under 5s. The 'mother and baby package' combines community-based obstetrics, district level hospital services and information, education and communication (IEC) services.

Maintaining current gains. It is important not to overlook the health gains which are already being achieved through cost-effective interventions. For example, if a country has an effective immunisation service in operation, then low mortality from those infectious diseases may lead to the suggestion that they are not priority areas (and to withdrawal of funding from the immunisation service). That would clearly be a mistake. A comparison with similar countries which have low coverage rates may allow a calculation of the cost per DALY gained by the established programme.

Future disease trends. Similarly, it would be a mistake to base prioritisation purely on the current burden of disease without taking into account the likely future trends. For example, in many developing countries smoking is predicted to become the major cause of premature deaths within the next two decades. Given the lag time involved, present day figures do not present it as such a major public health target. Nevertheless, prevention now is likely to be highly cost effective, even with discounting of future benefits. The same point applies to control of the spread of HIV, which has even larger positive externalities in the form of reduced onward infection.

Intersectoral collaboration. By focusing on health gains, the cost per DALY approach can facilitate intersectoral collaboration. However, some interventions produce health and non-health gains, and the latter will not be counted in this method. Improving water supplies and sanitation, for example, produce health gains, but the cost appears to be high if other benefits (such as reduced labour, especially for women and girls) are not counted. Other methods, such as cost-benefit analysis (see Chapter 7) may be appropriate for evaluating these interventions.

Public/political acceptability. It is likely to be politically controversial to focus public resources on a limited range of services. Even though a comprehensive free service probably did not exist in reality before, it is still hard to explicitly exclude services. Politicians, the professionals and the general public have to be won over to this approach and the view that it may be the least bad option.

What emerges out of this debate of use to developing countries? Under resource shortages, a number of strategies are appropriate:

1 Increase resources, using criteria such as equity (see Chapter 1)
2 Increase technical efficiency through improved management, reduced waste (see Chapter 13)
3 Allocate existing resources to best possible use. This will involve local managers (at national, regional and district levels) identifying the major health problems, cost-effective interventions to

prevent or cure them, and giving these priority. Issues of equity and affordability should also inform decisions about charging and coverage.

See Box 9.2 for a step-by-step guide to designing an essential package. Implementing an essential package is likely to involve a range of strategies. For example:

- Funding the right inputs: removing funding from specialist services, equipment and supplies outside the package, and redirecting these to staff and materials for the selected programmes.
- Changing training curricula, in-service training and work norms to reflect the desired pattern of services.
- Using media and public education channels to promote awareness of the package and redirect demand towards those services.

Box 9.2   Basic steps in designing a package of essential health services

1 Estimate the burden of disease due to premature mortality and disability for approximately 100 diseases and injuries, by age, sex and geographical regions.

2 Estimate the burden of disease for a selected number of proximate risk factors, for example, inadequate water and sanitation or tobacco consumption.

3 Select interventions which fulfil at least one of the following criteria: favourable cost-efficacy; ability to address diseases or risk factors with a high burden (more than 1 per cent of the total); high supply or demand; high recurrent expenditure; ability to address diseases of public concern. Health interventions should include public health measures; community outreach; and clinical services.

4 Estimate costs for the interventions and clusters of interventions which are justifiably grouped together. This includes making assumptions about technical efficiency and quality of care.

5 Collect information on efficacy of interventions and estimate expected effectiveness for the country's different health care facilities.

6 Define time frame and population coverage (current and targeted) to estimate incremental cost per intervention per year (including overheads and diagnostic services).

7 Combine information on the financial resources available with your estimates for incremental costs and expected effectiveness of different interventions to produce a package of high priority interventions that can be jointly delivered.

Source: Adapted from Bobadilla and Cowley, 1995.

• In countries where private providers or local municipalities are responsible for service delivery, the government should require that the essential package is provided by private insurance companies, or offered as a minimum package by local authorities.

It will not be simple. Resources may need to be shifted from tertiary to primary care level. Preventive services may claim a higher proportion of funds. Non-staff recurrent costs (such as supplies and drugs) may need to be protected against cuts, to ensure that services are effective. The public needs to be convinced that these services are indeed valuable. Donor resources need to be co-ordinated so that they support rather than undermine local priorities. All of these require skills and leadership.

However, the potential for health gain is significant – especially in countries with moderate or high mortality, where a few causes typically account for a large share of deaths (Bobadilla *et al.,* 1994). For example, in 1990 an estimated 55 per cent of the burden of disease was concentrated in children under 15, and of these, 71 per cent were caused by just 10 disease clusters. Apart from congenital deformations, all of these clusters could be treated by cost-effective interventions (less than $100 per DALY gained). Focusing resources in these areas should greatly increase the productivity of health expenditure. Whether it meets other public goals is debatable: we return to this point in the summary.

Capital investments

This chapter has largely dealt with issues relating to recurrent costs. Capital budgets raise slightly different issues. Traditionally, capital budgets have been donor dependent in developing countries, raising issues of sustainability. Planning for the recurrent cost implication of maintaining and running buildings and equipment is clearly vital. Otherwise, 'gifts' have a tendency to distort future public spending plans (as described in Chapter 8).

For planning purposes, the '*R coefficient*' is sometimes used. This is the ratio of average annual recurrent costs to the initial capital outlay on an item. (Actual costs will vary according to context, of course). Essential equipment lists can be developed at national level to promote appropriate technology, which fits in with disease control priorities, as discussed earlier.

One technique commonly used to make decisions on capital items is *option appraisal*. This is a defined process, including:

1 Set strategic context (demand for services, service gaps strengths of provider, etc.)

2 Identify objectives, criteria and constraints
3 Formulate long list of options
4 Reduce to short list of options
5 Assess and systematically compare costs and benefits of options
6 Consider uncertainties
7 Select preferred option

For more details of this technique, see Sanderson, 1997.

Summary

This chapter has covered a wide range of topics, reflecting the broad nature of priority setting in health at many levels.

Priority setting seeks to integrate 'objective' approaches, such as cost-effectiveness analysis, with the more subjective views of what are known as 'stakeholders' – i.e., people with an interest in the provision of health care. Although economics as a discipline is most commonly associated with quantitative/objective approaches, there is a sound theoretical justification for weighting estimates of benefits to reflect the values of a community. The question is how such values can be obtained, how representative they may be, and how to integrate them in situations of real choice.

Figure 9.2 shows the traditional division of functions in terms of priority setting between different levels in a public health sector. Notice, however, that the division is not so tidy in reality. Sometimes the deviation is positive – for example, when district level staff are consulted in the formulation of broad health policies. Other times, the examples are less productive – for example, when central level staff get unduly involved in management issues at the local level. These roles have also been influenced by recent reform programmes (see Chapter 11).

We have talked about the importance of listening to the users of services and responding to their priorities as shown by their behaviour. Issues of quality of services, cost, convenience and respectful treatment by health staff tend to rank high amongst users. Perceptions of need are also important, and these will influence and be influenced by encounters with clinical staff.

Clinical staff play a crucial role in allocating health care between individuals. Their perceptions of community health needs and the likely success of different health strategies should inform and be informed by the debates about priorities by health managers.

Distinguishing between the needs of different groups is the job of health authorities at national, regional and district level. In doing so, their two main goals will usually be to increase health

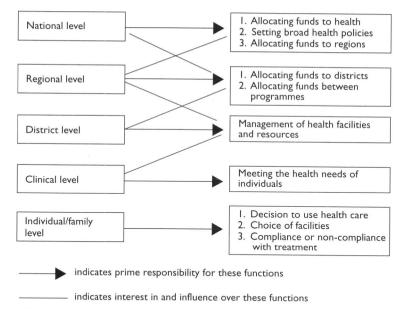

| National level | → | 1. Allocating funds to health
2. Setting broad health policies
3. Allocating funds to regions |

| Regional level | → | 1. Allocating funds to districts
2. Allocating funds between
   programmes |

| District level | → | Management of health facilities
and resources |

| Clinical level | → | Meeting the health needs of
individuals |

| Individual/family
level | → | 1. Decision to use health care
2. Choice of facilities
3. Compliance or non-compliance
   with treatment |

→ indicates prime responsibility for these functions

— indicates interest in and influence over these functions

Fig. 9.2 Priority setting in health: different levels

gain and to promote equity. One way of doing this is to allocate funds geographically on the basis of need. Different needs-based formulae are presented here. Another important strand is choosing more rather than less cost-effective interventions. The issues surrounding this are presented in the context of current efforts to promote 'essential packages' in developing countries.

Prioritising between programmes means taking politically charged decisions. The decision to focus on key primary health care interventions, for example, may be a decision to withdraw public funding from other important sections of the public (those benefiting from cancer treatments, for example). The decision to divert funds to the village health posts may mean cutting jobs at regional level. For every winner there is likely to be a loser, and so political skills and determination are called for. The timing and sequence of reforms are likely to be crucial to their success. Deciding how much to undertake is also very important. Where there is considerable political will (e.g., a new government, committed to change), change can be dramatic. More commonly, incremental and experimental changes are introduced.

An important point is not to let the best be the enemy of the merely good, as the saying goes. In other words, a small positive change is better than no change at all, even if it falls short of the wholesale change which the situation seems to demand. For example, if detailed data is lacking with which to calculate costs per DALY, use rough estimates. Talk to local physicians and communities about how to set priorities. Priorities are not set once and for all, but require continual information gathering, dialogue and decision-making. The initial outcome is less important than starting a process in which key players reflect on what they are trying to achieve, and how best to do so within the real constraints. This should also be linked to behaviour change, by health managers, doctors, patients and other 'stakeholders' in health.

Rationing – the controversial side of priority setting – is often perceived to be the evil work of health managers and economists. The simple answer is that rationing is all around. The question is not whether, but how. Should rationing be haphazard, *ad hoc* or hidden (e.g., the clinic runs out of drugs by mid-month; the doctor works till midday and then stops; the people who are well connected get the treatment, and others not; etc.)? Or should it be, as most economists argue, an open and rational debate? And if so, what are the criteria for rationing? By geography? By income group? By type of service? Underlying these choices are social values which have to be debated. For example, essential packages offer opportunities to improve health status for the population as a whole. On the other hand, they leave individuals uncovered for many chronic, incurable or catastrophically expensive illnesses (such as AIDS) – which also, incidentally, are often very hard to insure against. Which is more important? These issues need to be resolved locally and openly.

Questions for discussion

1 Ebul contains four regions. After setting aside money for national level health expenditure, an annual health budget of $30 million remains. You are asked to allocate the money between the regions. You may find the data in Table 9.1 helpful.
2 Which indicators do you think are most relevant? Why?
3 Using your chosen indicators, what is the final financial allocation?
4 What other information would you have liked to determine allocation of funds?
5 Assuming that your final allocation differs substantially from the current funding patterns, how do you plan to implement it to meet least resistance? How is this affected if the economy as a whole is growing/shrinking?

Table 9.1   Resource allocation exercise

Region	Total population	Infant mortality rate	Life expectancy	Average income (US$ per annum)	Cost index
North	700,000	102	49	250	1.5
East	1,200,000	90	57	270	0.7
West	1,800,000	64	62	300	0.8
South	1,300,000	60	67	310	1
Total	5,000,000				1
Total average		74.52	60.28	288.4	

References and further reading

General
Mays, N. ˙and Pope, C., (eds)(1996). *Qualitative Research in Health Care.* London: BMJ Publishing Group.
Murray, S. and Serani Pradenas, F. (1997). Cesarian birth trends in Chile, 1986–1994, *Birth*, 24, 4.
Witter, S. (1992). Vietnam: the challenge of development, *The World Today*, 48, 11.

Priority setting
Green, A. (1992). Setting priorities. Chapter 8 of *An Introduction to Health Planning in Developing Countries*. Oxford: Oxford University Press.
Zakus, D. and Lysack, C. (1998). Revisiting community participation: review article, *Health Policy and Planning*, 13, 1.

Purchasing
Drummond, M. and Maynard, A. (1993). *Purchasing and Providing Cost-effective Health Care*. London: Churchill Livingstone.
Ovretveit, J. (1995). *Purchasing for Health*. Buckingham: Open University Press.
Stevens, A. and Raftery, J. (eds)(1994). *Health Care Needs Assessment*. Oxford: Radcliffe Medical Press.

Resource allocation
Doherty, J. and Van den Heever, A. (1998). A needs-based, weighted capitation formula in support of equity and primary health care: a South African case study, in M. Barer, T. Getzen, and G. Stoddart, (eds) *Health, Health Care and Health Economics: Perspectives on Distribution*. Chichester: John Wiley.
Holland, S. (1996). Resource allocation: a theoretical overview, in *CARNET Central Asian Resource Allocation Handbook*. Copenhagen: WHO.
Kamanga, K. (1996). Can health system reform in Africa be driven by improving the efficiency of public hospitals? The case of Zambia, *World Hospitals and Health Services*, 32, 1.

Klopper, J., Bourne, D., McIntyre D., Pick, W. and Taylor, S. (1989). A methodology for resource allocation in health care for South Africa, *South African Medical Journal* , 76.

Selective/comprehensive primary health care
Rifkin, S. and Walt, G. (1986). Why health improves: defining the issues concerning 'Comprehensive Primary Health Care and Selective Primary Health Care', *Social Science and Medicine*, 23, 6: 559–566.

Walsh, J. and Warren, K. (1979). Selective Primary Health Care: an interim strategy for disease control in developing countries, *New England Journal of Medicine*, 301: 967–74.

Essential packages
Bobadilla, J. L. and Cowley, P. (1995). Designing and implementing packages of essential health services, *Journal of International Development*, 7, 3: 543–555.

Bobadilla, J. L., Cowley, P., Musgrove, P. and Saxenian, H. (1994). Design, content and financing of an essential national package of health services, *Bulletin of the World Health Organization*, 72(4): 653–662.

Murray, C. J. L. (1994). Quantifying the burden of disease: the technical basis for disability-adjusted life years, *Bulletin of the World Health Organisation*, 72: 429–45.

Murray, C. J. L., Lopez, A. D. (1996). *The Global Burden of Disease*. Vol. 1. Cambridge: Harvard University Press.

Murray, C. J. L., Kreuser, J. and Whang, W. (1994). Cost effectiveness analysis and policy choices: investing in health systems, *Bulletin of the World Health Organisation*, 72 (4).

Murray, C. J. L., Lopez, A. D. (1994). Quantifying disability: data, methods and results, *Bulletin of the World Health Organisation*, 72: 481–94.

Murray, C. J. L., Lopez, A. D. and Jamison, D. T. (1994). The global burden of disease in 1990: summary results, sensitivity analysis and future directions, *Bulletin of the World Health Organisation*, 72: 495–509.

Paalman, M., Bekedam, H., Hawken, L. and Nyheim, D. (1998). A critical review of priority setting in the health sector: the methodology of the 1993 World Development Report, *Health Policy and Planning*, 13(1): 13–31.

World Bank, (1993). *World Development Report 1993: investing in health*. Oxford: Oxford University Press.

Capital investments
Sanderson, D. (1997). Option appraisal in health care, in S. Witter and T. Ensor (eds) *An Introduction to Health Economies for Eastern Europe and the Former Soviet Union*. Chichester: John Wiley.

Western experiences of rationing
Ham, C. (1997). Priority setting in health care: learning from international experience, *Health Policy*, 42, 49–66.

Maxwell, R. J., (ed.) (1995). Rationing health care, *British Medical Bulletin*, 51, 4: 761–962.

PART 4

The organisation of health services

10

Public and private roles in the provision of health services

Sophie Witter

Introduction

One of the themes of health sector reform, which has taken place in both developed and developing countries, is a shift away from the assumption that the state should directly manage health facilities. The reality in most developing countries is that alternative providers of care have always existed – not least in the form of traditional medicine. Since the 1950s though there has been a strong view that it is the duty of the state to finance and provide all mainstream health services. However, supply in most countries has not been able to keep up with demand, either in quantity or quality. We have seen, in Chapters 4 and 5, that the burden of paying for health services has been shifting to individuals and families. In this chapter we focus on the question of how health services are provided. We ask the following series of questions:

- What are the problems with bureaucratically managed public health services?
- What evidence is there about the relationship between the private sector, competition, and the goals of efficiency, quality and equity?
- Quasi-markets in the public sector: what are the lessons?
- 'Privatisation': what does it mean and how is it done?
- Is there a consensus on roles for public and private sectors?

Problems with state provision

Mrs Darling, manager of the district hospital in Gamlan, is coming to the end of the financial year. It has not been an good year for her. The money she had been allocated by the Ministry arrived late and was usually less than promised. Some of her staff are spending more time treating patients privately than they do in their official clinics. Supplies of drugs and basic equipment like syringes keep running out and the patients are complaining. She asked for money for some new beds over a year ago but still has not heard back from the Ministry. It would be so much easier, she thinks to herself, if I were running a private business: I could organise myself as I liked and run so much more effectively.

Mrs Darling is facing a number of problems which we associate with 'command and control' style state-run bureaucracies:

1 *Overcentralisation:* decisions on relatively minor issues, like buying new beds, have to be approved by a higher authority. Local managers have little flexibility in use of resources.
2 *Poor management:* communication is poor between the levels; rigid norms are applied; the focus is on day-to-day survival rather than advance planning.
3 *Poor incentives:* quality and efficiency are not rewarded, either for the hospital as a whole or for individual staff.
4 *Resource shortages:* state budgets fall far short of what is necessary to meet demand with high quality services.

Many of these problems can be tackled by reforms within the public sector. The first problem has supported the policy decision to decentralise (see Chapter 11 for discussion of this issue). The second has led to a range of management-strengthening programmes (see Chapter 13 for discussion of increasing efficiency in provision). The third has prompted some reform of payment systems (see Chapter 12). The fourth has led to changes in health financing to increase revenues (see Chapters 4 and 5).

However, a disillusionment with public provision set in in the late 1980s, supported by the private-sector orientation of organisations like the World Bank, the collapse of communism in eastern Europe and the former Soviet Union and a number of market-style reforms in Western health sectors. The private sector was seen by many as more efficient, more responsive to customers and therefore likely to deliver higher quality services. Why?

Because competition between providers to attract customers is believed to drive quality up and costs down to a minimum (see Chapter 3 on markets and perfect competition). There was also a political agenda: at the general level, an ideological shift towards the misleadingly named 'free market'; and, at the more local level, an attempt to by-pass bureaucratic structures which were proving hard to reform from within.

Before we look at attempts to mimic private sector behaviour in the public sector ('internal markets' or 'quasi-markets') and attempts to hand over provision to the private sector proper (privatisations, of various sorts), let us consider what evidence there is for a general connection, in the health sector between:

- the private sector and competition, and
- competition and the goals of efficiency, quality and equity.

The private sector, competition, and health sector performance

> *If Lula compares the public and private sector in her village, what is she likely to find? The drug sellers offer reasonable prices in comparison with the health centre pharmacy, and generally have the drugs she needs. On the other hand, Dr Gonk's private clinic is more expensive than getting treatment at the health post (even allowing for gifts to the staff), though the quality seems higher. Some people borrow money to take their children there, if they are really ill.*

The old adage goes that 'the worst enemy of capitalism are the capitalists'. In other words, if a business can get into a monopoly position by driving out its rivals in some way, it will do, as this allows it to gain excess profits (see Chapter 3). Thus the private sector and competition are not synonymous, unless there is some regulation of the market to control anti-competition measures such as monopolies, cartels and price-fixing. This is true of health as of other markets. Particularly in the hospital sector, there is a tendency for local monopolies to occur because of the economies of scale and scope which exist and the high investment costs of setting up in that business. A monopoly in the public sector often leads to a fall in quality and responsiveness to patients; private monopolies still need to attract patients, so quality – at least quality as it can be judged by patients – is usually maintained, but at the cost of increased prices (especially when a third party is paying).

In the example given, the drug sellers may be operating in a competitive environment and so are under pressure to keep their prices low. However, if it is hard for patients to judge the quality of their products, then quality may suffer. For example, out of date or ineffective drugs may be sold. Dr Gonk, on the other hand, is in a monopolistic competition position: his is the only product of its type available, if he can distinguish it from the government health services on grounds of quality or convenience. He can afford to charge higher prices as long as he keeps a higher standard of service. This means, of course, that only richer or more desperate people will use his services. This challenges the goal of equity in access to health services (of equal quality).

Even where there is competition, there is no evidence that the private sector invariably provides greater efficiency or quality. For example, in the US competitive markets have been shown to have higher costs, more duplication of services, longer lengths of stay and higher staff ratios than non-competitive markets (Robinson and Luft, 1988). The indirect payment system (via insurance premia) can lead to price inelasticity of demand and an upward spiral of prices. Quality issues are often hard for the consumer to judge. For example, has the reduction in length of stay in hospitals in the US in the 1990s been a good or bad thing? It is not clear without further probing. There are also major issues of access both as a result of cream-skimming and the rising costs of health insurance policies.

Can we draw a general conclusion about the relationship between public or private sector provision of services and the goals of efficiency, quality and equity? We would argue not. Some simple positive and negative examples from both sectors are given in Table 10.1. What becomes clear on consideration of these examples is that it is not the ownership of facilities itself that matters, but rather a whole range of complex issues such as:

- how competitive is the market?
- what is the regulatory framework?
- how effectively are regulations enforced?
- what are the payment/pricing systems and what incentives do these provide?
- what is the overall level of resourcing of the system?

Table 10.1 Public and private sectors: how they are judged by our key criteria

	Efficiency	Quality	Equity
Public sector provision (the positive examples)	Because of economies of scale, purchasing of drugs and equipment can be done much more cheaply by the government and can be allocated according to real needs.	Health workers in the public sector (if adequately paid) can focus on appropriate treatments and prevention, rather than profit-making ones	Access to public services is usually a basic right: all can seek treatment at low or no cost
Public sector provision (the negative examples)	If you save money, your facility is likely to get less next year: there is no incentive to cut costs.	If you work hard at your job or give a good service, your salary remains the same. Why bother?	A limited supply of health care and low cost services can mean only one thing: rationing. Not all will be treated, and priority is unlikely to go to those in greatest need or with greatest ability to benefit.
Private sector provision (the positive examples)	Profits are retained, so any costs which can be cut without damaging business will be cut.	The customer is king: they shall have the services they desire, together with comfort and convenience.	Price discrimination may be introduced to attract poorer customers as well as rich.
Private sector provision (the negative examples)	Every facility has to have expensive diagnostic equipment to attract customers, even if this duplicates other local services.	Over-treatment may augment incomes, but it can damage patients' health, not to mention their wallets. It can also cause wider social problems, such as the spread of drug resistance.	Treatment according to ability to pay, combined with gross income inequalities, is not the way to ensure 'Health for all'.

- what is the culture/expectation/motivation of providers and consumers?

See Box 10.1.

Quasi-markets in the public sector

An obvious question to ask is whether (and how) we can keep the best of the public sector (in particular, accountability of services and the ability to impose public goals on them) *and* make private sector-type improvements in quality, efficiency and responsiveness to customers. One approach which has been tried, in the West and now in some transitional and developing economies, is to introduce competitive dynamics into a system which is still funded and, in some senses, managed within the public sector.

How has this been done? Let us take the example of UK health reforms in the late 1980s/early 1990s. There were a few main components:

1 *Purchaser-provider split.* Instead of providers being guaranteed to receive an annual budget, they were turned into self-governing (not for profit) bodies, which have to compete for funding from health authorities, doctors and private sources. As they remain in the public sector, they are governed by strict rules about use of assets, pricing and entry/exit from the market.

2 *Primary care fundholders.* Another innovation was to give the entire budget for a patient's care to the primary care doctor, who either provides services or buys the best deal from whichever secondary providers offer the relevant service. This ensures competition between purchasers as well as providers.

3 *Public/private barriers lowered.* With the introduction of service contracts and specification within the public service, it is an easy step to say that public purchasers can buy from private sources, just as public hospitals can provide services for private purchasers. Thus 'internal markets' may lead to a partial 'privatisation' of the kind discussed later in the chapter.

How successful has this been? No formal evaluation has been undertaken, and with so many changes, including in funding, occurring simultaneously, it has been hard to draw definitive conclusions (Maynard, 1994). However, it would appear that:

- there have been some gains, in terms of better services for fundholders' patients, and some rationalisation of hospital provision

- the gains appear to be less than expected, and there has been a substantial cost, in terms of one-off reform costs and ongoing *transaction costs* (contracting, paperwork, monitoring, increased information flows, etc.)
- there is an absence of real competition in many areas, and so dubious incentives to greater efficiency. Even contestability (the potential threat of competition) may be lacking, given the start up costs of the business and the advantage which that gives the existing provider
- there are real political problems about the idea of allowing an inefficient hospital to go out of business. Without this, are the sanctions against poor management real?
- tensions exist between the bottom up approach – allowing primary care doctors, say, to buy services – and an ability to plan services and avoid duplication and achieve economies of scale
- competition means market instability, and many purchasers have preferred to cultivate longer term relations with providers, assisting them to develop suitable services. Thus later reforms have changed the emphasis from short term contracts to longer term ones and the role of trust. Does this reverse the initial reforms?
- it is easy for providers to manipulate the system by, for example, cross-subsidising between services (e.g., between public and privately funded, if the latter is more price sensitive), or inducing demand
- as with decentralisation, the introduction of these market-based reforms has paradoxically stressed the need for stronger central control in the setting of standards and regulation of the market. The required money and competence may be more than before the reforms.

As a response to some of these problems, the new Labour government of 1997 has sought to change the emphasis of the health system, from competitive towards more co-operative behaviour (e.g., through the new primary care purchasing groups), while leaving many of the structures in place (such as the purchaser-provider split and the contracting system).

Note that many of the positive changes which these reforms have introduced into the public bureaucracy could be – and are being – tried out without the more far-reaching structural reforms. For example, it is possible to change payment systems and increase the flexibility of managers to use resources without the purchaser-provider split. (See Chapter 12 on payment systems and Chapter 13 on increasing efficiency for further discussion.)

Indonesia, for example, has followed the 'internal market' route by setting up Unit Swadana (self-governing) hospitals in the early 1990s. These were given considerable autonomy and the ability to attract private investment in facilities and equipment (as under the Private Finance Inititiative in the UK). Initial investigations suggest that these hospitals have been able to increase revenue and service quality, without excluding the poor (Gani, 1996).

In contrast to the UK, where reforms were introduced deliberately to shake up the system and improve efficiency, in some transitional and developing countries, public sector institutions have started behaving in a 'private sector way' (i.e., profit seeking) almost by default (commercialisation from the bottom up, rather than from the top down). In China, for example, because of the reduction in government funding and the high private demand for health services, many health centres and hospitals, while remaining in the public sector in terms of legal status, raise the bulk of their funds themselves by charging for services. This has been termed 'privatisation from within' (Smithson, 1993). Although nominally subject to policy direction by the Ministry of Health, these providers are effectively autonomous and highly responsive to 'the market'. It is debatable whether this arrangement is ideal, as the public sector is subsidising a profit-seeking group of providers without necessarily having much control over the scope, price or quality of their services.

The same occurs at the level of individual staff. In many developing countries wages in the government sector are lower than market equivalents and also below subsistence levels. In this situation, while formally continuing in government employment, staff have to become profit-seeking – by making formal charges, informal charges or by moonlighting as private providers. It is common for doctors to hold private clinics in the afternoon, for example, often using government facilities and equipment. Are they then working in the public or private sectors? If the public sector is taken to mean having non-profit-making goals, guided by government policies, non-discriminatory, taking a social perspective (Guisti *et al.*, 1997), then the answer is that they are working in the private sector, although administratively they may be treated as public sector employees. Public/private distinctions can no longer be based on ownership or formal employment alone, but should reflect a wide range of issues (see Box 10.1).

Box 10.1   Influences on provider behaviour: some questions to ask

Each provider, whether nominally private or public, will sit somewhere on a spectrum on each of these issues. Taken together these will determine the pattern of care provided.

Finance
- well funded ↔ poorly funded
- publicly funded ↔ predominantly privately funded
- progressive funding ↔ regressive funding

Motivation/outlook
- public health goals ↔ individual perspective
- guided by government policies ↔ guided by consumer pressures and desires
- concerned with equity/social solidarity ↔ individualistic
- universal access in theory ↔ ability/willingness to pay
- focus on health gain ↔ focus on profits
- emphasis on prevention/promotion ↔ curative services

Regulation
- clear legal framework for their operation ↔ deregulated
- minimum service quality standards ↔ none
- controlled entry into market ↔ none
- controls over pricing ↔ none
- regulator active and independent ↔ passive/coopted
- sanctions enforced ↔ not enforced
- informed public and consumer organisations ↔ none

Ownership and administrative rules
- owned by the government ↔ privately owned
- cannot go out of business ↔ can go out of business
- profits reinvested ↔ profits retained
- able to reallocate resources ↔ rigid rules/norms
- management autonomy ↔ centralised control

Context
- competitive market ↔ monopoly position
- clear specification of services ↔ unstated/unclear
- pay according to performance criteria ↔ fixed pay, regardless of activities or outcomes
- clear public priorities/policies ↔ unclear/changing

Different forms of privatisation

Private sector provision is substantial in developing countries, particularly in the primary care market. Some 70 per cent of health care in Pakistan is provided privately, while in Indonesia more than 60 per cent of health expenditure was spent on the private sector. In Ghana the figure is estimated at 40 per cent. In India, more than half the hospitals and nearly half of all dispensaries are privately owned, while in Kenya, 70 per cent of all doctors are working in full-time private practice. For drugs provision, the figure is nearer 80 per cent (Benett *et al.* 1997; Kumaranayake, 1997).

Hanson and Berman (1998) estimate that for Asia as a whole, private physicians constitute 60 per cent of the total number of physicians (population-weighted average), 46 per cent in Africa and 46 per cent in Latin America and the Caribbean. The average for developing countries is thus 55 per cent – more than half of the market. For the hospital sector the private share is smaller, as expected, but still very significant: private hospital beds constitute 28 per cent of the total number for developing countries as a whole (34 per cent in Africa; 31 per cent in Asia and 21 per cent in LAC). Generally, a more developed private hospital sector will be linked with the development of private or social health insurance.

By contrast, 'privatisation', in the sense of *actively* handing over publicly financed care to private sector bodies, has been more limited. There are a number of possible forms, which are quite distinct from one another. For example:

1 Government institutions, such as hospitals, are turned over to private management. They cease to be part of the public sector. This is the most traditional definition of privatisation (but rare in developing countries).
2 Government provides a subsidy to church or NGO health facilities providing services in underserved areas. This is quite common. Less common but growing is the use of subsidies to promote the provision of particular services (e.g., social marketing of condoms by commercial outlets).
3 A more formal way of buying services from the private sector is to contract for the provision of clinical or non-clinical services. This is becoming more common, although it is still relatively limited in developing countries.

4 While maintaining its role as provider, the government sets up regulations which encourage the parallel development of private services (e.g., legalisation of private providers). This has happened in a number of developing countries recently.

5 Finally, the ultimate method for promoting private services is for the government to withdraw from provision. This is relatively uncommon.

We will focus on forms 3–5, which are most prevalent in developing countries at present.

Subsidies/incentives

Where government facilities are lacking, it has been common, particularly in parts of Africa, for non-governmental organisations (usually non-profit-making, such as churches) to provide basic health care in an area with funding from the state. This often takes the form of the state providing recurrent costs, with capital costs being met from the provider's independent funding sources. This might be called 'implicit contracting' where the full costs of services are met, or a subsidy, where the costs are only partially covered by the state. Unlike in formal contracting out of services, there is rarely a clear specification of what services are to be provided, at what quality, etc.

This system offers advantages in spreading the financial burden, where government capacity to build and run facilities is poor. However, there can also be problems of accountability, co-ordination, and consistency between government-run and NGO-run services.

Another approach has been to use incentives or subsidies of various kinds to influence private sector behaviour. This follows from the recognition that private providers are the first point of contact for so many patients, including for diseases with significant externalities, such as tuberculosis. Rather than trying to curb private practice, many Ministries of Health have focused instead on the more positive question of how to increase private practitioners' awareness and use of cost-effective approaches.

For example, training and equipment can be offered to clinics providing preventive services or services with substantial positive externalities (e.g., treatment of sexually transmitted diseases). Alternatively, subsidised goods or tax breaks could be provided to private clinics which meet minimum standards of quality, or which comply with reporting standards, for example. In some countries, voluntary accreditation of private providers, which involves meeting certain minimum standards, has been linked with benefits such as eligibility for reimbursement by the insurance fund. This is a type of regulation, but one which offers positive incentives rather than the threat of sanctions (the carrot rather than the stick).

Another way of keeping private providers informed about government policies is to 'contract in' private specialists to provide a specific service in government hospitals, for example. In Zimbabwe and Malawi, governments allow private doctors to use public facilities for their patients in return for seeing government cases requiring specialist treatment free of charge (Bennett and Ngalande-Banda, 1994).

Studies of attempts to alter private provider behaviour in developing countries suggest that just providing information to practitioners is inadequate (Brugha and Zwi, 1998). A multi-faceted approach is advocated, which includes public education, incentives and mobilisation of local opinion leaders to change expectations in relation to particular treatments.

Contracting

Contracts are a legal agreement between purchaser and provider. They define the service to be provided and how much will be paid for it. They have usually been introduced either as part of a drive to increase efficiency (often encouraged by donors) OR as a result of changes in the funding system, particularly the spread of insurance programmes (see Chapter 4). They aim to introduce market-style efficiency, while maintaining government financing and policy control. They are sometimes signed after direct negotiation between purchaser and provider, or drawn up by the purchaser and put out to competitive tendering.

The elements generally included in contracts are:

- nature of the service
- minimum quality requirements
- price to be paid
- volume (and how to deal with over- and under-production)
- length of contract and renegotiation process
- information requirements: reporting to purchaser
- monitoring: how performance is to be monitored.

There are however different contract types. *Block contracts*, for example, leave the volume of services open. This may be appropriate where demand is unpredictable: for example, a contract may state that the provider will provide all emergency services for a certain area for a year. This shifts risk to the provider: if demand is high, their costs will increase without any automatic increase in income. *Cost and volume contracts* share risks more evenly. These specify a number of procedures (e.g., deliveries) and the price to be paid for them. This type of contract also needs to state what the penalties will be if providers do not reach the specified volume level, and how much (if anything) will be paid if they exceed them. Alternatively, a simple *cost per case* contract can be negotiated, which states the unit cost of each procedure. This runs the risk that the provider will induce demand and run up a huge bill for the purchaser, as no upper ceiling is specified. It has the advantage for the consumer, though, that they can choose which facility to visit; with the other two types that decision has been made on their behalf by the health authority, insurance fund or other purchaser. See Box 10.2 for some issues to consider in drawing up contracts.

In developing countries, contracting is at an early stage of development. What is the evidence so far about its appropriateness? To what extent has it increased efficiency or transparency of services?

The first point about efficiency is that many contracts are awarded without an open bidding process. This does not necessarily point to an absence of contestability. However, a number of case studies also suggest that contracts are renewed over long periods without proper review. In many cases, the purchaser may feel themselves to be in a weak bargaining position – perhaps because of the absence of alternative service providers in the area (what economists call a 'thin market') and the large investment costs of replacing existing providers. In such cases, providers may be able to provide poor services or increase their prices without fear of losing the contract.

What about transparency gains? The process of contracting usually involves a specification of the quantity of the services to be provided, their quality and cost. This offers an enormous potential advantage over an integrated public sector in which all of these details are usually vague (or, if specified, are often unrealistic and not adhered to). However, gaining accurate information on costs and outcomes costs money. In systems where resources are very scarce, the staff time, competence and inform-

---

Box 10.2 Important technical considerations in drawing up contracts

- How detailed should the service specification be (balance the need to give the provider autonomy against having a safeguard if things go wrong)?
- What is the appropriate unit of volume for that service (choose something which is relatively hard to manipulate)?
- What is the ideal contract length (keep the provider on their toes *but* minimise renegotiation costs and disruption to services)?
- How are services grouped for the purposes of contracting (balance between getting clear specifications and avoiding excessive costs of drawing up and monitoring contracts)?
- How are prices set? (Do not use average prices for that, as this rewards inefficient providers. See chapter 12 on payments systems.
- Which quality measures to use? Outcomes (e.g., readmission rates, operative mortality) are important, as are process indicators (e.g., following treatment protocols) and the patient's perspective (e.g., waiting times; patient satisfaction with the treatment).
- How are disputes settled? If either party to the contract is dissatisfied, what is the process for resolving the dispute?
- How to account for capital assets? If the provider is using public facilities, it is advisable to charge an annual rent, in order to put them on the same footing as other private providers and to create an incentive to use facilities efficiently.

(For further discussion, see Broomberg, 1994 and Piercy, 1997. England, 1997, contains a sample annual service agreement used in Trinidad and Tobago.)

---

ation technology are usually not available. In this context, contracts may produce a number of suboptimal results:

- no cost, no benefit: the information clauses of the contract are simply not fulfilled
- high costs, low benefits: the costs of collecting information outweigh its benefits (which also depend on it being well used, which is rare)
- high costs, no benefits: the information collected may be erroneous, either by accident or deliberate distortion to serve some provider aim.

In such a situation, the best approach is realism. Choose just a few essential indicators and monitor them effectively.

The same applies to the use of '*performance contracts*' in the public sector. These use contracts as a vehicle for setting clearer targets (and, presumably, rewarding their achievement or penalising their non-achievement) without the institutional separation which characterises contracting from the private sector. If they are successful, they may achieve transparency and efficiency gains. However, once again, there are financial and information costs to be counted, and indicators of performance have to be chosen carefully to avoid perverse incentives. For example, paying bonuses for numbers of patients treated will encourage low quality treatment, as it emphasizes process rather than outcomes.

There are also implications for the way in which services are organised. If, for example, managers are to be held accountable or penalised when targets are not met, then they must have control over the circumstances leading to non-performance – i.e., must be given the powers able to manage services effectively. Performance contracts or service agreements within the public sector are therefore complementary to a policy of decentralisation (see Chapter 11). They may also be linked with reform of resource allocation, moving from a historical funding system to a population-based one, and the introduction of an essential service package (both discussed in Chapter 9).

When is contracting appropriate in developing countries? For economists, the answer is, naturally, when the anticipated costs are likely to be outweighed by the benefits. Do not forget to consider the categories highlighted in Table 10.2. Studies of experiences to date of contracting in developing countries suggest that there is no systematic evidence of gains (Mills, 1998). Contracts tend to be re-awarded to the same providers and risks are commonly shifted to governments. Gains are most likely to be achieved in the richer developing countries, where there is a high level of resourcing and competence on the government side and greater scope for competition in the provider market.

Regulating the health sector

Lula's cousin, Bea, has been suffering from serious stomach pains for some months. First she visited the district hospital. The doctor there could not find any cause and sent her home. After a week of further suffering she decided to visit Dr Gonk's private clinic. He felt her stomach and gave her a prescription. It did not help; in fact, she now felt worse. When Bea returned to Dr Gonk to complain, he charged her for another consultation and gave her a different prescription, which does not seem to have helped

Table 10.2   The costs and benefits of reform

	Cost	Benefit
Efficiency	1 What will the start-up costs be? (One-off investment required by reform) 2 What *additional* management costs will the purchaser face, e.g., higher information costs in comparison with previous system (negotiating and monitoring contracts)? 3 What *additional* service costs will the provider face (for example, because of loss of central government purchasing)? 4 Might there be a shift in activity away from more towards less cost-effective services (allocative efficiency)? 5 Any other anticipated negative effects (such as limited ability to reallocate resources between services)?	1 Will there be reductions in the costs of running the service, or increased activity for the same cost (for example, because of increased productivity of labour in the private sector)? (N.B. Take broad view: have costs been displaced to patients, for example? These costs still count.) 2 Will there be any change in service provision towards more cost-effective services?
Quality	Will there be a reduction in quality of services (compared with previous level)? Consider all three dimensions: – medical outcomes – process – patient satisfaction	Will there be an increase in quality of services (compared with previous level)? Again, all three dimensions are relevant.
Equity	Do you anticipate a decrease in access to services? For which groups? Why?	Do you anticipate an increase in access to services? Why?

either. Bea is angry. She is sick, and feels that she has been treated badly.
She does not trust the doctors anymore, but who can she complain to?
What alternative does she have?

In Chapter 3 we discussed the 'principal-agent' relation between customers/patients and their health care providers. The patient relies on the medical staff for advice on treatment, but the staff have interests of their own to consider, in addition to those relating to the patient's well-being. They are therefore not perfect agents. The role of regulation is to control provider self-interest and protect patients against abuse by more powerful providers. This can be tackled by positive incentives (described under subsidies, earlier) or by negative sanctions, such as fines, losing your license to practice or even imprisonment.

There are three main groups which tend to be involved in regulating health markets. The first is *the providers themselves*, usually in the form of professional associations which set minimum entry standards in terms of training and accreditation and which are supposed to discipline members. The main issue with this form of regulation is that there is an obvious conflict of interests between protecting the public and protecting fellow doctors, nurses, pharmacists, etc. It is therefore rare for doctors to be disciplined by Medical Associations. In Zimbabwe, for example, the Medical Council failed to publicise cases of malpractice on the grounds that they might discredit the profession (Bennett and Ngalande-Banda, 1994). When they are disciplined, it is more likely to be for an offence such as 'gross immoral behaviour' than negligence or professional incompetence. Medical associations tend not to seek trouble: they do not usually actively seek to set, maintain and monitor standards, but rather sit back and wait for complaints. Patients who do complain do not generally find the system very responsive.

If providers wish to avoid outside regulation by, for example, a government body, they need to become more active in setting standards, informing patients about them and using both positive and negative instruments to see that they are upheld. From being the doctors' champion, they need to become the patients' friend. There will always be some suspicion about the conflict of interests, however, and so other regulatory systems will still be needed too. However, self-regulation can play an important part in maintaining the medical ethos of public service and hence the trust which the public places in health workers.

Note that the issues of self-regulation do not really distinguish between public and private sectors. Issues of minimum standards of training and practice apply equally to both. Given the increasing commercialisation of public servants, even such roles as setting normative fee schedules could be relevant in the public sector (for example, in relation to user fees or informal charges).

The government is the obvious second body with a regulatory role. Commonly its objectives are to limit charging, to avoid excess provision and to prevent poor practice. Minimum standards of training and premises are often enshrined in legislation, but the problem in most developing countries is poor implementation. This is particularly true of, for example, private pharmacists, who are often very numerous in relation to a small number of government staff entrusted with their inspection and registration. Apart from lack of resources and staff, there are often also problems of corruption: regulators receive bribes or gifts to 'turn a blind eye'. They turn their energies to 'rent-seeking', rather than enforcing good behaviour.

In the light of problems of self-interest by providers and 'capture' of official regulators by powerful lobby groups, the third element of *consumer empowerment* should be developed. Consumers are genuinely interested in their own welfare, but usually lack information, coordination and influence. Consumer organisations which are capable of monitoring provider abuse and assisting patients in making complaints and seeking compensation should be supported. If there is a legal framework for addressing medical incompetence and seeking redress, this can be activated by them. In many countries the media now plays a role in exposing incompetence and malpractice too, and media and consumer organisations can work together effectively. Public information and education on appropriate medical practice is also important, so that they can make informed judgements about the treatments which they receive.

Consensus on public/private roles?

As the distinction has becoming more blurred, it is not possible to say that the public sector should, in all situations, provide X service and the private sector Y. However, experience suggests some lessons.

1 A competitive environment is necessary (but not sufficient) if efficiency gains are to be made from switching to private

providers. This is often lacking, especially in rural or poorer areas. Poverty tends to reinforce risk aversion, which in turn leads to 'thin' markets. Access to capital is needed for firms wishing to set up in business, so developed capital markets make a competitive environment more likely. Private providers are likely to be able to offer efficiency savings if they have a competitive advantage, such as access to cheaper labour than government.

2 The public sector must have the resources, capacity and inclination to negotiate, set standards and monitor contracts with the private sector. Otherwise contracts or subsidies can simply perpetuate inefficient use of resources.

3 The link with financial sources is important here. Acting as a purchaser and contracting for services assumes that the state is the main funder of health care in that area. Where private finance predominates, it is harder for the government to influence provider behaviour (whether public or private, and whatever the instrument in question).

4 Privatisation in its various forms should not be viewed as a form of cost saving. An under-resourced system will produce distortions, whether in the public or private sectors. There are one-off costs and on-going information costs to consider, even if private providers are relatively efficient in their organisation.

5 Access must be monitored, especially to see if costs are being shifted onto patients.

6 Regulation of safety and quality becomes even more important, and the Ministry of Health is rarely capable of carrying out this role effectively. Regulations should be clear and simple and must be adequately enforced. This also means that legal systems must be accessible and reliable.

7 The issue of corruption must be considered. Will contracting out or subsidies increase the scope for corruption in government circles or the private sector? What kind of checks or audits are necessary to pre-empt such a development?

8 There is no evidence that private providers are unsuitable for preventive or promotive services, if contracts are appropriately structured.

9 The type of payment system is important (see Chapter 12), whatever the status of the provider.

10 It should be clear what the goal is in increasing private sector involvement. Possible goals might be to increase the quality of services, to increase the transparency of services, to achieve reforms in the public sector or to increase utilisation of services.

Summary

Private providers are not a new phenomenon in developing countries. However, this chapter started with an explanation of why there has been an ideological shift away from the view of the public sector as the 'right' (or only) provider of basic health services. It noted that many of the complaints could in fact be tackled by reforms within the public sector (such attempts are described elsewhere in the book). Arguments for private sector involvement have been motivated by political factors as much or, arguably, more than economic ones.

It then went on to examine the connection which is commonly made or assumed between the private sector, competition and the goals of efficiency, quality and equity. It argued that there is no necessary link between the private sector and competition, and also that competition on its own does not guarantee an increase in efficiency, quality or equity. It may do so, but only if other contextual factors are right.

We next looked at the many different interactions of public and private sectors (focusing on provision; clearly there is a link with funding systems, but that has been discussed in Chapters 4 and 5). One group of reforms have sought to bring private sector behaviour into the public sector ('quasi-markets'). These have been only partially successful, even in richer countries like the UK. What has occurred in many developing countries is more of a privatisation from within, in which public sector institutions and staff react to private opportunities to generate income more than bureaucratic control. This produces results which are far from ideal. It also calls into question traditional definitions of public or private, based on ownership of assets. Today we need also to examine the behaviour and motivation of staff and institutions, which will in turn relate to the local culture and the way in which the market is structured.

Experiences of wholesale transfer of assets from the public to private sectors (as has happened in some transitional economies, for example) are limited in developing countries. However, many services are purchased from the private sector, either through subsidies or contracts. Experience of regulating the private sector is also growing. Making gains of efficiency and quality are largely dependent on the level of development of the country: resources and management capacity are needed both on the government side and amongst providers to make the system work well.

The private sector, then, is neither the saviour nor the devil. It does not offer easy solutions to intractable problems in the public sector (underfunding, poor capacity, political divisions), but on the other hand it does not inevitably mean poor access and low accountability either. It, like the public sector, can be well or poorly managed. The discussion has therefore moved from inherent roles for public or private sectors, regardless of context, to 'getting the framework right'. This involves the whole range of measures, from ensuring adequate funding to institutional development, legal frameworks, promotion of a competitive environment, establishment of clear public health priorities, empowering consumer organisations, etc.

In the poorer developing countries, many of these features are not yet fully developed. In that situation, is market failure worse than government failure? It is hard to say, but it certainly suggests that a rush to privatisation may be inappropriate, given the absence of preconditions for its success. However, as health spending has shifted to individuals and households in many countries, so has the purchasing power, and this has increasingly favoured private providers or led to 'privatisation from within' of the public services. In this situation, governments cannot ignore commercial tendencies. Unlike in the West, where 'privatisation' was largely a top-down process, in developing countries, many governments have had belatedly to recognise and deal with what had been happening at the grassroots, where demand for health services was outstripping public supply, both in terms of quality and quantity.

This has had an impact on private and public sectors, and calls for wise use by governments of a range of approaches. For example:

- Where health markets and government capacity are relatively developed, contracting out clinical and non-clinical services may achieve efficiency savings.
- Regulation is also important to set minimum standards and protect consumers against abuse (regardless of whether public or private). This regulation should be kept to a minimum, should be appropriate and should be enforced.
- Within the public sector, competition for funds, performance contracts and performance-related pay can increase motivation and productivity, if the criteria used are consistent with public goals.
- There is also evidence that private providers can be effective partners in delivering appropriate services, where governments adopt positive strategies to train and motivate them.

Terms like 'public' and 'private' sectors tend to encourage simplistic thinking, often along political lines which see one as good and the other as bad. This does everyone a disservice. We should recognise that competitive forces and even commercial forces are found within public services; that regulation is required in relation to public as well as private providers because of the inherent features of health markets; that public services need not be a byword for poor quality; that private need not be a by-word for irresponsible profiteering. The old certainties are gone. The challenges remain.

Questions for discussion

1 Take some health service or facility, which you are familiar with, and consider the scope for introducing performance contracts.

- What would be in such a contract?
- How would volume and quality be specified?
- What information would you require to monitor it?
- Would it be effective in improving services with current levels of financing?
- What gains would you expect from it, and what problems?
- Overall, would you recommend introducing these, and if so, for which parts of the health system?

2 Consider the regulation of the health system in your country.

- which bodies act as regulators, and for which aspects?
- what means do they use?
- whose interests do they generally represent?
- how effective are they, in your assessment?
- what alternative regulatory strategies might work better (e.g., positive incentives, or partnership arrangements)?

References and further reading

Bennett, S., Dakpallah, G., Garner, P., Gilson, L., Sanguan, N. and Zwi, A. (1994). Carrot and stick: state mechanisms to influence private provider behaviour, *Health Policy and Planning*, 9, (1) (and other articles in that special edition).

Bennett, S., McPake, B. and Mills, A. (1997). *Private Health Providers in Developing Countries*. London: Zed.

Bennett, S., and Ngalande-Banda, E. (1994). Public and private roles in health: a review and analysis of experience in sub-Saharan Africa. Geneva:

WHO, Division of Strengthening Health Services. Currrent Concerns paper 6.

Broomberg, J. (1994). Managing the health care market in developing countries: prospects and problems, *Health Policy and Planning*, 9(3).

Brugha, R. and Zwi, A. (1998). Improving the quality of private sector delivery of public health services: challenges and strategies, *Health Policy and Planning*, 13(2).

England, R. (1997). *Contracting in the Health Service: A Guide to the Use of Contracting in Developing Countries*. London: Institute for Health Sector Development.

Gani, A. (1996). Improving quality in public sector hospitals in Indonesia, *International Journal of Health Planning and Management*, 11 (3).

Giusti, D., Criel, B., and De Bethune, X. (1997). Public versus private health care delivery: beyond the slogans, *Health Policy and Planning*, 12(3).

Hanson, K. and Berman, P. (1998). Private health care provision in developing countries: a preliminary analysis of levels and composition, *Health Policy and Planning*, 13(3): 195–211.

Hsiao, W. (1994). Marketization – the illusory magic pill. *Health Economics*, 3.

Kumaranayake, L. (1997). The role of regulation: influencing private sector activity within health sector reform, *Journal of International Development*, 9(4).

Maynard, A. (1994). Can competition enhance efficiency in health care? Lessons from the reform of the UK National Health Service, *Social Science and Medicine*, 39(10).

McPake, B. and Hongoro, C. (1995). Contracting out of clinical services in Zimbabwe. *Social Science and Medicine*, 41(1).

Mills, A. (1998). To contract or not to contract? Issues for low and middle income countries, *Health Policy and Planning*, 13(1).

Muschell, J. (1995). Privatization in health. Health economics briefing note. Geneva: WHO.

Musgrove, P. (1996). Public and private roles in health. Discussion Paper 339. Washington, DC: World Bank.

Perrot, J., Carrin, G. and Sergent, F. (1997). The contractual approach: new partnerships for health in developing countries. Macroeconomics, health and development paper 24. Geneva: WHO.

Piercy, J. (1997). Contracting. Chapter 7 in S. W. Her and T. Ensor (eds) *An Introduction to Health Economics for Eastern Europe and the Former Soviet Union*. Chichester: Wiley.

Robinson, J. C. and Luft, H. S. (1988). Competition and the cost of hospital care, 1972–1982, *Journal of American Medical Association*, 259.

Smithson, P. (1993). Health financing in Vietnam: sustainability case study. A report for Save the Children Fund (UK), London.

Witter, S. and Sheiman, I. (1997). The private sector and 'privatisation' in health, in S. Witter and T. Ensor, (eds) *An introduction to Health Economics for Eastern Europe and the Former Soviet Union*. Chichester: John Wiley.

11

Health system decentralisation

Matthew Jowett

Introduction

This chapter looks at the issues surrounding the decentralisation
of health systems, a term that has become closely linked with
health sector reform. In established market economies public
management theory has in recent years encouraged greater decision making at lower levels of organisations, and this movement
has increasingly influenced the way in which government ministries are organised in developing countries. An overview of what
is meant by the term, and its implications for the organisation of
health services is presented in this chapter, which covers the following areas:

- the objectives of decentralisation
- different types of decentralisation
- country experiences
- the impact of decentralisation

The objectives of decentralisation

Dr Fixit: *One issue that I would like to discuss is the increasing number
of tasks and responsibilities that myself and my team in Rungara
Province are being given to do. Whilst I welcome this move in principle,
I am unclear of why this reorganisation has suddenly been implemented
and what the thinking behind it is.*

Professor Bluff: Decentralisation has been promoted as part
of health sector reforms since the primary health care (PHC)

initiative in 1978. At that time it became an unwritten theme of the PHC movement, in the sense that it was considered a prerequisite for the greater involvement of communities in the planning of health services, and effective multi-sectoral collaboration. The specific objectives of decentralisation typically include:

- improved planning and management of health services (e.g., greater responsiveness to local needs and less duplication in provision)
- improved accountability in decisions about the use of resources (e.g., through setting up hospital management boards)
- achieving the goals of primary health care more effectively (e.g., through promoting effective inter-sectoral collaboration, and by providing the framework to allow communities to influence the organisation of local services, and ultimately to see the benefits)
- providing incentives to providers to collect private financing, and reinvest proceeds to improve service quality
- the introduction of quasi-market forces to increase efficiency in the provision of services

There are a combination of influences put forward as a rationale for decentralising health systems. The belief that communities should have greater control and influence over the way in which local health services are organised can be argued in terms of the right to representation, in particular where communities contribute to financing.

Secondly, from a more pragmatic point of view, experience has shown that the involvement of local communities in planning and organisation, and the close co-ordination of the activities of different ministries, can only be adequately achieved through enabling decisions to be made at the local level. In terms of theories of management within large organisations, it is believed that whilst decentralised systems may be more expensive, through the loss of economies of scale, they can also be more efficient by overcoming physical, administrative and other bureaucratic constraints, and facilitating links between ministries of health, and other sectors such as education and water.

Thirdly, a belief in the ability of market forces to increase efficiency and quality in service provision has in several countries mentioned been a driving force for a particular form of decentralisation. (See the last chapter, Conclusion, for a discussion of this argument.)

Different types of decentralisation

Initiatives to decentralise health systems have often focused on the restructuring of service–delivery around districts, which cover anywhere between 50,000–500,000 people according to the World Health Organisation. In turn these units of health system organisation tend to be based on local government administrative structures. Given the broad nature of the term however, several questions need to be answered about how the process of decentralisation will actually proceed (Mills *et al.*, 1991). These include:

• what specific responsibilities should be decentralised? Should they include administrative duties, control over budgeting and financial management, or more substantial powers such as the ability to raise taxes?
• to what level should this power be decentralised? Provincial, district, sub-district or to the individual facility?
• to whom should power be decentralised? Bureaucrats, elected officials, or health professionals?
• should budgets allocated to lower levels of the system have elements earmarked for key interventions (e.g., preventive services), in order to ensure progress towards nationally set priorities?

The term decentralisation is somewhat ambiguous, implying to some people the regionalisation of management systems i.e., reorganisation based on geographical areas. Alternatively it might imply the reorganisation of services based on a particular function, such as the financing or purchasing of health services. Decentralisation can be split into four different categories:

• *Deconcentration* is the term commonly used to refer to organisational changes that shift administrative responsibilities from the central Ministry to lower levels of the system, without letting go of political power. Such reforms do little to alter where decisions about the organisation of services are made.
• Changes that involve the more substantial shift in political responsibilities, often with tax-raising powers to lower levels, are termed *devolution.*
• *Delegation* refers to the relocation of a specific function to a quasi-autonomous non-governmental organisation (quango) to promote efficiency, cost-consciousness or flexibility (e.g.,

through setting up a semi-independent insurance fund to purchase health services).

● Some authors also include *privatisation* as a form of decentralisation, whereby responsibility for certain functions, such as the delivery of specific services (e.g., family planning) is shifted away from government altogether.

Experiences of different countries

A broad range of countries from across Africa, Asia and Latin America have conducted public sector reorganisation in recent years. The experience of changes in the Tanzanian health system has been widely documented (Gilson *et al.*, 1993; Gilson *et al.*, 1994; Gilson, 1995) and provides a useful illustrative example of the process of decentralisation. Throughout the 1970s and 1980s decentralisation was part of a broader developmental process in Tanzania, which linked in with democratisation in the early years of independence. Table 11.1 summarises the many different factors that influenced the way in which decentralisation took place. One of the key lessons from the experience of Tanzania and other countries is that the appropriate way for decentralisation to proceed is highly context-specific. Each country, and indeed region within countries, must adapt changes to suit their particular situation. For example the current problems a region may be facing in terms of weaknesses in management structures and procedures, or problems in terms of the skill mix of health professionals, should dictate the specific objectives of decentralisation established for that particular area. There is hence no single 'ideal' way in which the process should proceed.

Some authors have highlighted the potentially negative consequences of decentralisation in developing countries (Collins and Green, 1994). Stressing that whilst decentralisation is concerned with enhancing the differences between regions in a country, there is an inherent tension in achieving this with the broader objective of equity within health systems i.e., the promotion of equal access to services. In particular where regions are given the authority to raise taxes to finance services, inter-regional equity may suffer, with richer regions having the ability to invest in service improvements. A mechanism for redistributing funds under such a system is necessary to ensure subsidies to poorer regions (see resource allocation in Chapter 9).

Table 11.1   Factors influencing decentralisation in Tanzania

Organisational and administrative factors	– Decentralisation of responsibilities, without the development of necessary capacity to implement – Badly planned mix of centralised and decentralised duties – Multiple and confusing allocation of responsibilities between levels of the system – Confusing budgeting procedures
Behavioural factors	– Acceptance of a hierarchical system of making decisions constrained move towards greater responsibility at local level
Political circumstances	– Conducted within a broader policy of national development – Some bureaucrats and politicians resisted potential loss of influence and power – Party political base strengthened through centralisation of certain functions
Financial and human resource situation	– District managers had limited skills and low morale – Limited capacity and skills at central level – Low salary levels undermined motivation – Resources constraints led to continued dependence on central level and donors

Source: Adapted from Gilson, 1995.

In Papua New Guinea provincial governments were given the power to raise taxes, but this led to greater inequities between rich and poor provinces. The mechanisms to equalise resources to overcome this problem failed to function adequately due to overall resource problems nationally. Those poorer regions with very low tax bases were still as dependent on central government allocations as they were before the new system was put in place.

Counties such as Kenya and Sudan experienced the decentralisation of certain functions without the necessary strengthening of management skills, at times creating greater problems than under the previous system. In Papua New Guinea certain central functions such as human resource planning effectively collapsed, with few mechanisms available for planners to oversee the national situation (Newbrander *et al.*, 1989). Other practical problems that have faced the process of decentralisation include that of clientalism, whereby local power groups may become reinforced by the new responsibilities, exacerbating existing political problems. Systems of accountability and regulation may not function effectively in such a situation.

The impact of decentralisation

Dr Fixit: *You have pointed out some interesting issues and experiences of countries undergoing this process. I sometimes feel that the central MoH is asking us to take on responsibilities too quickly. Whilst several staff have moved from planning teams at the central level, to join my team, it will take a lot of time and extra effort for us to achieve what we are being asked to. It's also important that money is devolved and that we get all the necessary resources to implement our new role. I must admit though that with all this effort spent reorganising services, it is easy to forget the reason for doing it, and we must be sure to check that it is having the desired effect.*

Professor Bluff: This is an important point to stress. One of the dangers is that decentralisation might be interpreted as an end in itself, rather than as a means of achieving health policy goals more effectively. Let us look at the following checklist (also in Appendix 2) to find out what decentralisation has meant for health systems in developing countries. In particular, we will look at:

- how resources are raised to fund services
- how resources are allocated to services
- how resources are used in delivering these services
- how equity is affected

Raising funds: By enacting legislation that gives health facilities the power to raise money from user charges or community insurance schemes, and perhaps more importantly by allowing the retention of a substantial proportion of those funds, some decentralisation programmes have had a significant effect on the raising of funds. Whilst it takes time for staff to adjust to the new responsibilities involved with collecting, holding, managing and being accountable for funds, and while the level of funding raised does not at the macro-level solve the problems of financial sustainability, many new incentives are created at the facility level. Revolving drug funds for example have in many countries increased funding for the supply of medicines, whilst also creating the perverse incentive to over-prescribe medicines. Whilst improved drug supply has improved the perceived quality of health services and subsequently utilisation, there is little evidence evaluating their impact on clinical quality.

Allocating funds: The decentralisation process in Ghana initially exacerbated the negative and inappropriate allocation of resources to curative services, whilst in Papua New Guinea and Ethiopia pressures grew for each province to have its own regional hospital despite, in some cases, adequate access to existing hospitals. In such instances, the new feeling of autonomy in regions may also create a desire for self-sufficiency. Where regions fail to give the same emphasis to the funding of preventive services as previously, vertical systems managed from the centre may develop to fill the gap, probably funded by donor agencies as in Tanzania. The problems of inter-regional equalisation has already been noted, with few examples of countries redistributing resources from richer towards poorer regions.

Delivering services: In the case already described, the development of certain services with stronger centralised management may serve to confuse the multiple lines of accountability within the system, possibly undermining the authority and motivation of managers at the district level or below. Once again the problems highlighted here can be limited by strong and clear direction from central government, providing the necessary policy framework and support systems for regional administrations. Where staff have the appropriate skills, quality in services delivery can be greatly improved by greater authority over budgeting and staff. In Tanzania some key actions identified as necessary to improve service delivery included greater supervision of staff, and disciplinary action when appropriate, close monitoring of clinical practice such as prescribing behaviour, greater continuing education, and the flexibility to move money between supplies and salaries.

On the positive side, where extra funds are raised they may be used as incentives to staff to improve performance, and the funding of essential supplies such as medicines. On the negative side there may be an over-provision of unnecessary services, and a failure to fully implement exemptions if the drive to collect money is strong. The key to achieving the positive and avoiding the negative consequences is again adequate management skills at the facility level and effective structures of accountability.

Equity: There is little evidence to date that equity in access to health care, and the distribution of its benefits, has substantially improved as a result of decentralisation. Indeed the increase in private financing and the ineffectiveness of redistributive mechanisms may only serve to exacerbate existing inequities. The examples of Niger and Cameroon however show that where service quality improves, there can be a positive knock-on effect for equity in access.

Summary

What is clear from the evidence on decentralisation to date is that without strong planning, management and regulation capacity at the central level, and the necessary development of skills at lower levels of the system, the process of decentralisation may exacerbate existing inefficiencies and inequities. Ironically however, weakness at the central level may actually give impetus for pushing responsibility down the system, with political factors playing a significant part (Collins and Green, 1993). The importance of building capacity at the central level prior to shifting responsibilities down the system has been an important lesson learnt in order to achieve successful decentralisation.

Questions for discussion

Collins and Green (1993) highlight ten key questions to ask of the process of decentralisation. Think of a proposed policy in your country's health system, or a change in recent years relating to decentralisation and try to answer the following questions:

1 Why is decentralisation being introduced? Who is driving the process and why?
2 What form will decentralisation take and how will the authority relationships be set out? Deconcentration or devolution?
3 To which level in the government system should decentralisation of resources, functions and authority be made? For

example, do the appropriate skills and infrastructure exist at lower levels of the system?

4 What is the role of the central Ministry of Health within the decentralised system? Will it provide guidance, support and monitoring roles, and does it have the appropriate skills?

5 What resources, functions and authority will be decentralised?

6 How does decentralisation fit into the development of national health planning? For example, who is responsible for human resource planning and negotiations with donors?

7 What provisions have been made to ensure the compatibility of decentralisation and the principle of equity? How will funds be allocated? Will inter-regional inequities widen or narrow?

8 Has a programme of health management strengthening and sustainability in the decentralised unit been developed?

9 Does decentralisation facilitate the democratisation of health management and planning? Is community participation encouraged and facilitated in the process?

10 Does decentralisation contribute to the development of intersectoral collaboration? What are the existing barriers to intersectoral collaboration and does the process overcome them?

References and further reading

Collins, C. and Green, A. (1993). Decentralisation and primary health care in developing countries: Ten key questions, *Journal of Management in Medicine*, 7(2): 56–68.

Collins, C. and Green, A. (1994). Decentralisation and primary health care: Some negative implications in developing countries, *International Journal of Health Services*, 24(3); 459–475.

Gilson, L. Kitange, H. and Teuscher, T. (1993). Assessment of process quality in Tanzanian primary care, *Health Policy*, 26.

Gilson, L. Kilima, P. and Tanner, M. (1994). Local government decentralisation and the health sector in Tanzania, *Public Administration and Development*, 14.

Gilson, L. (1995). Management and health care reform in Sub-Saharan Africa, *Social Science and Medicine*, 40(5).

Mills, A. Vaughan, J. P. Smith, D. L. and Tabibzadeh, I. (1991). *Health Systems Decentralisation. Concepts, Issues and Country Experience*. Geneva: World Health Organisation.

Newbrander, W. C. and Thomason, J. A. (1989). Alternatives for financing health services in Papua New Guinea, *Health Policy and Planning*, 4(2) 131–140.

12

Provider payment systems

Tim Ensor and Sophie Witter

Introduction

Health staff and provider organisations are able to influence the pattern of care because of the agency relationship and information asymmetries discussed in Chapter 3. They are motivated to do so too because they are either profit maximisers or, at least, aiming to reach a target income which assures them an acceptable standard of living. The way in which they are paid will be important in providing incentives to certain types of care.

In most developing countries, until recently, there was little debate about different payment systems. Staff in the public sector were paid on salary and institutions with a fixed annual budget, which was usually calculated according to last year's budget, adjusted according to the total funds available and other factors, such as inflation. In the private sector, fee for service, or user fees, were and still are the norm. Now, however, there is a growing realisation that there are other possible methods of payment, and combinations of payment systems, and some countries have been reforming their payment systems to achieve a variety of objectives.

This chapter will cover the following topics:

- What are the different options?
- Evidence on the impact of different payments systems
- Which system is best for developing countries?
- General lessons and summary

What are the options?

Mr Egghead, another health economist from the Ministry of Health, has been visiting Rungara Province. He has noticed that different health

*facilities are paid in different ways, and thinks that there may be a
connection between how they are paid and the pattern of health care which
they provide. Dr Gonk charges a fee for every consultation, and he is very
attentive towards his patients. The assistant doctor in the local clinic is
paid a salary, and she is scarcely ever to be found at the clinic. At the
district hospital, meanwhile, some patients are covered by voluntary health
insurance, which pays according to the number of days of stay. These
patients seem to spend a long time in hospital. Mr Egghead is advising on
the development of a national health insurance scheme. The payment
systems which it might use are not yet fixed. He is therefore interested to
find which payment system will encourage the most effective patterns of
care. What would you advise him?*

There are three main systems for paying both individuals and institutions which provide medical services:

1 Payment for a fixed period of time
2 Payment for the amount of service provided
3 Payment for looking after a given group of people.

Each of these systems can be used for paying primary and
secondary medical practitioners and medical institutions (see
Table 12.1).

1 *Time-based remuneration* is where the payment is made according
   to the number of full-time equivalent staff employed based on
   some pre-set salary scale. So the assistant doctor in the government clinic would receive a salary based on standard medical
   (sometimes civil service) pay scales adjusted according to
   whether he is employed full or part-time. A hospital would
   receive a budget according to number of staff employed and,
   inflation-adjusted historic expenditure for other items such as
   equipment and medicines.
      At its most simple, time-based remuneration can encourage
   practitioners to do very little for patients. If budgets or salaries
   are paid regardless of performance – quality or quantity –
   there is little financial incentive to work well or work hard.
      The lack of positive incentives can be converted into a *per-
   verse incentive* when the number of staff is related to the size of
   the physical capacity. In this case there is a disincentive to
   reduce the use of the facility, perhaps through cutting the
   number of inpatient beds – even when patients can be treated
   as effectively as outpatients – since this will also reduce the
   number of staff positions and final budget.

216

Table 12.1 Main types of provider payments

	Individual practitioner	Medical institution
Time based	Salary	Fixed budget (based usually on historic allocations)
Service based	Fee for service Fee for patient Target payments	Fee for service Fee for patient Budget based on case-mix/utilisation Cost and volume contracts
Population based	Capitation payment	Block contract

But salaries and budgets need not be paid in such a mechanistic way. Staff can be employed on short- to medium-term contracts, the renewal of which is dependent upon positive evaluation of performance. Provided that the criteria for judging performance reflect overall health service objectives and the process of performance monitoring is seen to be transparent and fair, then salary system can be a positive instrument for ensuring quality.

Similarly, budgets can be related to performance criteria and their payment de-coupled from the size of capacity. The fairest way of doing this may be to relate the budget to size of the population served. This has the effect of converting a salary-based budget into block contract, as described in the following section.

2 *Service-based remuneration* – payments vary according to the level of service provided (as used by the private practitioner, Dr Gonk). There are four main types, which can be used for both practitioners and institutions:

- *Fee for service (FFS)* – reimbursement according to the number of services provided for patients. Services might include basic physician consultations, diagnostic tests, x-rays and drugs prescribed.

  In this case there is a financial incentive to over-provide services for each patient. This can be achieved by recommending too many tests or visits or prescribing too many drugs.

  The size of the incentive to over-provide is dependent upon a number of factors. One factor is the extent to which patients recognise induced supply. The complexity of much medical care makes such control difficult (see Chapter 3) but patients may be able to compare treatment received by other patients to gauge whether what is being provided is reasonable.

  A second factor is the extent to which doctors are willing to induce demand beyond what is medically necessary and perhaps in a way that would compromise their medical ethics. It has been argued that this is more likely when medical salaries are relatively low.

  A final factor is whether the user or a third party (insurance fund or budget authority) actually pays the bill. In the former case there is a natural brake on demand inducement through the consumer willingness and ability to pay. In the second case no such brake is present. In these circumstances the worst possible system – from a cost point of view – would be where doctors are paid by FFS and are relatively poorly paid, information on health services to consumers is poor and payment is by a third party.

- *Fee for each bed-day* – where providers receive a payment for each day a patient stays in hospital regardless of the amount of services provided to each patient. This is the system used by the district hospital in the earlier example.

  Payment for each day in hospital reduces the incentive to over-provide services but introduces an incentive to keep patients in for long periods. The reason is that most of the cost of caring for a patient is in the early stages of treatment – such as pre and post-operation – whereas later stages are mainly concerned with recuperation, requiring basic nursing and hotel services. It is, therefore, usually more profitable to keep one patient in hospital for 10 days rather than treat two patients for five days each.

- *Fee for each patient* – where providers are reimbursed according to the number of patients treated regardless of the number of services provided for each patient.

  Payment per patient treated regardless of how many services are provided or length of hospital stay reduces the incentive to keep patients in hospital a long time. Two important problems remain. First, providers have an incentive to treat too many patients. Second, if the same payment is made regardless of the complexity of the case they have an incentive to treat the simpler cases and not admit the more complex – a form of *cream skimming*.

The second problem can be reduced by introducing an adjustment for case mix. A simple way of doing this is to classify departments into low, medium and high complexity with different fixed payments for each patient treated in each. More complex methods exist, the most well-known of which is the diagnosis-related group (DRG), method for grouping procedures within diagnostic groups that have similar costs (see Bardsley *et al.*, 1987; Witter and Ensor, 1997). With simple and more complex systems there is always the risk that providers will 'play' the system by re-categorising simple cases into more complex and lucrative categories.[1] The administrative cost of

1 In this US this problem is known as DRG creep. In the early systems patients were categorised according to first medical diagnosis. There was an incentive to change this diagnosis to a secondary diagnosis if this meant the patient was placed into a group with a higher price.

establishing and maintaining/monitoring such a system can also be substantial.

At the primary level an additional activity-based system is the *target payment*. This is where institutions or practitioners are paid for achieving a target level of coverage for preventive care for a specific population group. Typical examples are payments for achieving a target level of vaccinations of a given population and screening for common diseases in an age-group. Target payments do not have the associated disadvantage of over-treatment since the objective is to cover as many people as possible and more than 100 per cent coverage is not possible. There is a small risk that the incentive may lead to falsification of records or sub-standard provision through, for example, the use of out-of-date vaccines.

Institutional contracts based on volumes of service can be developed in a number of ways. One way is a list of prices for each procedure – fee for service. Another way is to base it on patients treated – fee for each patient. More details on contracting principles are provided in Chapter 10.

3 *Population-based remuneration* is where providers are remunerated according to the size of the population served. In the case of primary practitioners and institutions this may be based on the population living in a certain geographic area or upon the number of people actively registering with the provider (often known as open enrolment). The later generates an incentive to search for patients since income increases with every person enrolled. Remuneration per person may be adjusted for population risk factors such as age and gender. For example if it is known that the elderly (over 65s) use services twice as much as other people then the capitation payment for each elderly person registered with the practitioner would be twice as much as other registrations.

In the case of secondary institutions, budgets can be allocated according to the size of the population served by the area. Some adjustment may required if the hospital receives many people from outside the geographic area. These are effectively block contracts for services and could be for the services of the entire hospital or for individual departments. There may be less choice for patients, in which case the incentives to provide an attractive service will be reduced.

With primary care enrolment, a competitive incentive can more easily be introduced to attract patients. There is a secondary incentive to provide the minimal treatment possible for each patient in order to allow time to serve as many patients as possible. But if bad care is provided the patient has the option of seeking care with another practitioner. There are two problems. First, if the provider holds a monopoly position then there may be no feasible alternative for the patient. Second, the patient may judge the quality of service using easily judged criteria that may be non-medical – for example, the quality of waiting area. So providers might invest in these observable characteristics at the expense of improving medical services.

Population-based remuneration with open enrolment can be used to finance primary care providers that also take responsibility for buying secondary care for the patient. In this case the payment per person includes an element for secondary as well as primary services. This is the basis of the Health Maintenance Organisation in the US, fund-holding general practitioners and Primary Care Groups in the UK, and budget-holding polyclinics in the Former Soviet Union. There is an incentive generated to restrict referrals to secondary institutions. This may reduce unnecessary referrals but could also affect necessary referrals. This requires careful monitoring.

Evidence on the impact of different payments systems

Mr Egghead: *This all sounds quite complicated. What has been the experience of introducing these different systems of payment?*

Empirical evidence on the effect of different payment systems is dominated by the US literature (see Table 12.2). Historically, the US relied on what is known as 'retrospective reimbursement'. This means that health facilities would charge insurance companies fees for each service given to patients according to the UCR principle (payments are usual, customary and reasonable). Such a vague approach to cost control has led to the well known problems of cost escalation. Variations in surgery rates between the US and countries with more controlled payment systems (Gerdtham *et al.*, 1992) are reported as a possible consequence. It has also led to considerable innovation in the types of payment

Table 12.2 Evidence on fee-for-service payment systems in a range of country and cross-country studies

	Country	Evidence	Reference
Impact of fee-for-service			
General impact of fee-for-service compared to other funding mechanisms	OECD	11% increase in expenditures	Gerdtham et al., 1992
Impact on diagnostics	China	Increase in purchase and use of expensive diagnostic equipment	Gellert, 1995
Surgery rates compared to other countries	Brazil	High rates of caesarian sections compared to other (similar) countries not using fee-for-service. Study not statistically controlled	Barros et al., 1986
Fee-for-service system for providers	South Korea	Fee for service blamed for escalation in costs	Barnum et al., 1995
Effect of fee-for-service on utilisation	Vietnam	Disproportionate increase in utilisation for insured group funded by fee-for-service compared to group funded out of the budget	Ensor, 1995
Fee-for-service compared to salary	US, UK and Canada	Higher standardised surgery rates for fee-for-service	McPherson, 1981

222

Table 12.2 *continued*

Effect of alternative payment methods on utilisation and outcomes

Change to DRG system	US	More than 9% reduction in length of stay and cost per admission by 14%, but DRG 'creep' a problem	Rosko and Broyles, 1987
Case based payment compared to per diem rates	Brazil	Introduction of a case mix adjusted per patient system in place of the per diem system. Fall in admission rates and patient stays. Study does not adjust for other factors	Rodrigues, 1989
Managed care (predominantly capitation) compared to fee-for-service	US systematic review	– Lower levels of hospitalisation and shorter hospital stays – No clear impact on prescription medicine – Little difference in quality and outcomes (mixed experience for different conditions)	Robinson and Steiner, 1998
Salaried members of HMO compared to fee-for-service members of medical aid scheme	South Africa	Medical scheme members saw doctors 33% more, 133% more radiological procedures, no evidence that quality is better	Boomberg and Price, 1990
Fee-for-service compared to capitation	Russia	One third increase in costs without substantial differences in health outcomes.	Barr and Field, 1996
Introduction of average cost per patient compared to fee-for-service	China (Zhenjian and Jiujiang province)	Expenditures reduced when fee-for-patient introduced	World Bank, 1995
Volume caps on fee-for-service (response to increasing expenditure despite limits on individual	Canada	Discounted payments (one third payment) on above ceiling expenditure. This has reduced the volume of services given	Naylor, 1992

systems. Because of the focus on an alternative system to fee for service, most of the studies have examined the transition from fee for service to other systems.

One important transition has been the development of a case based system for paying for all the care given to a patient (by diagnosis related group or DRG). This is a system for paying a fixed amount for typical patients within a diagnostic group rather for each service given to patient. It is a fee for patient (FFP) rather than a fee for item of service (FFS) system. The DRG has had influence on containing total expenditures on each patient although there is still an incentive to admit larger numbers of patients than necessary. There is also some evidence that hospitals place patients into more lucrative categories for payment purposes.

A second important change in the US has been a movement from fee-for-service to capitation funding. This has mostly been through the introduction of the Health Maintenance Organisation (HMO) and other similar organisations. There are a number of different types of HMO (see Robinson and Steiner, 1998 for a description). The basic principle is that patients pay an annual registration fee, that may be adjusted for certain risk factors, to the HMO which must then provide all the primary and secondary care for that patient either by employing staff directly or contracting with other practitioners or health care facilities.

Evidence in other countries follows a similar pattern and, in particular, suggest that fee-for-service systems tend to encourage more, and often inappropriate, use of services that are more lucrative to providers. Studies in Brazil have attributed the high rate of caesarian sections to the fee for service payment system, although other factors, such as accepted medical practice, are undoubtedly important but not controlled for. In China it is suggested that the rapid escalation of costs of care is due to the fee for service methods insurance companies use to pay health facilities, although the demand effect from a rapid rise in urban incomes is also a factor. Experiments going on in some Chinese provinces that have introduced fees for each patient have helped to contain costs (World Bank, 1995).

Mr Egghead: *Well, I am pleased that the evidence supports the theoretical suggestion that fee for service increases utilisation while budget and capitation reduce use. But what I really want to know is whether the quality is influenced. After all, if fee for service measures are increasing* *utilisation of highly effective treatments then this must be positive, at least in terms of efficiency, even if it makes cost containment more difficult.*

There is a paucity of evidence on quality of services and final outcomes of treatment. This reflects the difficulties of obtaining such data and making sure that any results are adjusted for other factors. A systematic review of the US literature (Robinson and Steiner, 1998) found that capitation-based systems, which included elements of managed care (see Chapter 5), were mostly indistinguishable from more expensive fee-for-service systems in terms of their impact on quality and outcomes of treatment. Less systematic studies in middle income countries suggest similar conclusions (see Boomberg and Price, 1990 on South Africa and Barr and Field, 1996 on the Former Soviet Union). There is very little evidence one way or another in low income countries.

It is important to realise that most studies in the payment field, led by the US literature, compare fee for service to capitation or similar systems. Few examine the opposite trend, looking at the impact of moving from a budget-based system to fee-for-service system. Most people that work in a system that pay health facilities fixed budgets and practitioners salaries regardless of the amount they work, know that this type of system tends to encourage low levels of activity and quality. Yet there is little systematic evidence on the impact of institutional budgeting and individual salaries on medical care. Wolfe and Moran (1993), for example, found that although an increasing number of OECD countries use budgeting systems to control costs, that there is little systematic evaluation of their impact on quality.

Which payment system is best for developing countries?

> **Mr Egghead**: *Very interesting! But now I am even more confused since all the payment systems mentioned appear to be flawed in one respect or another. How do I know which system to use?*

Each of the payment systems described have advantages and disadvantages. Many countries use a combination of payment methods to balance the opposing incentives. We should bear in mind a number of important factors when designing a payment system.

1 Payment systems have intrinsic characteristics but are also dependent on the context in which they are implemented. A capitation payment in one country may lead to strong competition to improve quality and attract patients. In another it may stimulate the provision of services that have little medical benefit but are attractive to patients such as excessive prescriptions.

2 The success of a payment method depends in large part on the ability to monitor and control the system. More complex systems that, for example, adjust for case mix of the provider can reduce the problems such as cream skimming. But the price of complexity can reduce the overall transparency of the system and make it more complex to administer. This is not only costly, in managerial terms; it can also increase the possibilities for providers to 'play' the system to get as much reward as possible.

3 Even if payment methods are designed that are relatively easy to administer, the system of monitoring can incorporate an increasingly sophisticated information system. Budgets for hospitals based on the local populations can be made contingent on the institution introducing a basic management information system that provides data on key indicators of activity and quality. The budget allocation process could be made contingent on the implementation of such a system and satisfactory indicators of activity. If, for example, the number of patients treated in a particular department fall or number of patients dying just after an operation increases, then the hospital would be required to explain the reasons.

4 The changes in payment methods may be affected by the presence of an unofficial market for health care (see Chapters 5 and 10). Specifically, if doctors receive substantial unofficial income on a fee-per-patient basis, it is unclear what effect a change in the way they receive their formal income will make – particularly if the formal part of income is small.

5 Financial incentives are only one part of the complete set of incentives that encourage particular provider behaviours. Other incentives could include:

- professional satisfaction from doing interesting work as opposed to routine (but perhaps well paid) procedures
- ability to pursue research and upgrading of skills
- area in which practitioners are asked to work, availability of good schools, social facilities, shops, etc. – it is usually difficult

to attract a doctor from an urban to a rural area even if a much larger salary is offered.

With these principles in mind we can now look at how methods of payment might be adapted in developing countries.

Payment of practitioners

In developing countries, in primary care, salaries are currently the dominant method of payment in the public sector and fee for service in the private. This produces the pattern which we associate with them, of poor service in the public sector and excessive, inefficient service in the private. Some improvements may be possible. For example, in urban areas where competition between primary doctors could be real, the introduction of capitation into the public system could give doctors an incentive to improve standards. Another important issue is the scope for promotion. Fixed salaries will not be a disincentive to performance if promotion prospects are real and are based on merit. Short term contracts with health staff, combined with regular evaluation of performance, offers a way of relating income to performance in a more controlled way than with fee per service. Reforms along these lines could do much to encourage staff productivity.

Some countries have had success with introducing bonus points systems, paid in addition to salary, to reward performance. Indonesia, for example, has a system which gives additional pay for doctors who take on extra responsibilities, undergo additional training, engage in research, etc. (Chernichovsky and Bayulken, 1995). In other countries, such as Nepal, Pakistan and Thailand additional payments are made to public doctors *not* working in the private sector. To be effective, these schemes have to (a) be administered fairly and simply; (b) offer significant rewards to high performers; and (c) be closely matched to priorities for the public sector. There is no point, for example, in giving high points for research and training, if what the health system actually needs is more competent doctors managing rural facilities or delivering community-level services.

It is harder to regulate the private market. However, target payments could be used for both public and private practitioners to achieve public health goals, as long as adequate monitoring of quality is in place, along with other positive incentives (described in Chapter 10).

Payment of health facilities

The desirability of a particular funding system for institutions depends so much on the context – the level of facility, availability of management expertise, existing information system and experience in using different systems of payment – that it is impossible to specify a generic system.

In the hospital sector, fee for service is not usually recommended because of its complexity, perverse incentives, tendency to escalate costs and to reduce affordability. Case-based systems of payment are probably too complex to administer for most low income countries. They also have perverse incentives of their own which will be difficult to monitor when the information systems are relatively undeveloped. But case-based systems could be seen as a way of developing the system in the future as resources and managerial capability increase.

Fixed budgets are therefore likely to remain the norm for the moment. But how are these budgets to be fixed and how tightly is resource use controlled within the budget?

Budget systems can be effective provided that they do not penalise attempts to economise on resources. In this respect a budget based on local population size would be preferred to a wage-based budget. The monitoring of a budget, whether based on population or number of patients expected to be treated, should require the facility to supply not only information on financial spending and patient numbers but also other indicators of activity such as lengths of stays in hospital and mix of patients by department. It could also collect information on various measures of quality. In time it may be possible to develop a system of rewards for the hospital based on the efficiency of resource use (see Chapter 13).

Once the budget is set, managers should be free to transfer money between budget categories, if they are to have an incentive and ability to be efficient. (These are sometimes known as *global budgets*.) They should be able to retain surplus monies for specified uses, such as capital investments, incentive payments, repair, or increased services. In return for this freedom, a system of independent financial and clinical audits must be established to check that services are of an adequate quality and that resources are not misused.

Services such as elective surgery, for which demand is relatively predictable in advance, may be negotiated and paid for separately, with activity and quality levels agreed in advance, if the health authority wishes to promote a particularly important activity. This requires some knowledge of the costs of providing different services, as a basis for negotiating price. Note however that the actual costs of a facility should not be used as the price for the service: this would encourage inefficiency on the part of the provider (a classic 'perverse incentive').

Summary

Payments systems are only one factor influencing patterns of health care, but they are an important one. Comparisons between salaries and FFS systems, for example, consistently find higher numbers of visits, rates of intervention, numbers of prescriptions, etc., compared to other systems of funding. There is no one ideal system: the context and the relative priority of different criteria should determine the choice for any particular service.

Whatever the changes introduced, there are some important general pre-conditions for success:

- *Adequate funding.* It will not help to alter payment systems if overall levels of payment remain below subsistence level. In that case, informal payments and/or inadequate services will continue.
- *Training/support.* Any new system requires support and training to establish, and this is particularly important if clinicians are being required to master new skills, for example in planning and budgeting.
- *Control of informal payments.* If informal payments continue to run in parallel with official payment channels, they are likely to confuse the 'signals' which the hospital or doctor receives, as well as undermining cost control and equity. It is therefore important that informal payments are replaced by new systems, not merely supplemented.

There are also a number of general points to note in relation to payment systems.

1 Assessing management competence is crucial to deciding which system to implement.
2 The degree of competitiveness in the market is also very important. Whatever the system, increased competition helps to maintain standards.

3 The level and source of funding will also influence incentives. For example, FFS paid through a third party (such as an insurance company) will have a higher tendency to cost escalation than if paid direct by the patient.

4 Different types of service will of course benefit from different payment systems, for example:

- FFS could be used for specific services, such as antenatal cover and immunisation, for which high coverage levels are desirable.
- More unpredictable services should probably be included in capitation, block contract or global budgets.
- Services which can be planned could come under a separate cost and volume contract.
- Services which are non-essential or to be discouraged could be charged direct to the patient (e.g., fertility treatment; extra hotel services; self-referral to higher facilities).
- Activities with a particular tendency to cost escalation, such as provision of drugs, might be best suited to a fixed budget, possibly with a level of copayment from patients, so that provider and patient both have an incentive to use them efficiently and effectively.

5 The bargaining power of providers and payers will also be crucial to the process of negotiating payment systems. Generally speaking, providers prefer systems such as FFS which are associated with a higher levels of income.

6 Although most of the comments above are conditional on context and specific design, it is generally agreed that FFS with a third party payment system is the least desirable payment system.

7 Although there are ways of mitigating the negative incentives of payment systems such as FFS, they tend to be rather complicated. An example of this is the system currently operating in Germany, where total expenditure on primary care is fixed, but incomes are still awarded according to activity. Activities have relative weightings, whose absolute value depends on the aggregate level of activity at the end of the period of calculation. This can lead to bankruptcies, where providers are active and incur costs, which are not covered when the value of the points are calculated at the end of the period. Another approach has been to reduce the fee levels once a practitioner reaches a certain level of income.

8 Co-ordination between different payment sources is also important. If insurance companies or private sources pay according to
   FFS, for example, it may distort the incentives set by government
   payment systems and undermine overall cost containment.
9 It is important that the method of payment for individual practitioners is consistent with the method for paying institutions. A
   fee for service system for practitioner, perhaps introduced as
   part of a bonus system, for example, sits uneasily with a budget
   system for institutions. The first will induce extra demand while
   the second attempts to control spending. Institutions may find
   they are unable to pay the bonuses promised from the income
   obtained through the budget system.

Questions for discussion

Think of a health programme or facility which you know well, in
your country.

1 What is (are) the current payment method(s)?
2 What incentives do they generate?
3 What are the public priorities in relation to the service?
4 Would any of the other options mentioned above serve those
   priorities better?
5 Would the benefits of changing systems outweigh the disadvantages, in your opinion?
6 How could change be implemented?

References and further reading

Bardsley, M., Coles, J. and Jenkins, L. (1987). *DRGs and Health Care, King
   Edward's Hospital Fund for London,* 2nd edition. London: Kings Fund.
Barnum, H., Kutzin, J. and Saxenian, H. (1995). Incentives and provider
   payment methods, *International Journal of Health Planning and Management,*
   10, 23–45.
Barr, D. and Field, M. (1996). The current state of health care in the former
   soviet union, *American Journal of Public Health,* 86, (3): 307–312.
Barros, F. C., Vaughan, J. P. and Victoria, C. (1986). Why so many caesarian
   sections? The need for a further policy change in Brazil, *Health Policy and
   Planning,* 1, (1): 19–29.
Boomberg, J. and Price, M. R. (1990). The impact of fee-for-service reim-
   bursement system on the utilisation of health services, *South African
   Medical Journal,* 78, 133–138.

Chernichovsky, D. and Bayulken, C. (1995). A pay for performance system for civil service doctors: the Indonesian experiment, *Social Science and Medicine*, 41(2): 155–161.

Donaldson, C. and Gerard, K. (1993). *Economics of Health Care Financing: The Visible Hand*, Basingstoke: Macmillan.

Ensor, T. (1995). Introducing health insurance in Vietnam, *Journal of Health Policy and Planning*, 10(2): 154–163.

Ensor, T., Witter, S. and Sheiman, I. (1997). Methods of payment to medical care providers, in S. Witter and T. Ensor, (eds) *An Introduction to Health Economics for Eastern Europe and the Former Soviet Union*. Chichester: John Wiley.

Gellert, G. A. (1995). The influence of market economics on primary care in Vietnam, *Journal of the American Medical Association*, 273(19): 1498–1502.

Gerdtham, U., Sogaard, J., Anderson, F. and Jonsson, B. (1992). An econometric analysis of health care expenditure: a cross-section study of OECD countries, *Journal of Health Economics*, 11, 63–84.

McPherson, A. (1981). Regional variations in the use of common surgical procedures: within and between England and Wales, Canada and the USA, *Social Science and Medicine*, 15A, 273–288.

Naylor, C. D. (1992). The Canadian health care system: a model of America to emulate? *Health Economics*, 1, 19–37.

Robinson, R. and Steiner, A. (1998). *Managed Health Care*, Buckingham: Open University Press.

Rodrigues, J. (1989). Hospital utilization and reimbursement method in Brazil, *International Journal of Health Planning and Management*, 4(1): 3–16.

Rosko, M. D. and Broyles, R. W. (1987). Short-term responses of hospitals to the DRG prospective pricing mechanism in New Jersey, *Medical Care*, 25, 88–99.

Witter, S. and Ensor, T. (eds) (1997). *An Introduction to Health Economics for Eastern Europe and the Former Soviet Union*. Chichester: John Wiley.

Wolfe, P. R. and Moran, D. W. (1993). Global budgeting in the OECD countries, *Health Care Financing Review*, 14, (3): 55–76.

World Bank (1995). China: health-care financing reform 1996–2001, Washington, DC.: Human Development Department, World Bank.

13

Measuring and improving efficiency in health care

Sophie Witter and Robin Thompson

Introduction

We have talked in a number of previous chapters about different approaches to allocating resources in order to achieve our health and other social goals. The chapters on economic evaluation, priority setting and programme analysis (Part 3) all focus on the issue of allocative efficiency (allocating resources to activities which should maximise health gain). Having selected and established health care activities, however, most managers and health economists will face the related but distinct and very important question: how well are we doing what we set out to do in this programme? This is what economists call 'technical efficiency'. Some other ways of asking the same question are:

- Could we achieve the same effect in this programme using fewer resources?
- Could we be more effective using the same resources?
- Could we improve the quality of our service without increasing the cost?
- Could we reorganise the service to achieve additional benefits without increasing the cost?
- If we increased the scale of activity in this programme, would the increase in benefits significantly outweigh the increase in costs?

Although managers often express these questions differently (e.g., 'are we providing a good service?'), at the heart of much of their concerns lies this question of technical efficiency. Efficiency is not just about cutting costs: it means doing whatever you do in the best possible way. Reducing waste is a key concern, but so should be providing a high quality service which meets customers' needs.

This chapter will cover the following topics:

- What is efficiency? How do we measure it?
- Common causes of inefficiency
- Possible strategies for addressing these factors

Measuring efficiency

Mrs Foresight is having a bad day at the office. The Minister is facing hostile questioning in the Council of Ministers about how well the health budget is being spent. He has asked her, as key planner in the Ministry of Health, to investigate how efficient Ebul's health sector is and to identify areas for possible savings. Where should she begin?

All efficiency studies have to look at three areas:

$$Inputs \longrightarrow Throughputs/process \longrightarrow Outcomes$$

In an industrial process, we could measure the cost of the inputs (labour, equipment, facilities, supplies, etc.); then measure the value of the outputs (finished product, at market price) and compare the value-added achieved by production with that of rival producers. If our product was more expensive to produce, we would re-examine the production process to see how it could be altered to produce our product more efficiently.

In health care, there are a number of complicating issues:

- The inputs are not always homogenous: a patient with TB at one facility, for example, is unlikely to have the same severity of illness and response to treatment as a patient diagnosed with the same disease at another facility.
- The 'production process' (i.e., health care activity) cannot therefore be uniform, but must be allowed to vary according to the specific needs of different patients.
- The outcome will be related to a number of factors independent of the treatment/prevention process itself, such as the overall level of health of the patient, the degree of their compliance with the treatment, their home environment, income levels, etc.
- Health care activities have many goals, not all of which are easy to measure. Palliative care, for example, aims to reduce suffer-

ing, but may have no effect on length of life. Its impact in terms of reduced suffering will be hard to measure.

Let us imagine that Mrs Foresight starts by collecting information on as many of the indicators in Table 13.1 as she can find.

It becomes clear pretty quickly that while these indicators, combined, may be suggestive of some features of the health system, they are not, on their own, conclusive. If health expenditure is relatively low in Ebul, is that because the health care sector is efficient, or just underfunded? If its outcome indicators are comparable with neighbouring countries despite lower expenditure, is this because the health sector is more effective, or because of other factors relating to income distribution, consumption patterns, infrastructure, etc.? Similarly, are low admission rates good or bad? They might be good if they reflected a well-functioning PHC system, or bad if they reflect the lack of confidence which the population has in the hospital system.

We also have to bear in mind the *quality* of the information (how was it collected? Is it accurate?) and *what information is missing* (e.g., we know how many were admitted, but how many were turned away? Or failed to be referred? Or were admitted inappropriately?).

Finally, because more health care is not always better, we should ideally connect information about inputs, throughputs and outputs to *need* and to the *health and welfare gain* which they produce. For example, in terms of need, do the services mirror the burden of disease and what is known about the effective ways for preventing or treating it? Similarly, can we make causal connections between general health indicators (such as mortality and morbidity) and the activities of the health sector? Generally, there are too many other influences, but in some studies where other factors are kept equal we can make a direct measurement of the impact of an intervention.

Taken together, these general indicators will suggest some areas of possible poor performance, and this can be the basis for more detailed efficiency studies at lower levels of the system.

Measuring efficiency within and between facilities

Mrs Foresight goes back to the Minister, arguing that this question cannot be answered without conducting some studies of specific districts and facilities. She is given permission to go ahead and gets in touch with her friend, Dr Eva Ready, Provincial Health Administrator in Rungara

Table 13.1   Possible indicators of health sector efficiency/productivity

Inputs
- Health expenditure per capita
- Health expenditure as percentage of GNP
- Public/private share of overall health expenditure
- Health expenditure as percentage of government spending
- Expenditure per admission, per bed-day, per procedure, or per outpatient visit
- Hospital beds per 1,000 population
- Doctor/nurse to population ratios
- Mix of health personnel (e.g., doctor:nurse ratios)
- Prescribing rates for drugs
- Allocation of spending to different levels of facility (e.g., primary, secondary, tertiary)
- Allocation of spending between different services (e.g., MCH/FP, AIDS care, etc.)
- Allocation of spending between service inputs (e.g., capital costs; staffing; supplies, etc.)

Throughputs
- Average length of stay in hospitals
- Bed occupancy rates (percentage of hospital beds filled, on average)
- Bed turnover interval (time that beds are vacant between patients)
- Utilisation rates of other facilities
- Admission rates (percentage of population admitted into hospital each year)
- Waiting times for different procedures
- Daily caseload per health staff at different facilities
- Coverage rates for immunisation, antenatal care and other preventive work
- Accuracy of diagnostic tests (percentage of false negatives or positives)

Outcomes
- Peri-operative mortality
- Post-operative infection rates
- Re-admission rates
- Success (or cure) rates for different procedures
- Patient satisfaction measures
- Effective immunisation coverage

Province, to ask for her help. They decide that a comparison of district hospitals will be most useful as these see the majority of patients. How should they go about analysing their efficiency?

The first question they need to ask is: *efficiency at doing what*? What are the main objectives of the district hospitals? Is it to see referred cases, or self-referred? And how should they group their many activities for the purposes of comparison: should they consider each procedure separately (more work, but more specific results), or group together into inpatient curative services, for example? The answer to this will depend largely on how services are organised: if they are provided in an integrated way, for example, it would be difficult and unhelpful to separate out components. If on the other hand services are provided by different staff, using different equipment and facilities, then it makes sense to look separately at how resources are being used and managed in these separate programmes.

Next comes the question of *how they are going to measure outcomes*. Ideally, they could compare inputs with the longer-term impact which they have had on health. However, this involves longer term follow up of patients. In many situations a 'quick and dirty' approach may be more realistic, in which throughputs (e.g., numbers of patients seen or number of vaccinations given) are measured.

They also have to think about *how to judge efficiency*. Is there a 'gold standard' that tells them that, for example, to perform a normal delivery without complications it should cost $5. Anything costing more than that can then be judged to be in some way inefficient. This is rarely the case, and most commonly judgements about efficiency are made by comparing across facilities. Some may then stand out as relatively inefficient, which is useful information, although it tells us nothing about the optimum level of efficiency (even the relatively efficient services may be inefficient in an absolute sense, but this is harder to judge).

If we are comparing average costs for a procedure, or group of procedures, we also need to consider the following three questions:

1 *Are we comparing like with like in terms of inputs?* Let us imagine that the team has decided to compare the cost of in- and outpatient services between district hospitals in the region. They would follow the step-down allocation of costs as described in Chapter 6 in order to get an estimate of cost per

patient admitted and cost per outpatient visit. (Note the point about *shadow pricing* where necessary to ensure that our estimates reflect the true social opportunity costs of resources used.) A direct comparison of these costs between districts assumes that *the case-mix is roughly the same* in both places, which may not be the case. If one district has a more complicated case-mix, then it may face higher treatment costs for reasons unconnected to its own efficiency. Comparisons between different level facilities often face the problem of a more demanding case-mix at higher levels (particularly if referral systems are working).

How do we allow for case-mix variation? One approach is only to compare facilities which should have similar case-mixes, in terms of the area and the function which they serve. Another is to collect cost information for the same type of procedure so that the comparison between two facilities is valid. Finally, some allowance for a more complicated case-mix could be made, although this would require an assessment of the real increased costs which that facility faced.

2 *Are we comparing like with like in terms of outputs?* The comparison also assumes that *quality is constant* between the facilities – for example, that outpatient visits, on average, produce the same positive impact in Gamlan district as in Mela district. The research team should investigate whether this is likely to be true before making such an assumption. One way of dealing with this problem (when we are comparing a specific intervention) is to set a minimum quality standard and only count throughputs or outputs which reach this level. (This must be done with care, however: is a stillbirth the result of a poor quality procedure, or of factors outside the control of the health services?) They would also need to assess the appropriateness of the services being provided: a well-performed caesarian is only of value when a caesarian was really required.

3 *Are we allowing for the relationship between cost and volume?* Finally, given that health services have many fixed costs (remember Chapter 6), there is usually a *strong relationship between volume treated and cost per unit.* If a hospital has a high occupancy rate, for example, then it is likely to appear more efficient in terms of cost per bed day. However, if this high occupancy results from inappropriate admissions, over-long lengths of stay or from poor quality treatment, then this is deceptive. Use these indicators with care.

Table 13.2   Costs for in- and out-patients in three districts

	Gamlan district hospital	Mela district hospital	Rungi district hospital
Cost per in-patient (US$)	$15	$20	$12
Cost per outpatient visit (US$)	$5	$10	$3

The research team come up with the figures in Table 13.2 for in- and out-patient services in three districts.

They have reason to believe that the case-mix and quality of services are not very different between these three districts. The figures therefore suggest that some services are being provided more efficiently than others. However, in order to verify this and realise the potential gains, the team need to know what are the underlying *determinants of efficiency (or inefficiency)*. How should they go about establishing these?

This is more of an art than a science. The following are the types of questions that they might ask in order to find out why costs are differing substantially:

• Do the facilities face the same input costs? (Usually they do, but in some cases, labour costs, for example, may be higher. In that case, are there ways in which labour inputs could be reduced without affecting outcomes?)

• Are facilities using the same input mix? Is one facility, for example, more wasteful of supplies and how could this be improved? As with staffing, this involves making normative judgements about the 'right' level of input. Higher staff ratios may be a sign of better services, or of overstaffing. Deciding which will involve an investigation of activity (how much staff do) and outcome (what effect it has).

• Are services organised differently, and, if so, are there any negative effects from the system which seems more cost-effective?

• Are there demand factors which need to be taken into account? We have concentrated here on supply side issues, but inefficiency can, for example, be caused by low service utilisation (generating high unit costs) where public demand is low. This is often the case at lower level facilities, if the public can self-refer to higher level ones.

Common causes of inefficiency

Mrs Foresight has established that there is very uneven performance by district hospitals. She suspects that the issues may be broader than just managerial incompetence. What is the next step? She calls together a meeting of people who she thinks might have some ideas about why the health facilities often seem to be badly run. Mr Egghead, the young health economist is invited, along with the provincial medical officer, the district hospital manager, some medical staff from the hospital and village health centres, and even a few villagers to represent patients. What do they think are the problems with the way the health services are delivered?

Hospital doctor*: How can I work effectively when there are never enough gloves for surgery, or drugs for the patients, and the electricity keeps going off just when we need to use the lights in the operating theatre?*

One of the most common causes of inefficiency in many developing countries is underfunding. Strategies for increasing funding were tackled in Chapters 4 and 5. Whatever the size of budget for a facility, though, there is usually scope for improving performance by ensuring that high priority items are funded first. In particular, recurrent budgets for supplies tend to be underfunded relative to other categories. If staff are paid but lack the materials with which to be effective, that is clearly inefficient and managers need to find ways of moving resources to where they are most needed. Some strategies will be discussed in this chapter.

Hospital manager*:   How can I concentrate on the quality of our work when I never know how much money I am going to have to pay to cover our bills from month to month? All I can do is to try to survive.*

Problems of poor financial planning, financial uncertainty and lack of control over finances by local managers is common in many developing countries. This means that it is difficult for staff at the local level to set priorities and plan services.

Patients*:   We are not made to feel very welcome in the health centre. The opening hours are not convenient for us and are very short. We are made to wait for long times, before seeing the nurse or doctor, and when we get into the consulting room it is very rushed and he has very little time to discuss our problems.*

Are services oriented towards the needs of their customers, or the convenience of staff? How can staff be made more responsive to patients? Although this is primarily an issue of quality, it also affects efficiency in a general sense.

• Extra waiting time for patients imposes a cost on them, as made clear in Chapter 6 on costs.
• They are less likely to use services in future.
• When they do use them, they may not be correctly diagnosed, if the staff lack time to question them properly.
• Opportunities for providing preventive, promotive and appropriate curative services may be missed.
• Communication with patients is likely to be poor; this will reduce compliance and transmission of health education messages.

> **Provincial medical officer**:   *I rarely get time to do my job, as so much of my time is spent taking donors and foreign consultants around. They need information all the time, and have to be kept happy if we are to keep their funding for our MCH and malaria control programmes.*

The multiple demands of donors are notorious for overloading local staff and information systems which are already struggling. What are the option for setting up monitoring systems which can meet local needs and generate a single set of information which will satisfy donors?

> **Health economist**:   *It seems to me that none of you is asking the most important question: how do you know that what you are doing is effective anyway? And if it is effective, how do you know that it could not be done using fewer resources?*

This is an important point. Not all health care promotes health: some of it even damages it. We do need systems in place which ensure that staff are kept informed about which procedures are effective and cost-effective and about recent developments in medical research and technology. Similarly, their performance needs to be monitored and supported so that incompetence is eliminated or reduced to a minimum. On the positive side, they should be involved in monitoring the quality of services and suggesting ways in which improvements might be made.

Strategies for increasing efficiency

Inefficiency has to be examined in its local context, so all strategies should begin with establishing a motive and a means for local managers and health professionals to tackle it. Start then with the following questions:

- Why should they care? What are the incentives which they face?
- What can they do about it? What tools might they adopt?

Many of the strategies fall more within the field of health management than health economics, and so will be referred to briefly here, with pointers to further reading.

Incentives

- *Payment systems* are an important instrument in setting incentives that promote agreed local priorities. See Chapter 12 for a discussion of different issues to consider here. Facility indicators may be developed, and additional payments made to facilities which meet the targets. However, great care is required to use appropriate indicators. Normative lengths of stay may be too crude, given the differing needs of patients (for example, if women who have had a caesarian are expected to stay in hospital for 7 days). It is also important not to set targets in relation to past performance, or managers will have an interest in keeping productivity low (the more you do, the more you are expected to do the following year). Similarly, in terms of rewards to individual staff, beware of systems which link promotion or pay to activity alone, without checking that quality is not suffering.
- *Decentralisation* can empower local bodies to use resources more efficiently. See Chapter 11 for discussion this issue.
- *Market-style reforms* are another strategy which aims to give an incentive and the means to achieve gains in efficiency. Financial autonomy for providers gives them the ability to change inputs and activities, while the retaining of profits provides a motive. See Chapter 11 on public and private roles for a discussion of the experience of quasi-markets and privatisation in general.

Tools

- *Planning, management and budgeting tools* may alleviate the problems raised by the hospital doctor and manager. Lack of skills, clear objectives and mechanisms for planning and managing services within realistic resource constraints are a common cause of poor and inefficient services. Human resource planning and management is particularly important, given that staff absorb an average of 7 per cent of the costs of running a health service (WHO, 1998). See Green (1992) and Collins (1994) for in-depth discussion of these areas.

Staff are usually the experts in what the problems of organisation are within a service, but their ideas for solving them are often not solicited by managers. See Cassels and Janovsky (1991) for an approach to team-based problem solving at the district level.

In terms of budgeting, the three most common problems for managers are:

1 *Unpredictability*: funds do not arrive in the amounts or at the times they are expected. This leads to a climate of chaos, with short-term survival strategies dominating longer-term planning. The solution is easier to say than achieve: better financial planning and organisation at higher levels and improved safeguards against and penalties for fraud.

2 *Inflexibility*: a common problem for managers is not being permitted to redeploy resources between budget headings (what is known as 'line-item budgeting'), so that important categories (such as maintenance) can become chronically underfunded. Although 'global budgets' require some trust that funds will not be embezzled, the increased freedom to manage which they permit can be complemented by improved financial auditing systems.

3 *Perverse incentives*: for example, when managers have any savings from their budget at the end of the year taken away from the next year's budget. An example of this is when any savings due to reductions in staff are clawed back by the treasury. This discourages efficiency and should be altered so that savings can be rolled over or reinvested.

Restructuring of budgets can also be helpful: for example, if budgets are related to objectives or programmes, rather than inputs, that can help to focus attention on what health services are seeking to achieve. Although 'output budgeting' (linking resources used to the final product or benefits) has proved rather ambitious to implement, a more limited approach of 'programme budgeting' (linking resources to the activities of different programmes) is fairly simple and allows managers to make judgements about relative efficiency and to identify areas of possible improvement. See Chapter 6 on costing for issues about how costs are allocated to programmes and Issaha-Tinorgah and Waddington (1993) for a discussion of improving efficiency through budgetary reforms.

- *Improved communication with and responsiveness to service users* is required to respond to the patient's complaints. If services do not meet the needs of their users, then they are neither effective nor efficient.

One aspect of communication is picking up what are the important issues for users. If, for example, the absence of drugs is a major deterrent to utilisation, then improving their availability may lead to an increased perception of quality, increased demand and thus increased efficiency (Barnum and Kutzin 1993). Consultation with users to establish their priorities and views on existing services should be part of the regular management structures. In addition, one-off surveys on issues of particular relevance can be carried out. See Oppenheim (1992) on different consultation methods.

Another aspect may be clearer communication about health benefits. Where demand for services with significant externalities is low, campaigns to communicate the benefits to households may also help to increase awareness and utilisation.

- *Donor co-ordination* is clearly being called for by the Provincial Medical Officer. Donor co-ordination is more often dream than reality, as each organsation has its own agenda and requirements for its funders. However, if local health managers and decision-makers have clear goals and priorities, then they will be in a stronger position to negotiate with donors so that the latter support their policies rather than vice versa.

The idea of 'sector-wide' approaches (SWAps) is that recipient countries play a more dominant role in preparing plans for the health sector, with the co-ordinated support and technical assistance of donors. The focus should be on sustainability of the sector as a whole, and on minimising the burden on recipient governments by a single agreed framework for reporting and financial flows. Whether they will work well in reality is yet to be seen. See Peters and Chao (1998) for more details on SWAps, and Cassels (1996) for a good summary of issues relating to aid in the health sector in general.

- *Treatment protocols and clinical auditing* are one tool to deal with the concerns raised by Mr Egghead, the health economist. Treatment protocols can be developed or adapted by local staff in order to promote current best practice in treatment of specific conditions. (See Jamison *et al.*, 1993, and the Cochrane databases, listed in Appendix 4, for details of these.) The focus should be on eliminating harmful or ineffectual practices and increasing the quantity and quality of effective procedures. Many should produce savings, as they allow lengths of stay to be reduced by quicker treatment and increasing the ability of patients to manage their condition in their home environment. This should benefit patients, as hospitals are a dangerous environment to stay in, with potential cross-infection from other patients. It should also increase efficiency, though overall costs may of course go up if the volume of patients who can be treated increases. Muir Gray (1997) is a good reference on evidence-based medicine.

Together with in-service training for health staff and regular supervision, this forms a positive approach to improving clinical skills. Clinical auditing involves looking retrospectively at the diagnosis and treatment of a sample of patients in order to assess to what extent correct procedures were followed. This is a way of identifying general or individual problems which require corrective action.

Dealing with his other point – not only to ensure that treatments work, but that they are the most cost-effective option available – there are a number of important tools.

- *Health information.* Information on inputs, throughputs and outcomes is needed if we are to be able to assess the effectiveness and cost-effectiveness of services. Without usable financial and performance data, managers have no basis on which to plan changes in service provision. However, generating too much information imposes an unnecessary cost on health services. Health information policy should therefore start by defining who needs to know, what they need to know and how that information can be collected at minimum cost. See Green (1992) and Austin (1997)for a discussion of the issues.
- *Reinforcing PHC provision.* Where patients are by-passing the primary health care centres and seeking basic treatments from hospitals, efficiencies in terms of both costs and qualitative aspects (such as continuity of care) can be gained by taking measures which reinforce PHC. These might include imposing charges for self-referral to hospitals or introducing differential fees which make lower level care more affordable; increasing resources to PHC centres; or improving supplies – taking what-

ever measures are indicated by local situation analysis as necessary to increase public confidence in the first level of services.
(This may, by the way, increase unit costs at the hospitals, which
should now face a more complicated case-mix.) See Barnum
and Kutzin (1993) for further discussion.

- *Technology assessment* focuses on decisions about new investments
  and how to ensure that they meet the criteria of appropriateness, acceptability, effectiveness and efficiency, relative to other
  possible approaches to the problem (see Banta, 1994). This is
  particularly important in developing countries because of the
  severe resource constraints and the problem of capital 'gifts'
  from donors which can distort services and generate substantial
  recurrent costs (see Chapter 8).

- *Essential drugs lists* are useful in limiting expenditure on expensive brand-name drugs and harmful or relatively non-effective
  drugs. For further details on how to establish and implement an
  essential drugs list, see MSH/WHO (1997).

Summary

This chapter has shown that finding ways of measuring and improving efficiency are central to the work of health planners,
managers and economists.

We argue for a broad definition which focuses not just on the
quantity of input to quantity of output, but also on the quality of
services provided and the extent to which they meet customers'
needs. While much of the chapter has focused on the supply-side
issues, we have also emphasised that low demand causes problems for efficiency and that providers either have to adapt to
meet demands or try to induce demand (for high priority services, such as control of infectious diseases).

In measuring efficiency, it has become clear that indicators
such as length of stay or utilisation rates have to be interpreted
carefully in a given context. They are not unambiguously bad or
good: we have to look at the causes behind them before drawing
conclusions.

Efficiency studies have to take into account the different goals
of health care programmes; the heterogeneity of health inputs
(different case-mix, differing health states on admission etc.); the
difficulty of measuring outcomes (especially where the follow-up
period required is quite long, for example, in determining

whether cancer has been 'cured' or merely halted); the qualitative difference between apparently quite similar activities or outputs; and the effects of changing volume on the average or marginal costs of programmes.

The efficiency studies described here focus on the ratio of input costs to output gains and make comparative judgements between different facilities or regions. This approach is relatively simple and cheap to carry out. In the West, econometric estimation of cost or production functions and techniques like data envelopment analysis (DEA) are also used to measure efficiency. For further information see the references on DEA listed at the end of this chapter.

Strategies to improve efficiency must address the motivation of individuals and institutions in the system as well as the means which they possess to improve the situation. Introducing market-style reforms, decentralisation and reform of payment systems are all ways of increasing the incentives and ability of staff to improve efficiency. The extent to which they have been successful has been discussed elsewhere in this book (see Chapters 10, 11, and 12). A number of other tools for increasing efficiency are introduced here, with pointers for further reading.

Questions for discussion

You are the provincial medical officer. You have been promised increased funding next year if you can make significant efficiency savings in the region's health services.

1 How would you go about establishing which services are relatively inefficient?
2 What are the likely main causes of inefficiency in your area?
3 How many of these are within your power to change?
4 How could you involve staff at higher and lower levels of the system in addressing problems? Would they feel threatened?

References and further reading

Andersen, P. and Petersen, N. (1993). A procedure for ranking effecient units in data envelopment analysis, *Management Science*, 39, 1261–4.

Austin, N. (1997). Information, in N. Austin and S. Dopson, (eds) *The Clinical Directorate* Oxford: Radcliffe Medical Press.

Banta, H. D. (1994). Health care technology as a policy issue, *Health Policy* , 30, 1–21.

Barnum, H. and Kutzin, J. (1993). *Public Hospitals in Developing Countries: Resource Use, Cost and Financing.* Especially Chapter 3 on hospital costs and efficiency. Baltimore: Johns Hopkins University Press

Cassels, A. (1994). Health sector reform: key issues in less developed countries, *Journal of International Development,* 7(3).

Cassels, A. (1996). Aid instruments and health systems development: an analysis of current practice, *Health Policy and Planning,* 11(4).

Cassels, A. and Janovsky, K. (1991). *Strengthening Health Management in Districts and Provinces: Handbook for Facilitators.* Geneva: World Health Organisation.

Charnes, A., Cooper, W., Lewin, A. and Seiford, L. (1994). *Data Envelopment Analysis: Theory, Methodology and Applications.* Boston: Kluwer.

Collins, C. (1994). *Management and Organisation of Developing Health Systems.* Oxford: Oxford University Press.

Green, A. (1992). Chapter 6 on information for planning, *An Introduction to Health Planning in Developing Countries.* Oxford: Oxford University Press.

Hollingsworth, B., Dawson, P. and Maniadakis, N. (forthcoming). Efficiency measurement of health care: a review of non-parametric methods and applications, *Health Care Management Science,* forthcoming.

Issaka-Tinorgah, A. and Waddington, C. (1993). Encouraging efficiency through programme and functional budgeting: lessons from experience in Ghana and the Gambia, in A. Mills and K. Lee (eds) *Health Economics Research in Developing Countries.* Oxford: Oxford Medical Publications.

Jamison, D., Mosley, W., Measham, A., Bobadilla, J. (1993). *Disease Control Priorities in Developing Countries.* Oxford: Oxford Medical Publications for World Bank.

MSH/WHO (Management Sciences for Health/World Health Organization) (1997). *Managing Drug Supply.* West Hartford, CT: Kumarian Press.

Muir Gray, J. (1997). *Evidence-based Healthcare: How to make Health Policy and Management Decisions.* New York: Churchill Livingstone.

Oppenheim, A. N. (1992). *Questionnaire Design, Interviewing and Attitude Measurement.* London: Pinter.

Parkin, D. (1991). Comparing health service efficiency across countries, in McGuire, Fenn and Mayhew (eds) *Providing Health Care,* Oxford: Oxford University Press.

Peters, D. and Chao, S. (1998). The sector-wide approach in health: what is it? Where is it leading? *International Journal of Health Planning and Management,* 13.

Salinas-Jimenez, J. and Smith, P. (1996). Data envelopment analysis applied to quality in primary health care *Annals of Operations Research,* 67, 141–161.

World Health Organisation (1998). *Evaluation of the Implementation of the Global Strategy for Health for All by 2000: 1979–1996: A Selective Review of Progress and Constraints.* Geneva: WHO.

14
Conclusion

Sophie Witter

Challenges for the new millenium

As we start the new millenium, it is clear that much has been achieved over the past few decades in health in developing countries. At the same time, there remain considerable challenges. While health indicators have been improving in many countries, in others life expectancy has been stagnant or falling, with the AIDS epidemic a key cause for concern in some regions.

At the same time, the financial burden of ill-health has been falling heavily on households and individuals. Their search for health is not assisted by health markets where private providers are profit-oriented, public providers are also having to support themselves through entrepreneurial activities, and information about the effectiveness of treatments is not widely disseminated. In this situation, people are still suffering and dying from preventable diseases, and exploitation and quackery (the selling of false remedies) still takes place. The challenge for health services in many areas is very basic (though difficult to achieve in practice):

- *Increasing coverage*: Unless people use their services, they cannot meet health needs
- *Quality*: Unless they provide a reasonable quality of service, customers will not be attracted
- *Effectiveness*: Once people have come, they should be given treatments which work and which are appropriate to their needs

The 'double burden' of disease, discussed in Chapter 2, highlights the need not only for improved performance by health services in preventing and treating the most common communicable diseases, but also for new skills in combating the risk factors underlying the 'diseases of affluence' (e.g., health promotion or use of incentives, such as taxes).Whereas smoking rates are stable or declining in most developed countries, for example, in developing countries the rates are increasing fast, bringing dramatic increases in mortality and morbidity over the next few decades (Murray and Lopez, 1996). Psychiatric illnesses are also projected as a major part of the burden of disease in developing countries over the next two decades.

We hope that this book has shown how health economics, used in conjunction with other bodies of knowledge in public health, management and medicine, can assist in addressing some of these important problems. It can make an important contribution to the following challenges, which have been discussed in the book.

- The achievement of socio-economic development in developing countries which favours the poor. This is potentially one of the most effective ways of improving health
- The application of cost-benefit measurements across sectors to inform resource allocation and to widen the debate about health from Health Ministries alone
- The development of stable sources of finance for health care which do not restrict access for the poor
- The improvment of the awareness of economic evaluation techniques and their use by local managers
- The development of positive interactions between public and private services, with an emphasis on improving the quality and focus on public health goals of all providers
- The stimulation of local debate on how rationing should take place: how best can limited public funds be used (both effectively and equitably)
- The implementation of fair systems for allocating resources between areas, allowing for differences in need and in local income generation capacity
- Improved planning for services, both through better co-ordination with donors and improved analysis of project and programme costs by local staff
- The reform of provider payments to stimulate productivity and cost-effective health care
- Increased awareness of staff and their involvement in measuring efficiency of services, analysing the causes of problems and developing solutions.

Key questions for health economics in developing countries

This book demonstrates that there is a growing body of knowledge in health economics which can be applied in developing countries to improve the way in which resources for health are generated and used. To date these have been of limited effectiveness, for two main reasons:

1 lack of dissemination and training in health economics
2 health economics has not been developed in or adapted to the context in many developing countries.

There are a number of reasons why a different emphasis is required – why some of the assumptions which Western health economists reasonably make cannot be sustained in many developing countries, leading to a different set of questions. We will give some examples from this book.

Financing patterns. It is accepted by most in the West that public finance should be a dominant source of funding for health care in order to ensure access and 'social solidarity' ('from each according to his ability to each according to his need'). In developing countries, as we have seen, the tax base is weak and the burden of financing health care falls heavily on individual households. Formal and informal charges proliferate and there is evidence that exemption schemes have not effectively protected the poorest. In the light of this, economists in developing countries need to focus on:

• how to develop credible risk-pooling schemes
• the development of intertemporal transfers such as savings schemes in areas where social cohesion and trust in institutions ('social capital', as it is increasingly known) is low
• effective local mechanisms to protect the poor from the costs of ill health.

The role of the state. It will have become clear in the course of the book that we cannot assume a dominant role in either health financing or provision for the state, or even that it is an effective market regulator. In all countries there are questions of to what extent the state is a 'perfect agent', promoting the best interests of its citizens. This problem is compounded in many developing countries where governments may be even less representative and more subject to capture by self-interested elites or even indi-

ViewById

viduals. Even if they are representative and benign, their competence as regulators is often severely restricted by financial and staffing constraints and the growth of the informal economy. This suggests the need for:

- more focus on the political economy of health care
- the strengthening of coalitions supporting public health goals
- the development of regulatory approaches which can be effective in this environment (e.g., using positive incentives and/or self-selection by providers)

Use of public money. Given that its funds are limited, how should the state be using its money? Should it continue to provide a low-level subsidy – as it is doing in many countries at present – to all services, with a focus on higher level and urban services which command more political clout? This is not very satisfactory, from either a cost-effectiveness or equity point of view.

What is the alternative and how feasible is it? For example, the 'basic package' approach targets resources by choosing services with the highest potential impact on the burden of disease in relation to their cost. Can this work in practice and how? Can it gain the support and understanding of the public? Another possibility would be to accept a (regulated) private market in health care for most, with public monies used to insure the poorest (the US model, though in a very different context). What would the implications of that be?

Public and private sectors. It has also became clear in this book that public and private sectors are not so clearly differentiated from one another in many developing countries, where public staff are increasingly acting in an opportunistic way. By seeking income through a variety of strategies (gifts in kind, voluntary donations, fixed fees, payments for quality, sale of drugs, etc.) they are in effect operating as private agents, though based in or benefiting from a public facility. Once this has occurred, there are a number of important issues. For example:

- How can government influence the activities of these 'staff'?
- How will changes to official pay interract with informal sources of income?
- To what extent are informal charges driven by demand (the search for quality) or supply (supply induced demand)?
- How do informal charges relate to the income level of patients?
- Can informal income be formalised and what would that mean for patients and providers?

Lack of central purchasing. If patients are to a large extent financing care directly, then this has a major implication for the role of the centre, region and district in planning services. Instead of a command-and-control system, what we are seeing in many developing countries is deregulated private health markets, with all the problems of information asymmetry and increased transaction costs which that brings. The focus therefore has to be on such questions as:

• How can consumers be informed about which treatments are effective?
• How can excessive or inappropriate treatment be controlled?
• How can information on the quality of providers be made available in appropriate form to consumers, etc?

Health markets. Whereas in many Western countries planned markets or quasi-markets in health have been deliberately introduced in order to stimulate competition and, it was hoped, increased efficiency, in developing countries health markets have either always existed or have grown up from the grassroots as a response to the limited quantity and quality of health care which the state could provide. The issues are therefore quite different – not how to stimulate competition but rather how the state can gain some strategic control over what kind of services are provided, at what cost and to whom. As stated earlier, this also raises some important questions about the nature of that 'state' itself.

These are some of the challenges which health economists in developing countries will grapple with over the coming years. As well as playing a role in meeting the health needs of their countries, they may contribute to the development of what has been, until now, a rather Western-dominated field.

References and further reading

Murray, C. and Lopez, A. (1996). *The Global Burden of Disease.* Geneva: WHO.

Appendix 1

The ethics and philosophy of health economics

Sophie Witter

Economists generally have a pretty poor image – seen as a group of heartless, mean-minded people, obsessed with saving money, no matter what the human cost. In the field of medicine it is particularly galling for doctors trained to save life *at all costs* to be confronted with a group of people who want to know *how much it costs*. However, there is an strong ethical reasoning behind health economics, and it goes like this.

1 Almost all actions consume resources and those resources are then not available for any other use.
2 By treating X patient you are therefore denying Y patient, unless your pot of resources is limitless (which it never is).
3 The cost of treating X is the worse health which Y will enjoy as a result.
4 By treating X patient without considering alternative possibilities you may be gaining less than you might have done.
5 It is therefore unethical to proceed blindly. Ignoring costs means ignoring the sacrifices imposed on others. Rather you should consider how much you can spend and how much gain can be produced by different interventions; from this you should be able to decide the mix of services which will produce the maximum overall benefit for society.

Health economics is therefore not uncaring. It does not proceed by cost minimisation alone. Nor does it create the resource constraints which people bitterly resent. It is nature that does this. Rather it works within them to find the best uses of existing resources. In doing so it has to be very concerned with benefits. Thus a very expensive service may well be justified, if it generates widespread and significant gains. If on the other hand it is expensive but largely ineffectual then it cannot be justified.

Having defended the discipline, we have to recognise and respond to some of the main methodological criticisms which have been levelled against it.

Rationality

Economics starts from an assumption that individuals are rational – that is to say, that they can process information in a orderly fashion and draw appropriate conclusions, and that they actually do so. Similarly, economists tend to assume that organisations merely need to be presented with 'the facts' to draw logical conclusions and act accordingly. However, critics argue, reality suggests that rationality is the exception rather than the rule! How can we deal with this?

Bounded rationality. Economists have long recognised that people, like computers, can get overloaded and there is a real cost to trying to acquire and process too much information, especially in a changing, uncertain world. It may therefore be 'rational' to consider a more limited set of information in day-to-day decisions. These issues can be built into the economic model by looking at factors like the degree of risk aversion of individuals, the costs which they face in gathering information and transactions costs which they face in continually renegotiating with health care suppliers.

Social animals. Similarly, a body of recent writing by economists (see, for example, Mooney, 1998) has recognised that people are social animals. To treat people too individually is to ignore the social side of our nature – that we are influenced by others around us, by our position relative to theirs, by the distribution of benefits as much as absolute levels etc. The group dynamics and politics of a situation are undeniably important in how and which decisions are reached. Moreover, individual tastes are influenced to a large degree by environmental influences, such as peer behaviour, advertising, etc.

Maximisers

The normal assumption in economics is that individuals will maximise their own welfare, which is usually interpreted as various types of consumption. While this may be accurate in some circumstances, critics argue, it leaves out some important elements of the human personality.

Satisficing/minimising risk. First, we may choose other decision rules, such as limiting the risk of loss. Thus, for example, with peasant farmers it has been observed that they may not act in such a way to produce the greatest harvests, but rather act conservatively to minimise the likelihood of total crop failure. Again, in an uncertain world without safety nets, that is probably rational.

Apparently self-destructive acts. If you smoke, knowing that it is likely to reduce your life expectancy, how can you be described as maximising your welfare? There are many issues here. First, you may judge the short-term pleasure to be worth the longer-term pain (i.e. have a high personal discount rate). Secondly, you may be unaware of the real risks, or have chosen not to be aware because of the nature of your addiction. Finally, even if there are some instances of genuine and conscious self-destructive behaviour, does this invalidate the useful generalisation that people maximise their own welfare?

Non-material factors. Our welfare is affected not just by what we consume but also often by what others around us consume; by how we consume; and by other non-material factors, such as our religious outlook. An example of the first is when we feel bad because we see someone else suffering. This feeling, known as *altruism* (see Chapter 3) can be very powerful and is the driving force behind the organisation of universal public health systems. An example of the second is when a person chooses not to obtain health care rather than face the stigmatising process of being exempted from fees. This demonstrates the importance of the *process*, not just the consumption itself. Finally, an example of the importance of religious or spiritual outlook is when an ill person chooses not to present themselves for treatment because they believe that it is 'their lot' to suffer, that something which they have done has caused the illness, etc.

Health economists do not (or should not) assume that people are purely narrow self-interested materialists. Our focus on equity is a recognition that fairness is a concept which motivates people, even when it works against their own self-interest.

Utilitarian approach

Economics tends to take the approach that the 'greatest happiness of the greatest number' is the goal. This is an almost mathematical rule by which the size of gain is multiplied by the number of gainers, and the approach which is thought to produce the greatest sum total is selected for implementation.

An assumption that this makes is that each individual's consumption counts equally. In fact, critics say, it is unlikely to be the case that an extra year of life is worth the same to Mr Smith as it is to Mrs Black. It is also questionable whether individual gains (assuming that we can calculate them) can simply be added together without any consideration of who is gaining them.

While this is true, it is a useful and morally appealing position to act as if each person has equal weight. Furthermore, where there is evidence for different social preferences (such as an increased significance attached to treatment of young people), then weights can be applied to benefits, as carried out by the World Bank in relation to their DALY calculations (see Chapter 9).

There are few moral positions which cannot be accommodated by economics, as long as the criteria and decision-rules are clearly expressed. The only position which leaves no scope for economics is one which takes the view that certain things are absolutely right or wrong, regardless of costs. In this case, there are no trade-offs and health economists can pack up and go home. Having said that, it is hard to imagine a society actually living by such absolute rules. Even where these are stated, the reality is usually more pragmatic compromises in practice.

Goals of health policy

This brings us on to the question of what are the goals of health policy, against which we make decisions? Economists are attracted to the notion of maximising health gains, because of the assumptions of their discipline. This has various factors in its favour:

- It focuses on health, the basic good, rather than health care activities, which are a route to that end
- It emphasises effectiveness and efficiency: not just that you try, but also whether you succeed in saving lives, prolonging life, etc.
- If health is defined broadly, as in the WHO definition, it includes issues such as reassurance, comfort and dignity, which are sometimes seen as 'process utilities'
- It is a technical rule of thumb which is in theory capable of being measured and applied objectively

However, the other big goal for health economists, which has admittedly received less attention, is that of reducing health inequalities. This recognises the importance of social solidarity and the role of altruism, as discussed earlier. As argued throughout this book, distribution of benefits will determine the social welfare derived from a given set of resources. There is also an economic argument against gross inequalities in the form of the principle *of diminishing marginal returns,* which suggests that the more of a good an individual has, the less will be the value to him of an extra unit of that good. This implies that, other things being equal, a more even distribution of resources will produce more welfare than an uneven distribution.

So health economics, we would argue, has an ethical basis, with certain customary assumptions, which can however be adapted to fit different moral positions, if these are clearly elaborated. As long as social criteria are clear, economists can advise on the resource implications of reaching those goals (the 'positive' role of economists). When social criteria are not clear, which is common, economists are forced to invent them (the 'normative' role). This is legitimate, if it is clearly stated.

In many situations, health economists find themselves pointing out that public decision makers, while claiming to be following certain public goals (such as maximising health) are in fact pursuing other agendas (such as maintaining public employment). These agendas may or may not be legitimate, but they should be laid open to public scrutiny and the costs and benefits associated explored. That is the role of the health economist.

References and further reading

Mooney, G. (1998). Economics, communitarianism, and health care, in M. Barer, T. Getzen and G. Stoddart, (eds) *Health, Health care and Health Economics: Perspectives on Distribution.* Chichester: John Wiley.

Rice, T. (1998). The economics of health reconsidered, Chapter 5 in *Equity and Redistribution.* Chicago: Health Administration Press.

Sen, A. (1977). Rational fools: a critique of the behavioural foundations of economic theory, *Philosophy and Public Affairs,* 6.

Williams, A. (1988). Ethics and efficiency in the provision of health care, in J. Bell and S. Mendus (eds) *Philosophy and Medical Care.* Cambridge: Cambridge University Press.

Appendix 2

A brief history of health policy and health sector reform in developing countries

Matthew Jowett

This appendix provides an overview of major developments in health policy in developing countries over the last four decades, and their impact in terms of health sector reform. This provides a background to many of the health economics topics covered in the book.

Common themes

Since the 1960s, which were for many low income countries the early years of independence from colonial powers, there has been significant reform to the organisation and financing of health services. The objectives of these reforms can be categorised into four broad themes.

1 Changes are being made *to the way in which health services are financed*. In Chapters 4 and 5 on health finance the range of different financing mechanisms have been examined, along with observations on the impact they have had on the delivery of health services. From the perspectives of financial sustainability and efficiency, many recent reforms focus on how to capture private finances to supplement tax financing.

2 Reforms concerned with the *allocation of resources throughout the system*. For example, which levels of the health system (hospital or primary) should be prioritised? Which services should limited

budgets be spent on? From a broader perspective of improving health, should more money be spent on education, the supply of clean water or income-generating schemes? Increasingly economic analysis and evidence about the effectiveness of interventions are being taken into consideration in prioritisation decisions. Part 3 examines these issues in some detail.

3 *The way in which health services are supplied or provided.* Recent changes in the organisation of public health services, particularly in the way they are managed, have been broadly termed 'decentralisation'. Part of this movement has promoted the increased involvement of non-governmental organisations (both non-profit and for-profit) in delivering services, and reforms in the role of government. These issues are considered in Chapters 10 and 11.

4 *Equity.* Chapter 1 introduced the concept of equity as a major health policy goal. Measures of differential physical and financial access to health services amongst sub-groups of a population are often used to estimate equity. Alternatively a more outcomes-based approach of the distribution of the benefits of health services may be used.

Throughout each of these four issues is the overriding issue of the public-private mix, and the shifting balance between the two (see Chapter 10). There are four roles that government can play potentially: financing, purchasing, providing and regulating services. Under changes in recent years, government ministries are becoming less dominant in the provision of health services, private finance is playing an increasingly important role, and governments are trying to strengthen their role in developing national health policy and regulating its implementation.

Health sector reform in low income countries since the 1960s

There have been three main periods of change in policy direction in developing countries since the 1960s, with some debate over whether these actually constitute reform or not. The initial period of independence for many countries was characterised by both economic growth and much needed investment in the hardware and software of health systems, i.e., the infrastructure and human resources. Countries such as the Democratic Republic of

Congo began rebuilding new systems almost from scratch, having few of the necessary skills to provide health services. Few doctors had been trained and investments had prioritised services for the military and civilian personnel of the colonial population. As a result efforts were concentrated largely on training doctors and building hospitals. In the euphoric wave that brought new leaders to power, services were in many countries provided free of charge as a reward to supporters.

Throughout this period several countries developed health care systems that achieved health improvements far greater than other countries with similar levels of income. The experience of Sri Lanka, China, Cuba, Kerala State in India and Cost Rica provided a focus for the first major push for reform, particularly in low income countries. The achievement of 'good health at low cost' prompted a reappraisal of the best way to improve health (Halstead, 1985), culminating in the Primary Health Care declaration in 1978. In the following sections we will look in more detail at this, and other, periods of change or reform with the following reform checklist, in terms of their influence on the way in which:

- resources are raised to fund services
- resources are allocated to services
- resources are used in delivering these services
- the distribution of health benefits/equity in access is affected

Global strategy for health for all by the year 2000

The countries that signed the declaration in Alma Ata, at the WHO International Conference on Primary Health Care (PHC), agreed on five principles to guide the future development of health systems. These were:

- community participation
- health promotion
- equity
- appropriate technology
- multi-sectoral collaboration

Several of the principles are significant from the perspective of health economics. In terms of the reform checklist the following summary provides an overview:

Raising funds: The PHC declaration was not particularly concerned with the raising of resources. Government generally dominated the provision and financing of formal health services, and whilst economic growth and aid continued the issue of raising funds was not a priority.

Allocating funds: PHC was concerned with the allocation of resources. One of the primary concerns of the conference was the issue of low access to health services by the rural poor, and this provided a strong motive for promoting the redistribution of resources. The concept of health was seen very much within the context of broader human development, and the eradication of poverty and inequality. Whilst many countries extended primary level services as a result, the quality of those services has generally been low, with limited effect on access to quality services amongst the rural poor.

Delivering services: The use of appropriate technology was a key theme of PHC, based on the belief that major health gains could made through relatively simple and cheap interventions, such as oral rehydration therapy for children with diarrhoeal disease. Extending the system to the village level through cadres such as community health workers were widely introduced, with widespread attempts to involve communities in the planning of service delivery. Each of these strategies aimed to improve the effectiveness of service delivery.

Equity: Equity was at the forefront of the declaration, overlapping closely with the push for the redistribution of funds. The declaration called for resources to be shifted away from hospital facilities that largely served urban populations, and towards the expansion of a network of primary level facilities ultimately to guarantee access for the entire population. In addition the declaration called for the participation of communities in the organisation of services, such as decisions about priority-setting.

The 1980s

During the 1980s, soon after the PHC declaration, the economic context for developing countries changed dramatically. The oil crisis in 1979 which led to a 300 per cent increase in fuel prices prompted a world-wide economic recession. Together with soaring interest rates in the US and Europe, and a fall in the market price of export commodities such as tea, coffee, rubber, tin and copper, many countries found themselves in a debt trap, having to devote increasing amounts of their national income to the servicing of debt.

The ensuing recession led to falls in per capita income levels across Africa and Latin America through the 1980s, and the deteriorating economic situation gave weight to arguments that a broad comprehensive notion of PHC was simply unrealistic in terms of what governments could afford. In response arguments were put forward to focus on those elements of PHC with the greatest impact on health for the limited resources available (Walsh and Warren, 1979). In 1982 UNICEF launched its child survival revolution based on the GOBI strategy[1] which epitomised a more selective, cost-effective approach to services delivery. Through the 1980s it became clear that tax-based financing alone was insufficient to provide essential services for growing populations. In 1987 the World Bank put the arguments forward for the introduction of user charges for health services (Akin, 1987), and one year later UNICEF launched the Bamako Initiative which promoted alternative sources of financing for health services, for example, through the development of revolving drug funds (UNICEF, 1988).

Raising funds: Initiatives launched in the 1980s were primarily concerned with increasing the private financing of health services, and in doing so it was expected that financial sustainability would be improved. Ghana gives an indication of the deteriorating economic situation during this period, with real per capita health expenditure falling from US$10 in 1978 to around US$1.50 in 1983. Such situations put severe pressure on government to find supplementary funds for health services.

Allocating funds: The way in which resources were allocated was still an important issue during this period. The pressure however came from a different angle. Whereas in the previous decade there was a call for reallocations that would specifically benefit the poor, the emphasis here was that reallocations were made in favour of cost-effective interventions which in many cases still implied the greater funding of primary services.

---

1   Growth monitoring, oral rehydration therapy, breast feeding and immunisations. Later three further strategies were added: female education, family planning and food security.

Delivering services: The main focus in terms of the delivery of services was again concerned with financing issues. The severe lack of recurrent funding for services, particularly at the primary level it was argued, could be improved through capturing private financing and earmarking them for key inputs.

Equity: Whilst the various documents didn't explicitly call for the redistribution of resources, it was considered that if improved financing could be achieved, then key services could be extended, improving equity in access as a result. In addition the Bamako Initiative specifically called for greater involvement by communities in decisions about setting fee levels, and the use of revenue. In practice however community financing has often meant little more than making additional payments for health services, often along with payments for education, water and other essential services at the community level.

'Investing in Health': The World Development Report (WDR), 1993

The report 'Investing in Health' was the first development report dedicated to the health sector by the World Bank. One reason for this was its increased lending to health sectors around the world. The report drew on the experiences of previous decades and developed a measure of the burden of disease, the disability-adjusted life year (DALY), as its starting point. Following the measurement of the cost and effectiveness of a variety of interventions that tackled priority health problems, an economic analysis was conducted. The result was the selection of a 'basic package' of health services comprising both public health and clinical interventions (see Chapter 9 on priority-setting for further details).

Raising funds: The WDR set out clearly the need to raise finance from private sources. However it also acknowledged the problems related to user charges, suggesting they should only be used to finance non-essential services, stressing that even then they would work only when service quality increased as a result. The development of insurance was seen as an important future method of health service financing.

Allocating funds: On the basis of the minimum package of services identified in the report, it was proposed that governments redirect their resources from the many inappropriate services currently provided, in particular at the tertiary level. It was estimated that even given typical levels of health expenditure in low income countries, by redirecting public funds to the package of services identified, the burden of disease could be reduced by 25 per cent.

Delivering services: The report was particularly interested in improving technical efficiency in the delivery of services, and called for increased involvement of the private sector. Possible strategies included selling public hospitals to the private sector, and contracting out services to autonomous providers in order to promote supply-side competition. In terms of the public delivery of health services it was proposed that the decentralisation of management would mean more responsive and less bureaucratic service delivery.

Equity: The WDR, 1993 was unequivocal in promoting universal access to a minimum packages of key health services. By publicly financing these key interventions, and providing them free at the point of service, access by the poor would be improved. Beyond this package of publicly affordable services however, private financing and provision, it was argued, should take over. The consequences of this would be the emergence of a two-tiered system (which, many would argue, was already the case).

Sustainability and the sector-wide approach (SWAp)

In addition to concern with strategies for improving the performance of health systems in developing countries, attention has in recent years turned to the process of giving aid itself. The introduction of the sector-wide approach in countries such as Bangladesh, Ghana and Ethiopia aims to harmonise and streamline the flow of funds and information between donors and recipient governments (Peters and Chao, 1998). The process of applying for donor funds, frameworks for the expenditure of funds, and reporting on activities, are agreed on by donors and governments together, in order to reduce bureaucracy and speed up the disbursement of funds.

More significantly, however, the sector-wide approach requires a change in the relationship between donors and recipient governments. The process is led by the recipient government, with technical support and additional analysis provided by donor agencies in a co-ordinated fashion, for example through joint-donor activities. Building planning capacity in recipient governments is also a specific aim of the sector-wide approach. Once an overall plan for the health sector has been agreed, donors funds will be channelled away from specific projects and into a national fund, together with government allocations (see Box A2.1). The aim of the approach is to move away from a focus on the sustainability of individual projects (e.g., expanded programmes of immunisation), and to adopt a system-wide view of sustainability. Whilst there is broad agreement on the goals of this process it will take several years for both donors and recipient governments to test the approach in practice.

Summary

The focus of reforms in recent decades have generally been in one of four areas, namely the financing of health services, the allocation of resources, the strategies used to deliver services, and equity in access to services. In the past ten years health reform has been closely associated with the introduction of markets in health care, including greater private financing and provision, and the introduction of supply-side competition. Despite this the common theme of allocating greater resources to primary level services has run through the major changes in health policy since the Alma Ata declaration in 1978, although the driving forces and strategies promoted in order to achieve them have differed.

The sector-wide approach currently being adopted in many countries has three main aims: first, to streamline the aid process, minimising the work involved in accessing and reporting on loans and grants, and hence speeding up disbursements; secondly, to strengthen planning and management capacity in the recipient governments; and, thirdly, to promote a more sustainable allocation of resources through the health system by ensuring a system-wide focus rather than one focused on individual projects.

Box A2.1   The Health Sector Development Programme in Ethiopia

In Ethiopia the Health Sector Development Programme was launched in 1996, with a 20 year vision, and detailed planning for the first five years. Given the extremely low access to health services of the population (48 per cent within 10kms of a health facility), low quality primary level services, and extremely low utilisation (0.27 contacts per person per year, compared with a common rate of 2.5 in developing countries as a whole), a major focus of the plan was to expand the number of primary health facilities. The plan was estimated at 5 billion Birr (approximately US$750 million) for the five years, and a process of three joint-donor missions, led by the World Bank, was conducted over an eight month period.

At the initial meeting, plans were presented by the each of the eleven provincial health authorities with separate plans for the central MoH, and the country as a whole. On the donor side a range of technical experts (e.g., human resource planners, architects, financing specialists) discussed and gave support to regional staff on the relevant section of the plan. Plans were further refined at the second and third meetings until a plan acceptable to all parties was agreed. A financial and economic analysis of the health system nationally was conducted, rather than at individual programme or region level. The affordability of the plan was based on two key assumptions: that donors would actually disburse the funds pledged during the time period, and that government forecasts of economic growth and income would hold true. It was therefore necessary to build flexibility into the system that allowed reviews and adjustments on an annual basis.

One of the main issues during the process was the balance of recurrent to capital funding. Once a more sustainable balance had been achieved, it became clear that donor pledges were greater than capital investments, meaning implying that their funds would be used for recurrent inputs, something donors were reluctant to do. In addition some donors wanted certain funds to remain outside the 'national fund', over which they would have more direct control. From the government side there was a strong desire to move very quickly to having full control over donor funds, which in effect would increase demands on them for financial accounting, which they had limited capacity to deliver.

Source: Adapted from Jowett, 1998.

References and further reading

Akin, J. (1987). *Financing Health Services in Developing Countries: An Agenda for Reform.* Geneva: World Bank.

Gilson, L. and Mills, A. (1995). Health sector reforms in sub-Saharan Africa: lessons of the last 10 years, *Health Policy*, 32: 215–243.

Halstead, B. (1985). *Good Health at Low Cost.* New York: Rockerfeller Foundation.

Jowett, M. (1998). Economic Analysis: Health Sector Development Programme 1997–2002, Ethiopia. Unpublished consultancy report to the World Bank.

Newbrander, W. C. and Thomason, J. A. (1989). Alternatives for financing health services in Papua New Guinea, *Health Policy and Planning*, 4(2): 131–140.

Peters, D. and Chao, S. (1998). The sector-wide approach in health: What is it? Where is it leading? *International Journal of Health Planning and Management*, 13: 177–190.

Sen, K. and Koivusalo, M. (1998). Health care reforms and developing countries – a critical overview, *International Journal of Health Planning and Management*, 13(3): 199–215.

Unicef (1988). *The Bamako Initiative.* New York: Unicef.

Walsh, J. A. and Warren, K. (1979). Selective primary health care – an interim strategy for disease control in developing countries. *New England Journal of Medicine*, 301: 967–974.

Appendix 3

Glossary of common health economic terms

Ability to pay   The capacity of an individual or organisation to pay for a good or service. See also *willingness to pay*, which may sometimes be higher than ability, leading to borrowing or indebtedness.

Acceptability   Degree to which a service meets the cultural needs and standards of a community. This in turn will affect utilisation of that service.

Accessibility   Extent to which a service is easy to use for its intended clients. This will depend on a number of factors, such as its costs (see *affordability*), its distance from them, the way in which services are organised, etc.

Adverse selection   A situation where individuals are able to purchase insurance at rates which are below actuarially fair rates, because information known to them is not available to insurers (see *asymmetric information*).

Affordability   Extent to which the intended clients of a service can pay for it. This will depend on their income distribution, the cost of services and the financing mechanism (e.g., whether risks are pooled; whether exemptions exist for the low-paid, etc.).

Agency relationship   A situation in which one person (agent) makes decisions on behalf of another person (principal).

Allocation (of costs)   Deciding how much of different inputs are involved in producing a given output, such as a specific treatment or diagnostic test. The purpose is usually to produce a realistic estimate of the full cost of providing the service, so that managers can identify efficiency improvements and prioritise between services or different delivery strategies.

Allocative efficiency   Inputs or outputs are put to the best possible use in the economy so that no further gains in output or welfare are possible. (See *efficiency*, *technical efficiency*).

Altruism   Caring for others. The implication is that my welfare will be affected not only by factors which affect me personally but also by changes in the welfare of others. At a group level this corresponds to 'social solidarity', which motivates the search for accessibility, affordability, equity, etc. of services.

Annuitisation   Process by which a *capital cost* is converted into an annual cost, by dividing the overall cost by the number of expected life years (annualisation), and adjusting for the *discount rate.*

Asymmetric information   Situations in which the parties on the opposite sides of a transaction have differing amounts of relevant information.

Audit   Originally the process by which the probity of operations and activities of an organisation was examined (*internal audit*) and a report on the annual accounts produced (*external audit*). Now used more widely, e.g., *clinical audit* evaluates the effectiveness of clinical activities; *management audit* the effectiveness and efficiency of organisational and management arrangements, etc.

Average cost   Average cost equals total cost divided by the quantity of output. Total cost represents the sum of all *fixed costs* and *variable costs.*

Average length of stay (ALOS)   The average number of days a patient stays in hospital.

Bamako Initiative   Programme promoted by UNICEF in the late 1980s to generate funds for drugs and other recurrent costs by developing a range of community financing schemes, including the operation of revolving drug funds by health centres.

Bed occupancy   The number of beds occupied by patients at a particular time, expressed as a percentage of available beds or as the number of days each bed is occupied each year.

Bed turnover   The average number of patients using each bed in a given period, such as a year.

Bias   Deviation of results or inferences from the truth, or processes leading to such deviation. Any trend in the collection, analysis, interpretation, publication, or review of data that can lead to conclusions that are systematically different from the truth.

Block contracts   Like *capitation* in a primary care setting, these specify which services are to be provided, and to whom, and the total payment to be made, but without fixing the volume of services to be delivered.

Burden of disease (studies)   Measurement of premature mortality (deaths) and morbidity (non-fatal illness) in a given area. The aim of the study is usually to define which illnesses or risk factors are most significant in causing death and disability and hence to inform decisions about which services should receive priority. On its own, however, it is inadequate as a decision tool as it omits the issue of effectiveness of prevention or treatment strategies and the cost of implementing them.

Capital costs   Expenditure on goods which last longer than one year, such as investment in equipment or infrastructure.

Capitation   A method of reimbursement under which a provider is paid a fixed amount per person, regardless of the volume of services rendered.

Case-based payments   Where providers are reimbursed according to the number of patients treated, regardless of the number of services provided for each patient. These may be adjusted for complexity of case.

Case fatality (or morbidity) rate (CFR)   The proportion of cases of a specific condition which are fatal within a specified period. CFR (given as a percentage) = number of deaths from a disease in a given period, divided by number of diagnosed cases of that disease in the same period.

Case-mix   A measure of the assortment of patient cases treated by a given hospital, indicating the degree of complexity of the cases.

Civil society organisations (CSOs)   Organisations which are not part of the government structure but which play some public role and which are not profit-motivated. Not-for-profit providers, such as mission hospitals, consumer lobby groups, and community organisations are all examples of CSOs.

Clinical audit   Also known as medical audit. The critical analysis of the procedures used for diagnosis and treatment, the use of resources and the outcome for the patient.

Coinsurance (rate)   The share of costs which are paid by the beneficiary of a health policy (often after some *deductible*).

Command economy   Where the government decides how much of each good should be produced, how and for whom. The opposite to the '*free market*' paradigm, in which prices are set purely by the force of supply and demand. In reality, though, few economies operate in either of these two pure ways: more common are planned markets, regulated markets or managed markets, with varying degrees of involvement of government in market operations and outcomes.

Commissioning   Refers to the role of the purchaser in a system where purchasers and providers are not in a vertically integrated bureaucracy (see *purchaser-provider split*). Their role includes assessing the health needs of the population; examining cost effective interventions to meet those needs; comparing this with the existing pattern of services and on the basis of that preparing health priorities; negotiating with providers to provide the relevant services or quality improvements; and monitoring the performance of those providers.

Community financing   A wide variety of risk pooling and prepayment schemes introduced in developing countries to fill in gaps in the financing of health care. (See also *Bamako Initiative.*)

Community participation   The involvement of community representatives in setting priorities in the health sector and promoting health. This is a major strand of the *PHC* philosophy. It is sometimes confused with two separate issues: (a) the pragmatic need to shift some of the cost of services onto households and individuals; and (b) the empowerment of individuals to take responsibility for their own health.

Community rating   Insurance term: all members of a scheme are charged the same premium, regardless of their risk status.

Complements   Goods which are normally consumed together, so that an increase in the price of one will lead to a decrease in demand for the other.

Compounding   The process by which $1 now is given its future value, calculated according to the number of years and the annual discount rate.

Comprehensive vs selective PHC   The debate over whether *Primary Health Care* has to be implemented as a whole, or whether, in resource constrained situations, certain priority programmes can be singled out for funding. This debate, which started in the 1980s as a reaction to the power of various vertically managed programmes, continues today in relation to '*essential (basic) packages*' of services.

Compulsory health insurance   Health insurance under an obligatory public scheme. Payment for such an insurance amounts to a tax. Employers may have to pay contributions on behalf of their employees. Contributions are usually income-related. CHI is usually, but not always, administered by a public body.

Contestability   A term used in 'thin' markets, where no actual competitor exists, but where there are potential competitors able to step in if a firm fails. It is argued that this generates pressure to perform, even though there is currently no rival.

Contingent valuation   A method of eliciting the value set by individuals on such goods as life and health. A variety of methods have been developed to convert such *intangible* benefits or costs into monetary figures, in order to compare with other possible activities.

Contract   A legally agreement between purchaser and provider, usually specifying which services are to be provided, at what cost and with what minimum quality. (See also *performance contracts, block contracts, cost and volume contracts,* and *cost per case contracts.*)

Contracting out   The process by which work which was previously carried out by public sector employees is shifted to the private sector, but with the state continuing to finance it and to lay down specifications about the type, quantity and quality of the service being provided. Commonly it is the non-clinical services which are easiest to contract out, but clinical contracts are becoming more common too.

Copayment   Amounts paid by the insurance beneficiary as a result of *coinsurance* and *deductibles.*

Cost-benefit analysis(CBA)   A method of comparing the monetary value of all benefits of a project with all costs of that project.

Cost and volume contracts   These specify the type and level of services required by the purchaser. If fewer services are provided, some of the payment can be withheld. On the other hand, if levels are exceeded, additional payments will be made to providers, according to some pre-agreed scale.

Cost per case contracts   These set the cost of specific treatments only, with no limits on total payments or eventual volume of services.

Cost control   Ability to limit the resources used in a particular service or sector. This is one of the criteria frequently used to judge health sector performance (along with *efficiency, equity, acceptability,* etc.).

Cost-effectiveness analysis (CEA)   A method of comparing the costs of a project with the benefits, measured in terms of a social objective. Something which is cost effective achieves relatively high gains for relatively low costs, compared with other possible ways of achieving that goal.

Cost minimisation study   This assumes that two strategies or interventions achieve exactly the same effect. The study therefore focuses on costing each option in order to find out which one is the least costly. This will identify the most desirable option, assuming that important alternatives have not been omitted and that the benefits are indeed identical.

Cost-sharing   Methods of financing health care which require some direct payments for services by patients. (See also *copayment.*)

Cost-utility analysis (CUA)   A method of comparing the costs of a social project with the benefits, measured in terms of an overall index of both quantity and quality of life gained (see, for example, *QALYs*). This avoids the need to convert social benefits into monetary terms, but at the same time allows for comparisons between programmes with differing social objectives. However, collecting reliable information on changes to quality of life is relatively difficult.

Coverage (rates)   The proportion of the estimated target population which has been reached. These are often used in relation to preventive programmes, where target populations can be more easily estimated.

Cream skimming   Practice by which insurers or doctors discourage patients with expensive needs from joining their scheme or practice in order to protect their profit margins. Even if illegal, it can be achieved by subtle means such as having poor access to facilities for the elderly or disabled.

Decentralisation   Shift of power and/or of functions from the centre to the local level, however defined. This policy, which can have many different motivations and forms, is commonly thought to increase the effectiveness and accountability of services.

Deductible The amount of health care charges for which a beneficiary is responsible before the insurer begins payment.

Demand The quantity of a good purchased at any given price.

Demographic transition Shift from high fertility (usually with high infant mortality rates) to families producing fewer children who survive longer. This change is associated with improvements in health status, education, the status of women and changing employment patterns.

Depreciation The change in the value of a good over time, due to its deteriorating physical state or it being superseded by new technology.

Derived need Health is a direct need, as people desire it in itself. Health care, by contrast, is not inherently desirable: people only seek health care when ill-health arises. It is therefore a need which is 'derived from' a direct need, and while the direct need is constant, the derived need is sporadic and hard to predict.

Diagnosis-Related Groups (DRGs) A set of case types established under the *prospective payment system,* identifying patients with similar conditions and processes of care. Used for setting charges for different health care interventions.

Diminishing marginal returns/utility The idea that, other things being equal, the more of a good an individual has, the less will be the value to him or her of an extra unit of that good.

Direct costs This term is used differently in different contexts. In allocating costs in hospitals, direct costs are the costs which are incurred by patient departments (producing final outcomes), as opposed to the paraclinic, support and overhead departments (which produce intermediary goods). In evaluations, however, the distinction is being made between costs which are actually paid by the health service or patients, as opposed to the *opportunity costs* of time and production lost as a result of treatment (termed *indirect costs*), which are also real but are often omitted from consideration.

Disability-adjusted life year (DALY) Concept developed by the World Bank and WHO to measure the burden of disease, in terms of both premature death and disability. With adequate data, it can be used to compare potential health gain from different disease control programmes and thus to prioritise resource allocation according to cost effectiveness principles.

Discounting/Discount rate The process of converting sums to be received at a future date to a present value. The interest rate which is used is called the discount rate. It should be based on the social *time preference* rate which applies in that group.

Economic evaluation   Systematic comparison of all relevant costs and benefits of a programme to inform decision-making and maximise technical and allocative efficiency.

Economics   The study of how a society with limited resources decides what goods to produce, how to produce them, and how to distribute them among its members.

Economies of scale   Situations in which the *long-run* average costs of a firm are declining as output is increasing.

Economies of scope   Situations in which a firm can jointly produce two or more goods more cheaply than under separate production of the goods.

Effectiveness   The extent to which a specific intervention, procedure, regimen or service, when deployed in the field, does what it is intended to do for a defined population.

Efficacy   The extent to which a specific intervention, procedure, regimen, or service produces a beneficial result under ideal conditions. Ideally, the determination of efficacy is based on the results of a *randomised controlled trial.*

Efficiency   When the firm produces the maximum possible sustained output from a given set of inputs this is known as *technical efficiency.* By contrast, *allocative efficiency* is used to describe a situation in which either inputs or outputs are put to their best possible uses in the economy so that no further gains in output or welfare are possible.

Elasticity   Percentage change in some dependent variable (e.g., quantity demanded) resulting from a one per cent change in some independent variable (e.g., price). Elasticities which exceed one in absolute value are considered elastic; elasticities less than one are inelastic.

Epidemiology   Study of the distribution and determinants of disease in human populations.

Equilibrium price (quantity)   The price (quantity) at which the quantity demanded and quantity supplied are equal.

Equity   At its most general, equity means being fair or just. How to judge that is subjective and controversial, and involves value judgements. However, one common understanding is that everyone should have equal access (both geographical and financial) to existing health care facilities and services. A common distinction is drawn between *horizontal equity* – which means treating people with the same needs equally – and *vertical equity* – which means that people with unequal needs should be treated unequally.

Essential drugs   A policy initiative to ensure that a minimal number of effective drugs is available to treat priority health problems at a cost which can be afforded by the community. A related aim is to save the resources used by prescribing more expensive or even unnecessary drugs.

Essential (or basic) package This developed out of the World Development Report of 1993. Given the shortage of resources for health in developing countries and the high burden of disease, it suggested that public funds be concentrated on a defined range of highly cost-effective services. These are often called 'essential packages'. The term is a relative one, as what is deemed essential in a wealthy context may be a luxury in a poorer one.

Ethics Branch of philosophy concerned with the concepts of right and wrong, and how we judge them.

Exemptions Rules allowing certain groups in society (often lower income groups) not to pay charges or insurance premia. The difficulty lies in defining which categories should be exempt and in monitoring the system.

Externality A case in which a consumer (producer) affects the utility (costs) of another consumer (producer) through actions which lie outside the price system.

Factors of production The inputs which are required to produce any good. At a general level, these are divided into labour, land and capital (both finance and equipment).

Fee-for-service (FFS) A method of payment under which the provider is paid for each procedure or service that is provided to a patient.

Firm Any entity that transforms inputs into some product or service that is sold in the marketplace.

Fixed costs Costs which do not vary with output. They are expressed either as total fixed cost (TFC) or average fixed cost (AFC).

Fixed budget Budget which is set in advance for a period. Traditionally health budgets were based on historical precedent and were not only fixed in total but also in their internal break-down by line item. This is likely to lead to inequity and technical inefficiency. Consequently some countries are now experimenting with budgets based on *case-mix* and with some freedom to shift resources within them. (See *global budget*).

Free markets A term used to denote an economy in which government plays little role in production and distribution of goods. It is misleading to the extent that all markets require rules and regulations to function effectively, and in that sense cannot be totally 'free'. (See also *command economy*).

Fundholding Refers to UK experiment whereby primary care doctors (GPs) were given the budget for their patients for secondary care so that they could either provide simpler referral services themselves or choose a suitable provider. This approach is now being modified with the introduction of 'primary care purchasing groups' .

General Practitioner (GP)   A UK term, meaning a general doctor, or family doctor, who is the first point of contact with health services for all non-emergency cases. GPs in the UK are self-employed but contracted by the government to provide a range of basic diagnostic, preventive and curative services. They refer cases as appropriate to hospital-based specialists. (See *fundholding*.)

Global budget   An aggregate cash sum, fixed in advance (usually for 1 year), intended to cover the total costs of a service, whatever the eventual work load. It is sometimes used to mean a budget whose sum is fixed, but where the budget-holder has discretion to re-allocate amounts between budget headings within it.

Good   Economic term, meaning a commodity whose consumption provides utility for individuals

Gross National Product (GNP)/ Gross Domestic Product (GDP)   GNP is the current value of all final goods and services produced by a country during a year. GDP is a closely related measure which includes the value associated only with domestic factors of production.

Health   Can be defined narrowly as the absence of illness, or more broadly as the 'state of complete physical, mental and social well-being', as the WHO Constitution declares.

Health care   Goods and services used as inputs to produce health. In some analyses, one's own time and knowledge used to maintain and promote health are considered in addition to conventional health care inputs.

Health economics   The study of the value of health and how it can be produced most efficiently and distributed to maximise social welfare.

Health Maintenance Organisation (HMO)   An organisation which, in return for a prepaid premium, provides an enrollee with comprehensive health benefits for a given period of time.

Health sector reform   A substantial change to the structure or processes of health services, with the intention of improving outcomes.

Health status   Measures of the physical and emotional well-being of an individual or a defined population. (See also *morbidity rate* and *mortality rate*.)

Homogenous product   Where goods are of a similar kind and quality, so that a comparison of their price is valid.

Horizontal equity   The principle that those who have similar incomes should contribute a similar amount (in financing health services), while those with similar needs should receive similar levels of benefit (in terms of access, quality of care, type of treatment, etc.). (See *vertical equity*.)

Hotel costs   The costs of food, heating, maintenance etc. for keeping a patient in hospital, excluding all medical and treatment costs.

Human capital   The durable labour skills obtained by investment in a person through education, training, health and so forth.

Human capital approach   Method of valuing lives gained in terms of the discounted productive capacity of the patients treated.

Incentives   Systems which reward and therefore tend to encourage certain types of activity.

Incidence   Epidemiological term meaning the number of new cases of a disease in a given population in a given period (usually per 1,000 people per year). (See also *prevalence.*)

Income effect   The effect on quantity demanded that results from the change in real income associated with a relative change in the price of the good or service under study. (See also *substitution effect.*)

Income elasticity of demand   Percentage change in quantity demanded resulting from a one per cent change in income. (See also *elasticity.*)

Indirect costs   Usually used in economic evaluation, to indicate the *opportunity costs* of production or leisure time lost in order to undergo treatment.

Infant mortality rate (IMR)   The ratio of the number of deaths in infants (aged one year or less) during a year divided by the number of live births during the year. The equivalent for under-5s is the child mortality rate (CMR).

Inferior good   A good or service for which demand decreases as income increases. (See also *normal* and *superior goods.*)

Informal payments   Payments which are not officially set by health providers. These take many forms. They may be monetary or in kind. They may be for clinical or non-clinical services (e.g., food). They may be voluntary or compulsory (i.e., treatment is withheld if they are not paid). They may be flexible or a fairly fixed tariff. They may go to individual staff or be used by the institution as a whole. They may provide a small top-up income or the largest portion of the facility's budget. Their shared feature is that they are not legally mandated and cannot be enforced in a court of law.

In-patient   A patient who has been admitted to hospital and is occupying a bed in an in-patient department.

Insurance   Pooling risks with others in order to spread costs of health care (or other commodity) over time and protect against catastrophically expensive illness. (See also *voluntary health insurance, compulsory health insurance,* and *social insurance.*)

Intangible costs   Usually used in economic evaluation, to indicate features like pain, anxiety or grief, which are very important, but hard to measure or value and compare with other costs and benefits.

Life expectancy   Average length of life for a population as a whole, ranging from 79 years in Japan (1991 figures) to 39 in Guinea Buissau.

Long run   A period of time sufficient to permit a firm to vary all factors of production. (See also *short run.*)

Luxury good   A good that people tend to buy proportionately less of as price rises, so that its *price elasticity* of demand is negative and greater than one.

Macroeconomics   Looking at the operation of the economy as a whole.

Managed care   A term encompassing a broad set of actions which a firm or insurer establishes to reduce costs.

Marginal   Produced by an increase of one unit.

Marginal cost   The increase in total cost resulting from a one unit increase in output.

Marginal utility   The extra utility gained from consuming one more unit of a good, holding others constant. Utility is a measure of the satisfaction from consuming goods.

Market failure   Refers to all the ways in which a specific market may not meet the conditions for social optimality. For example, if there are barriers to entry, or a lack of information about the product, then that market will fail to produce the best possible outcome. The equivalent for bureaucracies is 'government failure': the ways in which a bureaucratic approach may fail to optimise social welfare.

Market structure   How an industry is organised in terms of the number and distribution firms and how firms compete among themselves.

Merit good   A good which public authorities want to encourage people to consume.

Meta-analysis   Using statistical methods to combine the results of different studies. It involves qualitative measures to select the studies to be used, and quantitative methods in combining them to produce statistically significant results. It runs the risk of several biases.

Microeconomics   Looking at interactions in a specific market or for a specific good.

Monopoly   Literally: single seller. Situation in which a firm faces a negatively sloped demand curve. In a pure monopoly, there is no other firm which produces a close substitute   for the firm's product. Thus the demand curve facing the monopolist is the market demand curve.

Monopoly profit (rent)   The return over and above a normal profit resulting from monopoly power.

Monopsony Literally: single buyer. Situation in which a firm faces a positively sloped supply curve in the product or factor market.

Moral hazard An insurance term. Where services are not paid for directly by individuals, they may take risks or act in a way which increases the demand for health services. It is in insurers' interests to create disincentives to such behaviour (such as *copayments* or risk-rated *premia*).

Morbidity rate The rate of incidence of disease in a particular population.

Mortality rate The death rate for a particular population. The crude death rate is the ratio of deaths during a year divided by midyear population. Because age is so important, the age-adjusted mortality rate is a measure which takes into account a population's age distribution.

Multisectoral approach This is an important element of PHC. It recognises that health is determined by factors beyond health services and that promoting good health therefore requires action by many institutional players, including in the fields of education, water and sanitation, environmental safety, housing, employment, social security, and general economic management. Intersectoral collaboration on strategies for promoting health is, however, an ideal which is easier to state than achieve.

National health accounts Methodology for tracking all sources of finance for health-oriented programmes and how these funds are disbursed.

Necessity A good whose consumption does not vary greatly with changes in price – i.e., a good with an *price elasticity* of demand of less than (minus)one.

Needs What a person requires in terms of health care. Judged subjectively this is often called *wants*, to distinguish it from an objective judgement about appropriate treatment. Commonly needs are judged by a professional, which introduces a different kind of bias. These are distinguished from what is actually purchased, which is *demand.*

Needs assessment Collecting information about the pattern of illness in an area and matching this to the existing services to determine priorities for service development. The process should also take into account the quality of services and the factors underlying their current level of utilisation by patients (e.g., if they are not using them, why not?).

Net present value (NPV) The sum of benefits or cash flows in different years in the future, discounted according to the year in which they are due to take place.

Nominal value The money value measured in current dollars. (See also *real value.*)

Normal good   A good or service for which demand increases in proportion as income or price increase.

Normative   Involving value judgements about public priorities. This is contrasted with 'positive economics', in which economists advise on the implications of different strategies for achieving given public goals.

Opportunity cost   The value of the best alternative which is forgone in order to get or produce more of the commodity under consideration.

Optimality   A productive arrangement which produces the greatest possible welfare for a given set of inputs.

Option appraisal   A defined series of steps for reaching a decision on a given problem. It is a management tool which aims to ensure that all important options are considered in a systematic and transparent way so that the likelihood of choosing an appropriate solution is maximised.

Outcome   The effect on health status of a health care intervention, or lack of intervention.

Outpatient   A patient attending for treatment or a consultation, but not staying overnight in a hospital.

Payment systems   Way in which medical institutions or staff are paid for their work. These will set certain incentives and encourage certain patterns of health care provision. The most common types are: *salaries, fee-for-service, capitation, target payments, case-based payments, fixed budgets,* and *contracts.*

Payroll taxes   Taxes which are specifically earmarked for a sector, like health. Distinguished from *social insurance* because entitlement is not limited to those who have paid contributions.

Perfect competition   A market structure in which there are (a) numerous buyers and sellers, (b) perfect information, (c) free entry and exit, and (d) a homogeneous product, (e) equal costs faced by producers, (f) no economies of scale and scope, and (g) mobile factors of production.

Performance measures   These can be applied to institutions or individuals. For example, how well is one hospital doing, compared with another? How well is a doctor working, compared with his or her colleagues? These questions call for agreement on what the priorities are. For example, if cost-cutting is the key, then a low ratio of inputs to outputs may be the focus. If there is strong competition for patients, on the other hand, then patient satisfaction may feature highly. High levels of activity may seem a good thing, but what is the cost in terms of quality? In terms of outcomes, is the goal to have low rates of failure, or do you want to maximise health gain? It is a challenge to agree priorities and avoid *perverse incentives* in setting up performance measures.

Perverse incentives   Where your system of rewards unintentionally encourages behaviour of an undesirable kind (e.g., paying according to the number of patients seen. Its aim may be to increase staff productivity. One result will almost certainly be lower quality treatment for patients.)

Premium   Payment for voluntary insurance. These may be community-rated (averaged across a group of individuals) or risk-rated (tailored to the claims experience or actuarial risk of each individual).

Prevalence   Epidemiological term meaning the number of cases of an illness per 1,000 population per year. (See also *incidence*.)

Price discrimination   Supplying the same good at the same time, but at a different price, according to the consumer's willingness to pay.

Price elasticity of demand/supply   Percentage change in quantity demanded (supplied) resulting from a 1 per cent change in price. (See also *elasticity*.)

Price index   Expresses the current prices of a group of goods relative to the prices of these goods in a base year. A price index, often used to convert *nominal values* (i.e., current prices) to *real values*, shows how much prices of those goods have changed since the base year.

Primary care   In a system with a gatekeeper, all initial (non-emergency) consultations with doctors, nurses or other health staff are termed primary care, as opposed to *secondary care* or referral services. In systems with direct access to specialists, the distinction is usually based on facilities, with health centres, for example, providing primary care and hospitals secondary care. (See also *primary health care.*)

Primary health care (PHC)   According to WHO, PHC is essential health care made accessible at a cost which the country and community can afford, with methods that are practical, scientifically sound and socially acceptable. It is a normative concept, implying *accessibility* for all, *community participation* and the importance of health promotion and a *multisectoral approach* to the production of health.

Priority setting   Deciding the relative importance attached to alternative goals or activities in a given setting. It is often connected with resource shortages and the need to *ration* care.

Private sector   Usually refers to organisations which are not managed by the state. Covers a wide spectrum of profit and not-for-profit organisations; formal and informal; competing with public facilities for customers or complementary, etc.

Privatisation   In the West and transitional economies, this usually means an active process of transfer of facilities from public to private management, often accompanied by a change in financing systems away from general taxation. In developing countries, however, the change is often more passive and bottom-up. Constrained supply and poor quality often leads consumers to turn to the private providers, who may be public health workers moonlighting, drug sellers, traditional healers, mission hospitals or private clinics. The shift to private suppliers may be reinforced by *contracting out* or other policies designed to increase the role of the private sector.

Productivity   The output produced for a given input.

Programme budgeting   Structuring budgets according to the type of output, or programme, which is being produced, rather than the traditional approach which divides by input categories (staff, supplies, etc.).

Progressive (tax)   Tax or other form of financing in which the percentage of the contribution to be paid rises with rising income levels. (See *regressive*).

Prospective payment system (PPS)   The method of hospital reimbursement used by Medicare in the US from 1983 under which hospitals were reimbursed a fixed amount for each patient treated, according to their *diagnosis-related groups (DRGs)*.

Provider   An organisation which provides health care, such as a primary care doctor or a hospital, and sells its services to purchasers.

Public good (pure)   A good (e.g., national defence) that no one can be prevented from consuming (non-excludable), and that can be consumed by one person without depleting it for another (non-rival). The marginal cost of providing the good to another consumer is zero.

Purchaser-provider split   Where the purchasers and providers of health care go from being vertically integrated in a bureaucratic system to being autonomous bodies which deal with each other through contracts for work. This aims to introduce competitive pressures into the public sector (see *quasi-markets*), although it may also significantly increase *transaction costs.*

Purchasing power parity   Adjusting exchange rate conversions to reflect the fact that a US dollar, say, may buy more in terms of an basket of goods in one country than another. This is caused by differences in the price of non-traded goods between the two countries.

Qualitative surveys   These focus not on the collection of 'hard data' (how much? How many? How often, etc?) but on factors such as motivation, perceptions, beliefs. They therefore tend to use different techniques, such as semi- or unstructured interviews and focus group discussions. They are complementary to quantitative surveying in providing explanations for the figures gathered in the latter.

Quality How 'good' a service is – something which can be considered from different perspectives. There are objective medical standards: was the correct procedure followed? What about outcomes: did the patient get better/ achieve the expected health gain? From the patient's point of view, was the procedure well managed? Were staff courteous? Were they given appropriate information, etc?

Quality-adjusted life year (QALY) – a measure of health gain which aims to measure life years added but also the quality of life which is achieved in those years. This is one measure used in *cost-utility analysis*. Another is the *DALY* – a narrower definition, but easier to measure.

Quasi (or internal) markets Refers to reforms undertaken over the last decade in countries like the UK to introduce market-style competition into the public sector. The aim is to keep the virtues of the public sector (public health goals, universal access, etc.) while increasing efficiency.

Randomised controlled trial (RCT) A trial to establish the efficacy of a given medical treatment, in which patients are identified according to strict eligibility criteria and randomly allocated to a treatment or control group; the assessors of outcomes are also usually 'blind' – i.e., unaware of which group each patient belongs to. The aim of these procedures is to remove biases and increase the accuracy of the trial results.

Rational maximiser Assumption made in economics that individuals have two key characteristics: (a) they can and do make use of available information to draw appropriate conclusions; and (b) they seek to maximise their welfare by achieving the greatest possible consumption of goods valued by them.

Rationing Restricting supply of services according to implicit or explicit criteria, where demand exceeds supply. It implies the absence of fully functioning market mechanisms to link demand with supply.

Real value Monetary values that are adjusted for changes in the general level of prices relative to some arbitrarily selected base year. (See also *nominal value.*)

Recurrent cost ratios The ratio of the annual recurrent costs generated by a piece of equipment or a facility and its capital cost (i.e., purchase or replacement cost). Average cost ratios are sometimes used as a tool to plan for the costs of running a service, though the ideal is to work out actual costs for a given situation.

Recurrent expenditure Expenditure which has to be incurred during each budget period (usually a year), such as on salaries, drugs, supplies, provision and maintenance.

Regressive (tax)   Form of tax or other financing in which the proportion of income paid falls with rising income levels.

Regulation   Government intervention in the functioning of markets. Can be interpreted narrowly as bureaucratic measures such as rules, backed by legal sanctions, or more broadly to include economic signals such as subsidies, taxes and incentives.

Rent seeking   Parasitic activity – deriving revenue from a position of monopoly, rather than from productive activities.

Resource allocation   In a general sense, all of health economics is concerned with resource allocation issues. However, this term is often used more narrowly to refer to the system by which recurrent funds (and sometimes staff) are divided between different geographical regions. Some kind of population-based formula is preferable to infrastructure-led spending, which tends to perpetuate inequity.

Returns to scale (increasing, decreasing, or constant)   Refers to the relationship between the number of units being produced and their unit cost. If the unit cost remain the same, regardless of the number being produced, then that is called 'constant returns to scale'. If unit costs increase as production increases, then you have 'decreasing returns to scale'. Conversely, if unit costs decrease as production size increases, then you have 'increasing returns to scale' and a situation where large manufacturers have an inherent advantage.

Rigidity   Usually refers to prices, in situations where markets do not allow them to vary in the short term. For example, a fall in demand for labour in a recession may not result in immediate decreases in wages where long term agreements exist between employers and employees and where trade unions are powerful.

Risk aversion   The degree to which a certain income is preferred to a risky alternative with the same expected income.

Risk pooling   Process by which people contribute to a general fund, from which they can be reimbursed if the need arises. This is the basis for all insurance funds. The costs of illness are then shared between members of the fund (thus risks are pooled).

Risk rating   Insurance term by which an individual's premium is linked to the likelihood of them incurring health expenditures in future (i.e., their expected ill health, based on information about their past record, genetic factors or lifestyle). Risk rating can also be applied to a larger group, such as a community.

Salary   Monthly payment to health staff which is fixed, regardless of the quantity or quality of their work. To counter the low incentives for productivity, bonus schemes are sometimes added to reward performance (however defined).

Secondary care   Care provided by medical specialists, usually in a hospital setting (see *primary care*), but also some specialist services provided in the community.

Sector wide action programmes (SWAps) Instruments for co-ordinating national plans for health sector development with funding by international donors. SWAps aim to increase the involvement of recipient governments in planning health sector development, reduce the burden of multiple reporting requirements of donors, and focus on the sustainability of the sector as a whole.

Semi-variable costs Costs which increase as output increases, but unevenly, as certain levels of output are reached.

Sensitivity analysis Testing how a result might change if key variables are altered. Relevant variables to test are ones where there is uncertainty about their expected range of values. A range of realistic values is then drawn up, and the end result recalculated to see whether its broad conclusion would be altered if those values were realised.

Shadow prices Market prices adjusted for distortions, for example in the price which can be charged for the good, the value of foreign currency, the cost of labour or cost of capital in a given sector or economy. Shadow prices are supposed to reflect more accurately the opportunity cost of the good being produced.

Short run Situations in which the firm is not able to vary all its inputs. There is at least one factor of production that is fixed. (See also *long run*.)

Social insurance Government insurance programmes in which eligibility and premiums are not determined by the practices common to private insurance contracts. Premiums are often subsidised and there are typically re-distributions from some segments of the population to others.

Standardised mortality ratio (SMR) The number of deaths in a given year as a percentage of those expected for that age and sex group (based on national data, usually).

Subsidy The opposite of a tax: the government funds a portion of the costs of a good. This will benefit producers and/or consumers, depending on how competitive the market is.

Substitutes Substitutes in consumption are goods that satisfy the same wants (e.g., beef and chicken) so that an increase in the price of one will increase the demand for the other. Substitutes in production are alternative goods which a firm can produce (e.g., corn and soybeans for a farmer) so that an increase in the price of one will lead to a decrease in the supply of another.

Substitution effect The change in quantity demanded resulting from a relative change in commodity prices, holding real income constant. (See also *income effect*.)

Superior good A good or service for which demand increases as income increases. (See also *inferior good*.)

Supplier induced demand (SID) The change in demand associated with the discretionary influence of providers, especially doctors, over their patients. Demand that is provided for the self-interests of providers rather than solely for patient interests.

Surplus (consumer or producer) A theoretical notion which measures gain to consumers (or producers) as the difference between the price which has been paid for a product and the willingness to pay for (or supply) that product expressed by the demand (supply) curve.

Sustainability Used in different senses, but in the health field it generally implies the ability to maintain a system over time, at a reasonable level of operation and using the resources that are likely to be available. Sustainability has various dimensions, including financial, institutional, and social.

Target payments Payments which are made to health care providers once they have exceeded a specified coverage level (e.g., for antenatal check-ups or other preventive programmes).

Technical efficiency The maximum possible sustained output from a given set of inputs. (See *efficiency, allocative efficiency*.)

Third party payment Refers to situation where the first party (patient) does not pay directly for the activities of the second party (providers), but this is done through a private insurer, sickness fund or government agency (third party). This set-up will affect the quantity (and possibly quality) of the service demanded and supplied.

Time preference The degree to which a sum, say $1, is worth more now than it would be in one year (excluding the issues of inflation or uncertainty).

Transaction costs The costs which are incurred by the process of negotiating between buyer and seller – for example, the cost of collecting information about products, drawing up contracts, negotiating prices, etc. These reduce the profitability of doing business in that market.

Transfer payments Payments which are passed on to a different group of the population (such as sickness benefits). These are not included as costs of a programme in carrying out economic evaluations.

Transitional economy Term used to describe economies which used to be run on *command* lines, but which are now giving an increased role to market forces. As the term implies, they are still in the process of reform, and not yet fully established market economies.

Treatment protocol Written guidelines for the management of a given condition, specifying actions to be taken by different professionals and, where appropriate, the patient. These are intended to encourage continuity of care between different professionals involved in a case, clearer communication with the patient, and consistent application of 'best practice' by the professionals.

User charges   Direct payment for services by patients, though not necessarily covering the full costs of that service. These are often introduced to supplement public finance for health services which used to be free. Charges can be officially sanctioned and their levels controlled, but commonly they develop informally and vary between facilities and even members of staff. (See also *informal payments.*)

Utilisation   Use of existing capacity, often measured as an average over a period (e.g., bed occupancy, or theatre usage).

Utilitarian   Adopting the philosophy developed by Jeremy Bentham in the nineteenth century, which suggested as the overall social goal 'the greatest happiness of the greatest number'.

Utility   Economic term indicating the welfare gained by individuals through consumption. The assumption is that individuals 'maximise utility', so that in general, more consumption is better than less, other things being equal.

Variable Costs   Costs associated with factor(s) of production which change in quantity according to the quantity of output. Often expressed as a total variable cost (TVC) or average variable cost (AVC).

Vertical equity   The (Aristotelian) principle that those with differing ability to pay for services will contribute different amounts, and similarly that those with different needs will be treated differently. This complements the principle of *horizontal equity*, but is harder to interpret in practice. (See also *equity*.)

Voluntary health insurance   Health insurance which is taken up and paid for at the discretion of individuals (whether directly or via their employers). It can be offered by a public or private company.

Wants   Subjective description of *needs*; what a person requires in terms of health care.

Weighted capitation   Sum of money provided for services to each resident in a particular locality. The three main factors commonly reflected in the formula are: age structure of the population; its morbidity; and the relative cost of providing services.

Willingness to pay   The maximum amount of money that an individual is prepared to give up to ensure that a health care intervention is carried out. (See *ability to pay*.)

World Bank   Set up after the Second World War, together with the International Monetary Fund (IMF), the World Bank's function is to promote recovery and development globally. It is currently the largest donor in the health field (although it makes loans, they are highly concessional to the poorer countries, and therefore count at least partially as aid). It plays a major role in developing thinking about health and development and also in setting agendas in-country for reform in the health and other sectors.

World Health Organisation (WHO)   United Nations organisation, based in Geneva, responsible for promotion of health throughout the world.

Source: Adapted from Witter, S. and Ensor, T. (eds) (1997). *An Introduction to Health Economics for Eastern Europe and the Former Soviet Union.* Chichester: John Wiley.

Appendix 4

Useful Internet resources for health economists

Cochrane collaboration

The Cochrane Collaboration was established in 1993 to provide fast access to the best evidence available internationally on the effects of health care interventions. It maintains four main databases covering:

1 Systematic reviews
2 Abstracts of systematic reviews
3 Register of controlled trials
4 Methodology for carrying out research synthesis and systematic reviews.

These are available from the UK Cochrane Centre,
Summertown Pavilion, Middle Way, Oxford OX2 7LG, UK
Tel. (44) 1865 516300
Fax (44) 1865 516311
email general@cochrane.co.uk
website http://update.cochrane.co.uk

UK NHS Centre for Reviews and Dissemination

Established in the University of York in 1993, its role is to

1 Carry out reviews of the effectiveness and cost-effectiveness of health care interventions, management and organisation of health services
2 To disseminate its results via databases, published reviews and studies, and an enquiry service.

It can be contacted at the NHS Centre for Reviews and
Dissemination, University of York, York YO1 5DD, UK
Tel. (44) 1904 433707
Fax (44) 1904 433661
website http://www.york.ac.uk/inst/crd

Useful websites

You can find the Centre for Health Economics (CHE), University
of York

Home page at:	www.york.ac.uk/inst/che
and the International Programme at:	www.york.ac.uk/inst/che/internat.htm
The international programme maintains a links page at:	www.york.ac.uk/inst/che/intlink.htm

which you can use to access many of the websites for donor and
non-governmental agencies, as well as other key sites listed. As
many website addresses change and become quickly out of date
this link site will be updated regularly.

For those interested in a variety of journals and databases with a
greater focus on OECD countries go to the general CHE links

page on:	www.york.ac.uk/inst/che/links.htm
Another general link is:	www.healtheconomics.com/
British Medical Journal: (you can read all the BMJ online)	www.bmj.com/bmj

International agencies

The addresses listed here are the 'home pages' for different organisations. Within each it is often possible to search for specific
information of interest to you. Try, for example, connecting to
the World Bank home page, selecting search and then typing in,
for example, health financing. Good luck!

World Health Organisation	www.who.ch
PAHO (WHO)	www.paho.org

World Bank	www.worldbank.org
World Bank, Health, Nutrition and Population	www.worldbank.org/html/extdr/hnp/hnp.htm
Asian Development Bank	www.asiandevbank.org
UK Department for International Development	www.dfid.gov.uk
USAID	www.info.usaid.gov
UNICEF	www.unicef.org
Burden of Disease Unit, Harvard	www.hsph.harvard.edu/organizations/bdu
London School of Hygiene and Tropical Medicine	www.lshtm.ac.uk
International Division, Nuffield Institute for Health	www.leeds.ac.uk/nuffield/id/id.html

Other sites

Many of the non-governmental organisations involved with health in developing countries, along with campaigning organisations can be found on the following website: www.oneworld.org

And also:

Health Sector Reform clearing house	www.insp.mx/ichsri/
Public-Private Mix network	www.healthlink.org.za/ppmnet/
HealthLink database	www.healthlink.org.uk/database.html
Devline – general development database	www.ids.ac.uk/index.html

Index

Abel-Smith, B., 66
acute respiratory infections (ARIs), 171, 172
Africa, 69, 84, 93, 191; *see also* sub-Saharan Africa
AIDS *see* HIV
Ainsworth, M. *see* Shaw and Ainsworth
allocation of costs, 99–103, 268
allocation of resources, 98–179, 251, 258, 261, 262, 263–4, 284
  cost information for, 98–114
  ethics of, 253
Alma Ata declaration, 260, 265
altruism, 40, 255, 257, 268
appraisal of health care projects, 133–56
Argentina, 67, 69
Asia, 69, 81, 93, 191;
  Central, 90
  South East *see* South East Asia
  see also individual countries
Asian Tigers, 67
Asiime, D., 90
Australia, 80
average costs, 100–2, 269

Bamako Initiative, 83, 84–5, 262, 263, 269
Bangladesh, 50, 51, 90, 264
Bolivia, 69
Brazil, 67, 81, 221, 223
budget restructuring, 242
Burkina Faso, 50, 51, 75
Burundi, 69

Cambodia, 93
Camcho, L., 70
Cameroon, 78, 212
Canada, 66
capacity to benefit, 10
capital investment, 175, 266
Caribbean, 69, 191; *see also* Latin America
case mix, 237–8, 270
central purchasing, 252
Centre for Health Economics, York, International Programme, vii, viii, 290
Chile, 67, 80, 82, 163

China, 19, 22, 68, 88, 146, 189, 223, 260
  hospitals in, 140
cigarettes *see* smoking
clinical auditing, 243
Cochrane Database of Systematic Reviews, 116, 289
Collins, C. and Green, A., 208, 212–13
commissioning health care, 163–4, 270
communication with patients, 240, 243
community
  benefits of health care projects, 149–54
  financing of health care, 82–88, 93, 271
  participation, 260, 271
  workers, 9
Congo (Dem. Rep.), 83, 85, 259–60
consumer protection, 81, 82
consumer surplus, 35–6
cost
  allocation, 103–4
  assessments, 105–9
  average, 100–2, 269
  -benefit analysis (CBA), 107, 118, 119–22, 130, 148–54, 272
  concepts and definitions, 98–102
  per DALY, 173, 175; *see also* disability-adjusted life years
  effectiveness of health benefits, 117–19, 129:
    effectiveness ratios (CER), 119
  impact of health projects, 134–48
  information for resource allocation, 98–114
  marginal, 100–1
  minimisation study, 129, 272
  opportunity, 105, 128
  recurrent, 146–7, 266
  -utility analysis (CUA), 122–5, 129, 272
  variable, 100
  see also remuneration
contracts, 193–6, 271
Costa Rica, 22, 67, 260
criticisms of methodology, 254–7
Cuba, 67, 260
currency problems, 50–1

decentralisation of health systems, 6, 165, 183, 205–13, 241, 272
  different kinds of, 207–8
  impact of, 210–12
  objectives of, 205–7
decision making tools, 126–9
definitions
  of health, 14–25
  of health economics, 2
Delcheva, E., 90
demand, 273
  curves, 31–3
  elasticity of, 30–2, 274, 281
  for health care, 26–9, 30–2, 75